Disability Life Stories

I0094961

Based on a 10-year longitudinal study in the United States, this much-needed text offers insight into the developmental trajectories of people with disabilities from childhood through adulthood using their language and amplifying their voices. Through in-depth interviews with 14 disabled people, the authors learned important lessons about how each individual developed and enacted a sense of life purpose. Their experiences are illustrated through rich and unfiltered narratives about childhood, family interactions, primary and secondary education, college, and work experiences. These life stories also illuminate growth over time, capturing details of educational, identity, relationship, and career trajectories. Featuring discussion questions at the end of each chapter, the book stimulates individual and group reflection and invites readers to engage in action as allies and advocates for equity and inclusion for disabled people. *Disability Life Stories* is essential reading for everyone—especially educators (in-service and pre-service), disability scholars, families, community organizers, healthcare professionals, and disabled people themselves.

Annemarie Vaccaro, Ph.D. (she/her), is a Professor and Associate Dean in the College of Education at the University of Rhode Island (URI).

Adam M. Moore, Ph.D. (he/him), is an Associate Professor of Special Education and Coordinator of Special Education Graduate Programs at the University of Rhode Island (URI).

Barbara M. Newman, Ph.D. (she/her), is a Professor emeritus in the Department of Human Development and Family Science at the University of Rhode Island (URI).

Philip R. Newman, Ph.D. (he/him), is a social psychologist whose research has focused on the transition to high school as well as on group identity and alienation.

Ezekiel W. Kimball, Ph.D. (he/him), is a Professor of Higher Education and Interim Dean of the College of Education & Human Development at the University of Maine.

Alexis Carlson, MA (she/her), is an educator at a public high school in Rhode Island. She also teaches education courses as a part-time instructor at the University of Rhode Island (URI).

Emily Doffing, MA (she/they), is a scholar-activist conducting critical Participatory Action Research (PAR) with disabled graduate students' lived experiences at California State University in Long Beach.

Wanting to be seen and heard is a universal desire, yet one the disability community rarely experiences. The history of disability is rife with assumptions made by those who are not disabled. In this ground-breaking text, the authors offer authentic insight into the lives of 14 disabled persons. Their 'unfiltered advice' for meaningful inclusion makes this compelling book a must-read for educators, policymakers, politicians, and community members.

Dr. Wendy Murawski, *Eisner Endowed Chair, Center for Teaching & Learning, California State University Northridge, USA*

Disability Life Stories comprehensively presents the school, career, and interpersonal experiences of 14 young adults with disabilities. Hearing these voices is critically important to examining environments, systems, and factors that enhance, and impede, positive adult outcomes. These stories and suggestions provide an invaluable framework for a range of audiences to examine, evaluate, and act on a range of points to promote successful outcomes for young adults with disabilities.

Dr. Joseph W. Madaus, *Director of the Collaborative on Postsecondary Education and Disability and Professor in the Department of Educational Psychology, Neag School of Education, University of Connecticut, USA*

This *compelling* exploration of the lived experiences of 14 individuals with disabilities captures their triumphs and challenges in navigating school, family, and careers. Drawing from a decade-long study, this book provides invaluable perspectives on resilience and life's purpose through authentic narratives tracing journeys from childhood to adulthood. A great choice for book studies!

Dr. Julie Irene Bost, *Clinical Associate Professor, University of North Carolina-Greensboro and 2025 Council for Exceptional Children (CEC) President, USA*

Vaccaro and colleagues have crafted a beautiful text that celebrates and centers the authentic voices and developmental journeys of individuals with disabilities! This masterfully curated collection of unfiltered, first-person life stories that demonstrate the diversity of the disabled experience is a critically poignant read for families, educators, employers, and others who care about disabled people.

Dr. Adam R. Lalor, *Vice President for Neurodiversity Research and Innovation, Landmark College, USA*

This book does a rare thing—it shares stories of disabled college students in all their complexity, individuality, and nuance. For the 21% of undergraduates with disabilities, this book offers understanding, validation, empathy, and encouragement. This book also asks higher education faculty, employees, and researchers to consider how their work can better address ableism and treat disabled students and fields of disability with the same respect these authors demonstrate.

Dr. Wendy S. Harbour, *Director, National Center for College Students with Disabilities, Association on Higher Education And Disability (AHEAD), United States*

Disability Life Stories

Unfiltered Voices on School, Family, Career, and Finding Purpose

Annemarie Vaccaro, Adam M. Moore, Barbara M. Newman, Philip R. Newman, Ezekiel W. Kimball, Alexis Carlson, and Emily Doffing

Routledge
Taylor & Francis Group

NEW YORK AND LONDON

Designed cover image: Getty Images

First published 2026
by Routledge
605 Third Avenue, New York, NY 10158

and by Routledge
4 Park Square, Milton Park, Abingdon, Oxon, OX14 4RN

Routledge is an imprint of the Taylor & Francis Group, an informa business

© 2026 Taylor & Francis

ISBN: 9781032801544 (hbk)
ISBN: 9781032782225 (pbk)
ISBN: 9781003495703 (ebk)

DOI: 10.4324/9781003495703

Typeset in Times New Roman
by KnowledgeWorks Global Ltd.

Contents

About the Authors

Annemarie Vaccaro, Ph.D. (she/her), is a Professor and Associate Dean in the College of Education at the University of Rhode Island (URI). She earned her bachelor's degree in social sciences from Castleton State College and a Master's degree in student affairs in higher education at Indiana University of Pennsylvania. She also has a MA in sociology and Ph.D. in higher education from the University of Denver. Annemarie's scholarship focuses on equity and justice in higher education. For the last decade, her research has focused on collegiate and career success for diverse students, including those with disabilities. Her qualitative research has been published in higher education, psychology, and human development journals. Annemarie is also the co-author of three books: *Centering Women of Color in Academic Counter-spaces: A Critical Race Analysis of Teaching, Learning, and Classroom Dynamics* (with Camba-Kelsay); *Decisions Matter: Using a Decision Making Framework with Contemporary Student Affairs Case Studies* (with McCoy, Champagne and Siegel); and *Safe Spaces: Making Schools and Communities Welcoming to LGBT Youth* (with August and Kennedy). She has received a number of professional awards for her scholarship including the: 2018 NASPA Pillar of the Profession Recognition; 2017 NASPA George D. Kuh Award for Outstanding Contribution to Literature Award; 2010 ACHE Alex Charter's Research Award; and "Recognition of Service Through Disability Scholarship and Research" from ACPA in 2013.

Adam M. Moore, Ph.D. (he/him), is an Associate Professor of Special Education and Coordinator of Special Education Graduate Programs at the University of Rhode Island (URI). Prior to teaching in higher education, Dr. Moore was a National Board-Certified special education teacher in the Boston Public Schools. As a national leader in the Teacher Education Division of the Council for Exceptional Children (CEC), Dr. Moore has worked to support teacher educators in special education programs for the last six years. Spanning over 20 years in the field, his area of expertise includes special education teacher preparation program design, accreditation, and program improvement. He currently serves as one of seven national experts on the CEC Accreditation Commission, as a member of the CEC Teacher Candidate Support Network working group, and as a member of the Rhode Island CEEDAR Center Collaborative. Dr. Moore served on the advisory board of the Institute of Education Sciences (IES) Regional Educational Laboratory for the Northeast and the Islands Teacher Preparation Research Alliance from 2017–2022. Dr. Moore is the Co-PI on a $1.1M Department of Education Office of Special Education Programs (OSEP) grant, *Project SUSTAIN*, aimed to diversify the special education workforce (2023–2028). Dr. Moore has been awarded several awards for his research, service, and teaching, including the New England Educational Research Organization (NEERO) Schmitt Research Award (2015), the URI Kappa Delta Pi Outstanding Teaching Award (2016), and the Roger Williams University Faculty Advisor of the Year Award for advising RWU Best Buddies (2023).

Barbara M. Newman, Ph.D. (she/her), is a professor emeritus in the Department of Human Development and Family Science at the University of Rhode Island. Dr. Newman received her Ph.D. from the University of Michigan and has held faculty positions at Russell Sage College and the Ohio State University, where she served as department chair in Human Development and Family Science and as Associate Provost for Faculty Recruitment and Development. She has taught courses in life-span development, adolescence, family theories, and the research process. An active researcher, Dr. Newman's interests focus on parent-child relationships in early adolescence, factors that promote success in the transition to high school and the transition to college, and the sense of belonging in early and later adolescence. Her most recent research focuses on the development of the sense of purpose among college students with disabilities. Barbara and Philip Newman have co-authored 14 books in the fields of psychology and human development including *Development Through Life: A Psychosocial Approach* (13 editions); *Theories of Human Development* (3 editions); and *Theories of Adolescent Development*.

Philip R. Newman, Ph.D. (he/him), is a social psychologist whose research has focused on the transition to high school as well as on group identity and alienation. He has taught courses in introductory psychology, adolescence, social psychology, developmental psychology, counseling, and family, school, and community contexts for development. After obtaining his Ph.D. from the University of Michigan, he served as the director for Research and Evaluation of the Young Scholars Program at the Ohio State University and as the director of the Human Behavior Curriculum Project for the American Psychological Association. He is a fellow of the American Psychological Association, the Society for the Psychological Study of Social Issues (SPSSI), and the American Orthopsychiatric Association (now called the Global Alliance for Behavioral Health and Social Justice). Barbara and Philip Newman have co-authored 14 books in the fields of psychology and human development including *Development Through Life: A Psychosocial Approach* (13 editions); *Theories of Human Development* (3 editions); and *Theories of Adolescent Development.*

Ezekiel (Zeke) Kimball, Ph.D. (he/him), is Professor of Higher Education and Interim Dean of the College of Education & Human Development at the University of Maine. His research focuses on: (1) disability identity development and disabled student success; (2) knowledge use and production in higher education; and (3) the relationships between identity, identity development, and postsecondary learning environments. To-date, he has authored or co-authored 46 journal articles, 2 scholarly monographs, and 19 book chapters. Additionally, with Dr. Karla Loya (University of Hartford), he is the co-editor of the New Directions in Institutional Research volume *Using Qualitative Research to Promote Organizational Intelligence.* He is a past executive editor of the *Journal of Postsecondary Education and Disability.* His work has been funded by the National Science Foundation, Department of Education, Spencer Foundation, and the Agency for Healthcare Research and Quality.

Alexis (Alex) Carlson, MA (she/her), is an educator at a public high school in Rhode Island. She also teaches education courses as a part-time instructor at the University of Rhode Island (URI). Alex earned her Bachelor of Arts in Secondary Education and English from URI where she graduated with honors in 2015. She also earned a Master of Arts in Education and a graduate certificate in digital literacy from URI in 2017. Her thesis explored the relationship between admission requirements and student teaching performance. In 2017, she co-presented *"I Am Not My Disability: Professional Identity Development of 6 Pre-Service Teachers"* at the Council for Exceptional Children International Convention and Expo. She is a co-author of "Constructing a Sense of Purpose and a Professional Teaching Identity: Experiences of Teacher Candidates with Disabilities" (2020). She has a decade of diverse education experiences, ranging from teaching students in kindergarten, twice-exceptional students, and students in 5th–12th grade. Alex also worked for the Johns Hopkins University Center for Talented Youth program as an instructor, course developer, and project-based learning mentor.

Emily (Em) Doffing, MA (she/they), is a scholar-activist conducting critical Participatory Action Research (PAR) with disabled graduate students' lived experiences at California State University in Long Beach. They earned their Bachelor of Arts in Psychology with minors in Sociology and Political Science with university and departmental honors at the University of Kansas (KU) and their Master of Arts in Psychological Research at California State University, Long Beach. They are certified as a proactive disability inclusion ambassador from KU's Disability Inclusion Program. They implemented five initiatives of accessibility to transform KU's Counseling and Psychological Services (CAPS). Using their identities of being low-income, Mad/psychologically disabled, and queer, they co-created and co-led three of CAPS' first free peer support groups. They then mentored three faculty to improve their workplaces. They have provided ten oral presentations and eight posters at local, regional, national, and international research conferences and local community colleges. They currently manage a disability justice research lab while being a communications manager for DARN! (Disability Activism, Research, and Networking), and the coordinator for DREAM's (Disability, Research, Education, Activism, and Mentoring) online disability cultural center.

Foreword

"Nothing for us without us" is a refrain that has long been proclaimed by many leaders in the disability community. Yet, far too many professionals and others continue to recommend policies and services for individuals with disabilities with limited knowledge of their situations and without much input from them.

This book shatters these glaring omissions. "Disability Life Stories: Unfiltered Voices on School, Family, Career, and Finding Purpose" incorporates the narratives of 14 individuals living with disabilities focusing on various stages in their growth and development. Professionals and others interacting with disabled persons need to be more aware of their real life experiences. They also need to collaborate more with them on the design and implementation of appropriate programs and services.

The lack of understanding and insensitivity around persons with disabilities impacted me. When I started losing my vision in my early 30s, my doctor and local superintendent both told me that I needed to stop teaching and get out of education. Fortunately, I soon connected with many individuals living with blindness and other disabilities. Without their recommendations and support, I never would have developed the vision or fortitude to continue as an educator.

Throughout this book, the authors share many real life stories from persons who have disabilities. Readers will see/hear/or touch many candid descriptions of challenges and joys experienced by individuals at different stages of their lives. They will learn more about both barriers and paths for success. Readers will gain a deeper understanding of the complexities of living with disabilities, and they will be better informed for their future interactions and support.

The commitment of the authors of this book to champion the perspectives of individuals with disabilities through extensive interviewing is powerful. By interweaving their many stories along with current research on disability policies and practices, professionals, family members, persons with disabilities and their allies will be better informed with specific actionable strategies. With this book, we will all be better prepared for more meaningful interactions and for more collaborative and effective support.

Bill Henderson

Bill Henderson was an educator in the Boston Public Schools for 36 years. From 1989–2009, he served as principal of a school which was renamed the Dr. William Henderson Inclusion School. Bill continues to advocate for inclusion and quality education through consulting and by presenting at universities and conferences. His book, "The Blind Advantage," shares examples and strategies of how including students with disabilities can improve a school for everyone.

Preface

Any time an author writes a book, they know that the information may become outdated to readers sometime in the future. Life moves on. Policies change. New technologies appear. Society evolves. However, the struggles, successes, barriers, and opportunities captured in the 14 stories in this book are in many ways timeless because they are fundamentally human. No matter when you pick up this book, we are confident that you will be moved by the powerful, extraordinary, and ordinary disability life stories shared here.

As we write this preface in the spring of 2025, we want readers to know a few things. Given the rapidly evolving nature of policy in the United States, we've decided to add a preface to alert you to some ways that the contemporary context might shape how you understand the stories, as well as the policies and practices, referenced in the text.

First, this book will be printed at a time of great uncertainty. As we mention in the text, anti-DEIA (Diversity, Equity, Inclusion and Accessibility) legislation continues to proliferate at the state and national levels. In some cases, restrictions on DEIA initiatives have meant closure of programs, services, and curricula designed to support a host of diversity issues–including disability. For many disabled youth, including the 14 whose stories you're about to read, DEIA programs, services, and protections were important sources of support. The closing of disability cultural centers, cancelling of disability studies courses, and elimination of disability-related social activities will likely have negative repercussions for disabled people in the future. They may not have access to many of the disability-related support systems enjoyed by our participants.

Second, many proposed policies could undermine fundamental protections in federal civil rights laws related to access and service delivery for disabled people. At present, three federal laws primarily define how people with disabilities are protected across the lifespan. (See Chapter 2 for more detail). The Americans with Disabilities Act (ADA) of 1990, and the 1998 amendments, protect the civil rights of persons with disabilities, including protection from discrimination within places of employment, public spaces, and services (U.S. Congress, 1990, § 12101). The Individuals with Disabilities Education Act (IDEA; 1990,

2004) is a federal law that ensures children with disabilities are provided with a free appropriate public education from birth to age 22. Section 504 of the Rehabilitation Act of 1973 requires that federally funded agencies (including schools and workplaces) provide reasonable accommodations to disabled people (U.S. Congress, 1973, § 504). If recent executive orders, organizational restructuring, and court challenges succeed, many of the enforcement provisions of these laws will largely be rendered ineffective. Some of these changes will mean that *even if* the legal protections for disabled people remain formal policy, the implementation or enforcement of these protections may be severely limited or non-existent. For example, reduction in staffing, and the possible elimination of the Office of Civil Rights in the Department of Education, will make proactive federal enforcement of disability rights—especially in school settings—much less likely. Historically, disability protections have been driven by data showing disparate outcomes for disabled students—ranging from school discipline, to educational attainment, to access to highly-qualified educators. Expertly and ethically conducted national surveys and anonymized datasets that demonstrate inequity (and justify support for disabled people) have been disrupted or deleted from public view. In the future, it will be challenging to show evidence of inequitable treatment of disabled learners without accurate information showing exactly what youth are experiencing in school settings. Finally, recent policy changes also threaten the training of special educators through the elimination (or reduction) of grants focused on recruiting and retaining special educators. We are concerned about the kinds of educational, workplace, and community barriers disabled youth—now and in the future—might face without accurate information, strong federal policy, and actively enforced protections.

Third, we remain steadfast in our admiration of the young people who shared their stories with us. Their narratives reveal a host of systemic hurdles in schools, communities, and workplaces—all that occurred during a historical moment when disabled people had the *most* legal protections and systems (albeit not perfect) to ensure the implementation of those protections. Even though these 14 stories were collected in a more hopeful time, the advocacy and activism you'll read about was not without a cost. Asking disabled people to fight for *basic* needs and to succeed within systems that were not built for them requires disabled people to work *harder* for the same opportunities as non-disabled people. For some disabled people, having to fight for equity causes frustration, anger, or despair—and requires significant energy, time, and money. Sometimes, though, it fosters a desire to help others, which is the case for the 14 people whose stories you're about to read. They shared their struggles and triumphs in hopes that other disabled people would know that they are not alone.

Finally, as authors, educators, parents, grandparents, and disability activists, we don't know what the future holds. But, we believe that the inspirational stories and advice shared in this book will prompt readers to want to take action. Everyone can engage in small and large actions that promote change.

We encourage readers to support non-governmental organizations (NGOs) and politicians that actively fight for disability justice. In this historical moment, we also hope that readers will take action in local, state, and national realms to ensure that present and future generations of disabled people have not only legal protections, but also families, schools, communities, and workplaces where they can thrive.

Acknowledgments

This book would not have been possible without the support of countless people in our personal and professional lives. Over the years, we received support from our families, friends, and colleagues who listened to our ideas and offered invaluable suggestions and insights. We are deeply grateful to our loved ones—especially during those times when this research project took us away from other life commitments. We appreciate their patience and unwavering support while we spent countless hours doing our best to ensure that the powerful stories told to us were shared with audiences far and wide.

Over the course of a decade, a number of emerging scholars participated in our research team. Without their help, this project could not have been possible. They all played unique roles—from conducting interviews, to coding data, to reviewing literature, and more. No matter the role or length of time they spent on the project, every graduate student who joined our research team was incredibly helpful in their own unique way. We are incredibly grateful to the graduate students from Roger Williams University, University of Rhode Island, and University of Massachusetts who supported different stages of this project since 2013. Specifically, we wish to thank the following individuals who played critical roles in this project while they were graduate students: Joseph Argueta, Denny Bobot, Athina Chartelain, Meada Daly-Cano, Jennifer Castro, Lindsay Costa, Dominique Dame, Abigail Higgins, Tiffany Hoyt, Victoria Kern, Melanie Lee, Hyenjung Lim, Mackenzie Maitland, Bay Naples, Jacob Reilly, Brandis Ruise, Cynthia Spinola, Hanni Thoma, and Nina Tissi-Gassoway. We thank you for your time, energy, and insights. We learned as much from you as we hope you did on this project.

We also appreciate the expertise offered by Dr. Peter F. Troiano who was a key member of the team when the project began. Peter helped us design the study and was actively involved in collection and analysis of the early interviews.

We express our deepest gratitude to Rebecca Melrose whose keen editorial eye and thoughtful feedback helped us move our rough drafts into a polished final book. With each review, she expressed excitement and interest in the stories—giving us hope that the book would also resonate with readers too.

We express our gratitude to Bill Henderson for writing the Foreword to this book. As authors we admire his scholarly work as well as his steadfast advocacy for inclusion and quality education for disabled people. His support of this book means so much to us.

We appreciate the financial support provided by a number of educational and non-profit organizations. Specifically, we would like to thank the following four organizations for supporting our project through small research awards: University of Rhode Island; University of Massachusetts, Amherst; Roger Williams University; and NASPA, Region 1. Their fiscal support provided much needed resources to pay for interview transcription. We also used the funding for gift cards. Although the gift card amounts were certainly not nearly enough compensation for their time and energy over the course of a decade, we are grateful for funding that allowed us to offer participants a small token of our appreciation.

As we note multiple times throughout this book, we are thankful to our participants who graciously gave us the gifts of their time and stories. Due to ethical guidelines regarding confidentiality, we cannot thank our participants using their real names. So, we thank them here by their pseudonyms. (Luckily, they know who they are!) Thank you so much Alice, Justice, Juno, Kalani, Kennedy, Landers, Mercedes, Peter, Poppy, Tippi, Titus, Willa, Willow, and Yolanda. You inspired us at every stage of this project. And, we have no doubt that your stories will inspire readers too.

1 Introduction

"When I talk to people and I share my story, I think about the little girl who maybe just started school; the young man in high school trying to make his way; or somebody that's in college just losing their sight and doesn't know how to navigate the system. I try to put myself in other people's shoes because I know how it is when people haven't done that for me, and how hard it is. We can learn from the good stuff. We can learn from the bad stuff. I think in order to make change people need to hear. That's how, over time, change happens. No matter what I do, I will help people with disabilities, help advocate, raise awareness about issues that they go through, and be a positive impact."

—Alice

Words matter. Stories matter. Disabled voices matter. When talking and writing about something as complicated as disability, finding the right ways to capture the nuanced and varied experiences of people with widely different disabilities and life histories can seem daunting. Finding the right way to talk about how people with disabilities navigate ableist environments and systems that create unnecessary challenges and barriers can seem nearly impossible. But the words with which we open this chapter—words that came from the disability life story of Alice, a blind college graduate—captured a sentiment shared by many of the people with disabilities we've talked to. Over the last decade, young people with disabilities shared their experiences and perspectives with us. From them, we learned that the best way to help prepare people with disabilities to navigate an unwelcoming world is by listening to those who have successfully made their way through the same challenges and barriers. We also believe that by listening to disabled voices, all of us can become better parents, relatives, teachers, supervisors, friends, and allies. In this volume, we invite you to experience

DOI: 10.4324/9781003495703-1

firsthand the life stories of 14 people with disabilities as they transitioned from early childhood to high school, to college, and then to adulthood. These stories were told in their own words. Their successes. Their struggles. Their hopes and dreams. And through these disability life stories, young people shared their expertise on how to make a better world for disabled people.

While we sincerely hope that everything that we have shared in that first paragraph seems like commonsense. Unfortunately, it goes against a long history of the medicalization and regulation of disabled bodies and minds. Diagnostic tests determine who has a "legitimate" disability and who does not. Medical professionals and educators create "treatment" and "intervention" plans intended to support people with disabilities. Bureaucrats, policymakers, and corporations make life-altering decisions about access to spaces and opportunities that nondisabled people take for granted. The end result is an experience of reality that can seem compartmentalized and detached from the daily needs of people with disabilities. In this book, unfiltered disability life stories challenge such realities and tell the experiences, perspectives, and lived realities of people with disabilities in their own words.

Most educational writing about people with disabilities captures their experiences at one moment in time (usually in primary/secondary education, higher education, or the workplace). And, many writings about disabled people substitute the expert knowledge of highly-trained professionals for experiences and hard-won wisdom of people with disabilities. Our book is different in that it seeks to simultaneously reject the compartmentalization of disability life stories *and* centers disabled voices in the telling of their stories. By placing disability at the center of the developmental trajectories and experiences that everyone engages as they move from early childhood through adolescence and into emerging adulthood, this book offers a uniquely holistic perspective on pivotal transitions and experiences in the lives of people with disabilities. The stories come from a decade-long qualitative study with disabled college students. Our work began with a question: how do college students with disabilities craft their sense of life purpose? Starting from an asset or strengths perspective, we hoped to learn how students defined their disabilities, how their disabilities figured into their broader sense of self, and what they envisioned as desirable goals for the future. The first interview occurred during college, and included reflections on childhood, family interactions, and college experiences. As the project evolved, we were impressed and delighted with how willing these students were to talk with us, not only once, but two or three times over the span of almost a decade. The second and third interviews documented growth over time—capturing rich educational, identity, relationship, and career trajectories. Through these in-depth interviews with disabled people, we learned important lessons about how they experienced educational systems, found support (or lack thereof), made meaning of their disability, navigated relationships, developed life goals, and worked to achieve their dreams. You'll read about all of these topics, and more, in the forthcoming stories.

A Note on Language

When you are trying to represent people's experiences, words matter a great deal. And, in the case of people with disabilities, the importance of language is even more in the foreground. In the United States, there is a fraught history of language used to demonize, dehumanize, or otherwise distance people with disabilities from public view. Often, this language has been *applied to* rather than *chosen by* people with disabilities. There is also a long history of disabled reclamation of language or linguistic innovation intended to lead to greater inclusion, representation, and accuracy of the experiences of disabled people. Digging into that history is vitally important, but ultimately, it is not the work of this book. We offer a brief overview of disability history, law, and policy in Chapter 2. Without that extended, and ongoing, examination of the words we use to describe disability, we had to make a choice as authors about how to describe people with disabilities. Throughout this chapter, you have already encountered some of the results of that choice. To understand this choice and what it means, we briefly share a contemporary debate about the language of disability.

At present, one of the great fissures of debate in the disability community is whether to use person-first language, identity-first language, both, or neither. Most often, traditions within academic disciplines and usage by non-disabled people point toward person-first language rather than identity-first language (i.e., person with a disability vs. disabled person). Meanwhile, a growing number of disabled activists have argued that doing so creates distance between a disabled person and what is likely for them a primary identity that fundamentally shapes their world. The argument most commonly made for this approach is that, since disability is generally a medicalized identity perceived as unwanted by many, person-first language is used as a distancing technique—quite literally to say "this is a person ... but they have a disability." For disabled activists, a shift to identity-first language reflects a broader effort to reclaim disability as an affirmative part of their self-concept. Yet, even among politically engaged people with disabilities, this usage is contested. Many culturally Deaf people—those who sign fluently and who engage with Deaf cultural productions such as American Sign Language literature and Deaf View Image Art (typically abbreviated De'VIA)—do not describe themselves as disabled. Likewise, many autistic self-advocates regard neurodiversity as a fundamental feature of human experience rather than a single definable or even constellation of definable disability diagnoses. Still others, disabled activists—for example, those who work within crip cultural frames or those who participate in various forms of mad activism (e.g., Jenks, 2019; Kafai, 2021; Milbrodt, 2018; Schalk, 2013)—have sought to reclaim terms originally designed to pejoratively label disabled people. These activists treat disability terminology as part of an affirmative self-definition—much as activists from other marginalized social identity groups have reclaimed and re-signified labels originally intended to stigmatize them (see Chapter 2 for an in-depth discussion of these concepts).

As authors we knew of this ongoing debate over the language of disability, and some of us even have participated in it actively as scholars and disabled people. Yet, we still found the choice about language for this book more daunting than expected. The simple truth is that we disagree among ourselves on philosophical and practical grounds, in part, because we come from different personal, professional, and academic backgrounds. We are also a team of people with and without disabilities. Yet, where we find common ground is in our commitment to honor the words, stories, and voices of the people with disabilities who participated in our study and whose disability life stories we share in this book. When we began interviewing people, we did not require that they think of themselves as disabled to participate. We did not require that they had an actively constructed disability identity or documentation of a disability. Instead, we asked anyone who was a person with a disability—and provided a wide-range of suggestions regarding what they might include—if they would volunteer for an interview and tell their stories. Some of our participants thought of themselves in terms of a diagnosis, others identified within a disability cultural framework, and a few identified with a specific disability subculture. They all would say that they were people with disabilities according to the definition we provided, but they would not all say that they were disabled people. In fact, some even eschewed the terms disability and disabled. As a result, our commitment to let their words, stories, and voices be the primary focus of this book won out (as will always be the driving principle of this book in the pages that follow). When we are talking about a group of people or our participants, we use both people with disabilities and disabled people. When we are talking about a shared experience or phenomena (e.g., disabled voice, disability life stories), we adopt the utilization that makes sense contextually. However, and most importantly, we always follow the words, stories, and voices of our participants and use the terminology that they used to describe themselves and their experiences. Participants in our study used their own words to describe their disability. We did not ask them to fit themselves into a box or predetermined category. As such, their self-reported disabilities are exactly that—self-reported and self-chosen. More details about the study and participants can be found in Chapter 3.

Having interviewed our participants several times from early in their college careers well into their adulthood, we have had an opportunity to illustrate how individuals weave their disabilities into a broader sense of self across multiple complex contexts. The disability life stories explore ways that our participants define their disabilities rather than having disabilities defined from the outside by medical, psychological, or educational professionals. What is more, the direct prose from young people sheds light on how they perceive the responses of others, and what they make of those responses. These reflections bring to light the nature of educational, familial, workplace, and community environments, which can accentuate the challenges a person faces, introduce new roadblocks, or complement and highlight one's strengths. We came to appreciate the variety of ways that a person's disability becomes integrated into a personal identity and influences the formation of a sense of purpose. The narratives remind us to resist generalizing about the potential costs or benefits of disabilities, but rather to let each individual tell us who they are, how they will (or will not) be defined or categorized, and the extent to which disabilities reduce or expand opportunities for self-fulfillment.

In crafting this book, we have been the recipients of two rare gifts in academia. First, we found a group of college students with disabilities who were both extraordinary and profoundly ordinary. They were extraordinary in their willingness and capacity to render in words their deepest thoughts and feelings about their own disabilities *and* to freely share stories that meant a great deal to them (and sometimes which caused them great pain). Collectively, their stories give voice to experiences shared by many people with disabilities. And yet, they were ordinary in the things that they talked about—including the experiences that they had prior to, during, and after college. They succeeded and struggled. They made and lost friends, started new jobs, and followed new career paths. They had great joys and great regrets. They experienced the things that happen in most people's lives between early childhood and adulthood. In their willingness to share these things with us, they offered us a gift of time and care to which we are endlessly indebted. Second, we present the disability life stories in this volume with little context or interpretation. What little that exists is relegated to introductory and closing commentary from us. Throughout the bulk of this book, centering the voice of our participants means decentering our own. That is fairly uncommon in academic writing, which tends to prioritize researcher voices above those of research participants. As such, our editor and publisher offered a rare gift that makes this book possible: the ability to disrupt scholarly norms by presenting disability life stories in a largely uninterrupted way. As authors we are deeply appreciative of these two rare gifts and we hope that this type of storytelling style becomes more common inside and outside academe.

Who Should Read This Book? And How?

We believe everyone who is disabled or who knows or loves someone with a disability should read this book. We are confident that the lessons that can be learned from unfiltered disability life stories in this book would benefit anyone who has ever interacted with a person with a disability. By definition, that population is everyone. Disability is everywhere in our lives, but it is often hidden by people in positions of power who feel discomforted by the reality of its pervasiveness. Or, by people with disabilities who seek to pass as non-disabled so that they might not be subject to stigma attached to disability. Typically, it would not be possible to have as many candid conversations with disabled people as are shared in this book. Even trying to do so raises troubling ethical questions about the labor required for disabled people to educate others. Anyone can benefit by reading this book. We encourage you to engage with the stories in the same way you might listen to the account of a friend or loved one—with trust and care.

Ultimately though, we did not create this book for everyone. We developed it with very specific audiences in mind: the people who have positions of formal or practical power over the educational, work, and life trajectories of people with disabilities. That includes, but is certainly not limited to educators, employers, healthcare professionals, service providers, and caregivers. This book is designed to help them center disabled voices in their spheres of influence (e.g., homes, schools, offices, etc.) by providing a holistic narrative of multiple disability life histories. It is intended to help these audiences compare and contrast lived realities of disabled people across the accounts, as well as across the life course of a single person. Reading the stories this way highlights that disability is rarely static, nor is the way that people with disabilities understand themselves. This book shows that there is no single experience of disability, but there *are* common patterns associated with ableism that play out in the lives of most people with disabilities. And most significantly, it is intended to center disabled voices in hopes of providing the advice that families, educators, employers, medical professionals, community resource professionals, and social workers need to hear. We also wrote this book in hopes of helping parents, caregivers, and loved ones recognize the power of the disabled voices and individuals currently in their lives. Relatives of disabled people all too often perform key roles in mediating both the harms and the joys of being disabled—in fact, as authors, some of us know this firsthand. In our participants' life histories, family emerges as both the single greatest source of support for people with disabilities and a potential threat to their self-determination, agency, and the emergence of an affirmative sense of self. In nearly every one of those negative cases, major problems could have been avoided by simply making space for the disabled voice struggling to be heard, read, or witnessed.

In writing a book to help families, educators, medical and mental health professionals, community resource professionals, and social workers, we recognize that we are also writing a book that we hope that people with disabilities will read and find at least one version of themselves within. Our goal in this book is to center disabled voices such that, even when people with disabilities feel that their voice has gone unnoticed in their daily life, they know that there are people who care about what they have to say. There is an audience for their struggles and successes, hopes and dreams, and all the things that make them ordinary and extraordinary.

Whose Stories Does This Book Tell?

As social scientists, our research is always intended to collect and analyze data about one small group of people in order to understand much larger phenomena. Qualitative researchers do this work primarily by seeking to understand the stories that people tell about what they have experienced and how the world works. We started by asking 59 college students to tell us about how their experience of disability shaped their lives from early childhood until the day that we first interviewed them—typically during their undergraduate college years and usually from ages 17–23. We then asked for volunteers from among that initial group to participate in a follow-up interview two years later and then another nine years after that. Those interviews garnered narratives that began in early childhood through adulthood. By the third interview, most people had graduated from (or left) college and gone on to do some of the things we typically associate with adulthood (e.g., started careers, moved away from home, gotten married, had children). Throughout these later interviews, we maintained a primary interest in how disability shaped their experiences. As a result, we cannot, and do not, claim that we understand our participants' full life histories. Instead, we understand how they share a subset of their experiences from the perspective of their disabilities. As such, we think of these accounts as disability life stories—a *partial version* of their own personal histories from childhood into adulthood contextualized by their attention to disability.

In shaping the disability life stories in this way, we also began a process that means that the resulting narratives neither fully belong to our participants nor to us. For clarity and brevity, we curated and organized the prose that you will read—taking direct quotations from three sets of interviews to best capture the life stories shared with us. We collected disability stories by asking our participants to reflect on, and describe, their experiences from childhood into adulthood. We present disabled life stories by illuminating particular examples and pieces of their narratives that best reflect the shared *and* divergent experiences of our original participant pool and of college students with disabilities more broadly. It is very important for us to acknowledge that we are not the authors of these stories in a traditional sense, but we like to think that we revealed them. During our interview process, we told study participants the broad parameters of where we hoped our interviews would lead and then we followed them on a journey through hours of individual interviews. In crafting this book, our participants reviewed their chapters to ensure their authentic story was presented accurately. See Chapter 3 for more details about the research project.

In the pages of this book, we try to do justice to the stories that participants shared with us rather than the stories that we might wish to tell. This is especially important, as we have learned from disability justice activists who contend that stories told by disabled people are a form of cultural activism. In fact, some consider disabled storytelling a radical act, as it can challenge ableist dominant narratives by asserting that disability stories are valid, have worth, and can inspire change (Kafai, 2021). Piepzna-Samarasinha (2018) calls for a reimagining of traditional activism to include disabled ways of knowing and being, which is held in stories. The first step in activism is usually creating awareness (Kafai, 2021). This book serves to bring awareness to disabled joy and growth as well as embodied trauma and grief. By sharing their stories, the participants demonstrate everyday activism. We hope that readers might experience what Mingus (2011) describes as access intimacy—which can be experienced when someone reads and understands someone else's story, including their access needs. It is through storytelling that activists, like our participants, dream of, and enact equitable, educational futures that are accessible and inclusive to all.

In their stories, our participants recount their acts of self-advocacy, a necessary and essential form of activism. Not only do disabled people who practice self-advocacy demand their individual access needs but, they also help facilitate change for future disabled people's rights (Kimball et al., 2016). By recounting their stories, our participants mitigate the harms of stigma, silence, and stereotypes. Connected to their activism, they share their purposes, passions, and lived reality situated in their intersecting identities (Kimball et al., 2016). Throughout this book, the life stories illuminate just a few of the innumerable ways that disabled people, who *also* hold other minoritized identities, experience not only ableism, but other forms of discrimination (e.g., racism, classism, sexism, heterosexism, religious oppression, etc.). This focus on intersectionality is rooted in a deep history of disability justice writing which built upon wisdoms of Black, Indigenous, and brown communities (Berne et al., 2018; Kafai, 2021) as well as queer femme activists of color (Acevedo et al., 2022; Berne et al., 2018; Kafai, 2021; Mingus, 2011; Wong, 2020). In sum, the disability life stories in this book are a form of cultural activism that we hope will inspire readers to identify, resist, and end not just ableism, but all forms of oppression.

Who Are We to Share These Stories?

Collectively, we have worked in a wide variety of educational settings ranging from 6–52 years. Members of our research team have experience as: a special education teacher, a director of disability services, a student affairs professional, college faculty, college administrator, high school teacher, disability cultural center coordinator, and disability activist. Many of us also consider ourselves disability and justice activists. We each have a variety of social identities that afford us access to power and privilege as well as social identities that serve to minoritize, marginalize, or render us suspect within educational spaces. Some of us have disabilities and some of us do not. We've navigated educational, medical, and social systems ourselves, and with disabled family members. As parents and grandparents, we've advocated for, and with, our own children with disabilities. In our classrooms and research settings, we have strived to enact, and role model, inclusive and equitable practices. But, none of us know exactly what our participants have experienced. A person's experience of their disability status is shaped by their other social identities (e.g., race, class, gender, sexuality), their relationships, the communities and geographies within which they reside, and their own personal history. One thing that we remind ourselves on a regular basis is that we know only how *we* experience the world: every person's experience is unique. That is why providing space for disabled voices to come to the forefront is so very important. In doing that, the similarities and differences in the ways that people with disabilities experience the world become more clear. We are confident that readers will be deeply moved by the uniqueness, and also the patterned experiences, in the disabled life stories in this book.

Organization of the Book

As previously noted, we center disabled voices in this text. However, as authors, we bookend the stories with introductory and contextual prose. Chapter 2 contextualizes the disability life stories in prior research and practice literature. That chapter offers a brief summary of key concepts and research findings on ableism, disability models and laws, and research regarding the experiences of disabled students in primary/secondary school, higher education, and post-college contexts. It is in no way comprehensive. Instead, we aim to give readers some background knowledge of disability scholarship to situate some of the issues that emerge in the individual stories. Chapter 3 provides a description of our research project including orienting questions, methods, and a demographic overview of the participants. We used everyday language to help you understand how we conducted our research study and how this book came to be. For those looking for more scholarly descriptions of our research, we encourage you to read the scholarly papers we've published in the past (Kimball et al., 2018; Moore et al., 2020; Newman et al., 2019; Vaccaro et al., 2018, 2019a, b, 2020, 2024).

The majority of the book, Chapters 4–17, centers the voices of the participants via individual disability life stories. In each of these chapters, the disability life story begins with a brief introduction to the participant (written by us) followed by an extended first-person narrative drawing directly from participants' responses to interview questions. The disability life stories are formatted loosely for consistency. However, the uniqueness of each individual story produced chapters that focus more or less on specific topics that participants described as most salient to their experiences and life paths. Each disability life story concludes with three or four questions for reflection. We think of these questions as our opportunity to call your attention to major themes in the book or formative experiences in a person's life. By focusing on these questions across the 14 disability life stories, we hope that you will come to understand disability differently, more fully, or even more personally. Moreover, these questions—while focused by our curation—ask the reader to take responsibility for analyzing and interpreting the disability life stories in this book—opening possibilities for insights that we may never have thought of ourselves. We hope you share this book with others and, in doing so, discuss these questions.

In Chapters 18 and 19, we bring the book to a close. Chapter 18 offers advice given by the participants. Aligned with the nature of this book, the advice is in first-person language drawn directly from participant interviews. Individually and collectively, participants had such important advice that we decided a stand-alone chapter was warranted. In Chapter 19, we provide a conclusion. Here, we shift our approach and use authorial voice to synthesize highlights from participant stories into overarching insights and lessons learned. Building upon knowledge from prior chapters, the final chapter concludes with a list of questions for people with disabilities, families, educators, employers, and community organizations to inspire action.

2 Prior Research that Informs Our Work

In this chapter, we introduce concepts from theory and research about disability to provide a background to the stories you will read in Chapters 4–17. It is not a comprehensive summary of the important theories and research about disability, school, family, career, or purpose; such a review would be impossible to cover in one chapter. However, as educators, we believe it is important to introduce some of the literature that informs our perspectives, the research project, and this book. We intentionally selected topics, concepts, and issues that appear in the stories you will read in forthcoming chapters.

Throughout this book we've tried to write in a clear and readable style so that all readers can fully engage with the material. Our commitment to using an accessible writing style was a challenge in this chapter. Reviewing academic literature always tends to sound a bit formal. We also recognize that readers will have a range of pre-existing knowledge of the topics we cover. For some, the information in this chapter will be new and thought-provoking. For others, the information won't be new, and may even feel rudimentary. If this is the case, by all means, skip ahead.

We encourage you to approach this chapter based upon how you learn best. Are you someone who likes to read about theory and research to better understand and apply those concepts to people's stories? If so, you might want to continue reading. Or, are you someone who likes to hear powerful stories and then go on to learn more about topics, issues, and concepts that arise from those stories? If this is how you learn best, you may want to skip this chapter for now and dive directly into the personal stories. You can revisit this chapter later to learn about an unfamiliar topic, issue, or idea that you read about in a story. No matter which option you choose, we hope that you ultimately find this brief overview of existing scholarship illuminating and useful.

Chapter Overview

As you will discover throughout this book, the idea of disability means different things to different people and can vary in significance across times and space (Dolmage, 2017; Friedensen & Kimball, 2017). It can simultaneously

DOI: 10.4324/9781003495703-2

be understood as an identity that a disabled person can choose *and* as a label that is applied by others in ways that can be both harmful and helpful (Egner, 2019; Schalk, 2013; Schalk, 2017). In this chapter, we discuss the complexity of disability—anticipating some of the ways that our participants' stories reflect a diversity of disabled experiences and varied ways of thinking about their identities.

The chapter provides a very basic overview of topics readers might find helpful when reading the forthcoming stories. First, we explore how people and institutions define disability. Then, we summarize some of the common conceptual models used to understand disability across time. Next, we offer a brief discussion of human development concepts related to adolescence, early adulthood, identity development, and purpose. Following that, we present a very short description of disability law within the United States that existed at the time we composed this book. For brevity, we focused on policy most related to developmental and educational services—with most of the focus on the transition from high school to college and the workforce. Finally, we summarize some of the literature related to the roles that families play for disabled youth. Collectively, this literature provides a brief snapshot of where scholarship about disability and education is at present and where it might go in the future.

How People and Institutions Define Disability

This section provides a review of some of the many different ways that scholars think about disability. These definitions include those based on expert classifications such as medical and diagnostic identifications as well as those rooted in self-identification (Evans et al., 2017; Friedensen & Kimball 2017). A consideration of different ways of thinking about disability can be useful for understanding how disabled people, and those who work with and/or care about them, make sense of disability.

The way people think about the idea of disability is based on two interrelated social phenomena. First, human beings have powerful normative ideas about how people's brains and bodies are meant to look, function, and perform in social environments (Dolmage, 2017). By normative, we mean that within a culture or society, people have common, shared expectations about the characteristics or behaviors associated with certain roles. Second, human beings exist within larger social structures, especially family, school, and work, through which normative expectations are communicated (Friedensen & Kimball, 2017). When someone has a body or mind that does not align with normative expectations set by these social systems, they may be labeled as disabled or they may themselves identify in that way.

The processes of labeling and identification are never simple or straightforward. Kimball and Friedensen (2017) explored the many ways that we define disability—eventually identifying six different definitions that all inform a holistic understanding of what disability is in our social world. These definitions include: medical, diagnostic, legal, environmental, economic, and cultural. It is important to know that, like Friedensen and Kimball (2017), we do not believe that a disabled person must be labeled, or identified as such, according to any or all of these definitions.

Medical Definitions

A medical definition of disability refers to a health condition that significantly limits a person's physical, mental, or sensory abilities to perform major life activities. The medical condition may prove to be a disability depending on the context in which a person is required, or desires to, participate. As Tom Shakespeare (2012) notes, even attempts to define disability ecologically must acknowledge the underlying reality that disabled bodies and minds differ from their non-disabled counterparts. Moreover, those differences often represent real challenges for disabled people—regardless of the way that physical and social environments are constructed. For example, a person with a chronic health condition that compromises their immune system faces risks in interacting with other persons regardless of how well these interactions for universal inclusion are designed (Creasman, 2021; Variono, 2024). Masking, air cleaning, and other public health strategies can reduce, but never eliminate, the reality that an immunocompromised person is more likely to get sick or have more prolonged or severe illnesses than a person who is not managing this chronic illness. Shakespeare (2012) contends that we will never be able to shed the underlying medical dimension of disability. Indeed, some disabled people argue that we should not try. Although medical providers can gatekeep who gets to count as "disabled," they also can provide life-affirming, life-sustaining care needed for a disabled person to flourish (Shakespeare et al., 2009).

Diagnostic Definitions

To access the life-affirming, life-sustaining care practices described in the section on medical definitions, disabled people typically require a formal diagnosis rendered by a diagnostician deemed appropriate by a community of practice related to a particular disability or type of disabilities (Brueggmann et al., 2008; Watson et al., 2011). For example, assessment from an audiologist is typically required to diagnose a hearing impairment but cannot typically diagnose dyslexia. Conversely, a school psychologist can typically diagnose specific language learning disabilities such as dyslexia, but not hearing impairments. In both cases, however, the diagnosis does not change the underlying physiological reality for a disabled person. They do not hear or read in the way that aligns with the normative expectations for society (Moser, 2000). Yet, without a diagnosis, a disabled person is unlikely to be able to access needed care or support (Son et al., 2019; Whittle et al., 2018). While not universal in the forthcoming stories, many of our participants revealed that a disability diagnosis functioned both as an important catalyst to help them understand their own identity, and as a powerful tool in opening access to needed services, especially in their PreK-12 learning experiences, via an Individualized Education Program (IEP) or an accommodation under the Americans with Disabilities Act (ADA) or Section 504 of the Rehabilitation Act of 1973.

Many disability rights and protections under the federal laws are explicitly, or implicitly, linked to a formal diagnosis (Thomas, 2000). That linkage can be problematic, however, when the diagnosis is criterion-based. A criterion-based diagnosis means that diagnosticians use specialized instruments—for example, an educational test or a medical device—to determine whether a person has a disability. In that measurement, there is typically a particular score above which a disability is diagnosed and below which it is not (Maddocks et al., 2018; Mac-Nicholas et al., 2018). As has been shown in other contexts, however, there is rarely a stark difference between someone scoring one point above an established threshold and a person scoring one point below (Angrist & Pischke, 2009). This means that a person can experience some hearing loss without being diagnosed as hearing impaired or some difficulty in skills of decoding without being diagnosed as dyslexic. We should also note that over time, with changing leadership, and policy alterations, the scores which serve as thresholds for diagnoses, may change—and in turn dramatically impact the services and support a disabled person is entitled to.

Measuring and diagnosing a disability is not always clear cut or effective. For example, there is no single diagnostic test to reach a diagnosis of autism spectrum disorder (CDC, 2024). The diagnosis may involve clinical interviews, standardized diagnostic tools, multidisciplinary assessment by a team of professionals, a detailed history of the child's progress in reaching early milestones, observations of the child's social interactions, communication skills, and behavioral patterns. Many sources of information are needed to reach a diagnosis and to determine the appropriate accommodation and modifications that would support an individual on the spectrum.

Given the complexity (and cost) of reaching any diagnosis, there has been pushback on the use of diagnostic criteria to determine who may self-identify as disabled within the disability justice community (Parekh & Brown, 2020; Watson, 2002). Nonetheless, the establishment of a diagnostic criterion remains important in a whole host of legal, medical, bureaucratic, and educational contexts.

Legal Definitions

Disability is a protected status in the United States (Thomas, 2000). Three federal laws primarily define how people with disabilities are protected across the lifespan today. The Rehabilitation Act of 1973, which requires any agency or organization which receives federal funding, such as institutions of higher education and public PK-12 schools, to ensure that people with disabilities are not discriminated against. The Act broadly defines disability as any mental or physical impairment that limits a daily life activity. The Section 504 of the Rehabilitation Act of 1973 requires that federally funded agencies provide reasonable accommodations to disabled people (U.S. Congress, 1973, § 504). In 1975, the Education for All Handicapped Children Act (public law 94-142) was signed into law after a number of lawsuits found students with disabilities in PreK-12 settings were not being provided with an appropriate education. This law was later renamed the Individuals with Disabilities Education Act (IDEA) (1990, 2004) and currently serves as the contemporary federal law that ensures children with disabilities are provided with a free appropriate public education from birth to age 22. IDEA narrowly recognizes 13 disability categories of which a student with a disability can be found eligible for services (U.S. Department of Education, 2004, § 1400). Finally, the Americans with Disabilities Act (ADA) of 1990 is to protect the civil rights of persons with disabilities, including protection from discrimination within places of employment, public spaces and services, while also ensuring access to legal remedies (U.S. Congress, 1990, § 12101). The ADA has a specific definition of what is considered a disability under the act. To learn more about what is meant by a physical or mental impairment that substantially limits major life activities, we recommend going to the website of the ADA National Network (adata.org) and read the fact sheet on how disability is defined. Later in this chapter we further explore these legal protections as they relate to transitions from school, post-secondary education, and employment.

In the United States, a lot rests on the shoulders of the disabled person or, in the case of a minor, the person's parent/guardian, to pursue a claim of discrimination and to seek legal remedies. Claims of discrimination typically require a demonstration of a specific and actual harm (Thomas, 2000). For example, lawsuits brought to challenge inaccessibility typically happen at the expense of the disabled person who brings it and are often settled out-of-court or via a non-public consent decree (Krieger, 2010). The net effect is that the legal definition of a disabled person under the law is reduced to those with formal diagnoses required to meet the legal standard, the knowledge that their rights have been violated, and the economic resources to pursue the enforcement of those rights. While all that plays out, the conditions of inaccessibility are allowed to persist. And even once adjudicated, organizations must only provide accommodations to the disabled person that are absolutely necessary for access and which are reasonable given the financial realities of the organization (Thomas, 2000).

Although well-intentioned, the resulting Americans with Disabilities Act actually requires non-disabled people to change very little. Moreover, a subset of privileged disabled persons gain substantially more rights than other disabled people, and the majority of disabled persons benefit little (Davis, 2015;

Peters, 2022). For example, disability advocates—both those with and without disabilities—have long-argued for universal design approaches to disability such that most physical and social spaces are accessible by design (Rose, 2000). However, legal frameworks in the United States are largely reactive (McNicholas et al., 2018). New buildings may be required to meet some minimum standards for accessibility, which are themselves insufficient, but older buildings are not. During renovations, spaces may be required to meet minimum accessibility requirements. However, if the organization doing the renovation decides that complying with the law may be too expensive, they may opt not to renovate, evade compliance, or risk the consequences for ignoring the law outright (Krieger, 2010). This pattern occurs on many college campuses when students, faculty, and staff in inaccessible spaces are simply reassigned to offices or classrooms that they can access. Campus administrators often argue that simply shifting classrooms, or locating an office in a different building altogether, would be a sufficient means to address the underlying inaccessibility of campus spaces. Of course, this process only happens when a disabled person knows to complain and takes the time and energy to do so. The insufficiency of these solutions is certainly a problem, but a bigger problem still is that only a narrow subset of disabled people will ever be able to pursue them.

Environmental Definitions

Disability can also be defined environmentally based on the key role that physical and social spaces play in determining the experiences of disabled people (Nathan & Brown, 2018). Environmental definitions of disability assume that people do have underlying variations in their bodies and minds. They also acknowledge that most variations in physiology can be accommodated with sufficient advance attention to accessibility including the concept of universal design. Environmental definitions of disability suggest that physical and social spaces can be disabling when inaccessible or not inclusive. When they are accessible, it makes potential underlying variations in physiology less important in producing disability than the choices of others within the environment.

By way of example, many neurodivergent people struggle with things like excessive stimuli, unclear instructions, and the hidden norms regarding social interactions across power differences (e.g., how to interact with a teacher, how to behave around a police officer) (Kennedy et al., 2000). Neurodiverse people do have underlying differences in the ways their brains work relative to neurotypical peers, but those variations only become a problem in an environment when physical and social spaces are constructed to normalize the experiences of those neurotypical peers rather than being inclusive of neurodiverse persons (Dwyer, 2022). Framed from this perspective, inaccessible, unwelcoming, and even hostile environments create disabling conditions. The variations in bodies and minds which could function well in more accessible spaces, only become problematic when environments are chaotic, noisy, inaccessible, or where instructions for behavior are unclear.

Economic Definitions

A person's economic resources play a powerful role in determining how they will manage the costs associated with their disability. A person's socioeconomic status may impact access to needed medical care and may determine whether or not a disabled person can pursue legal protections to which they are entitled (Friedensen & Kimball, 2017). Moreover, given the realities of inadequate financial support in places like schools and the workplace, required accommodations may not be provided. Economic factors can also determine whether disabled people are likely to incur what has been called the "disability tax," which refers to the hidden monetary costs associated with being disabled (Olsen et al., 2022). These can include things like specialized technologies, additional supportive care, or access to specialized equipment (Shaheen & Lohnes Watulak, 2019). Disability taxes can also include copays for medical care and additional costs for transportation for the routine demands of daily life.

Studies have consistently shown that, even controlling for level of preparation, disabled people are much less likely to be employed, and when employed, they are far more likely to be underemployed than non-disabled peers (Sevak et al., 2015; U.S. Bureau of Statistics, 2024). There is a long history of public policy that actively discourages high-wage work for disabled people. Legislation authorizing the creation of sheltered workshops permits disabled people to be paid pennies on the dollar to provide low-skilled labor for manufacturing industries (Gill, 2005). Social security and healthcare policies allow needed benefits to be withdrawn if a disabled person earns too much to qualify but earns too little to meet their basic needs (Malli et al., 2018).

Even more significantly, the economic dimensions of disability extend both backward and forward generationally. Given that some disabling conditions are inherited, parents of disabled children may be more likely to be disabled themselves resulting in suppressed career outcomes relative to parents of non-disabled children. What is more, parents of disabled children are more likely to miss work more frequently for childcare-related reasons, choose to work in less demanding roles, and realize lower take home pay on average than parents of non-disabled children. When disabled people have children, these economic forces extend to the subsequent generation. The quality of schools is strongly correlated with the income of community residents. Since disabled people have lower incomes on average than non-disabled persons, the children of disabled parents are likely to attend less well-resourced, lower quality schools (Horowitz & Souza. 2011). Moreover, since these schools may not be fully accessible, disabled parents may not be able to participate fully in the school-based activities. For example, disabled caregivers might miss out on participation in parent-teacher conferences, volunteering in the school, or joining parent organizations (Rivera Drew, 2009). Schools are the primary site for diagnosing disabilities in children. Yet, the frequency and accuracy of those diagnoses are themselves correlated with how well-resourced the school is (Son et al., 2019). When a school district has limited resources for comprehensive diagnostic services, families with greater economic means have the opportunity to seek non-school diagnostic services. Paying for such services are far more challenging, and in some cases impossible, for low-income families to afford.

Cultural Definitions

Disabled activists have argued that disabled people should have the capacity to determine how they will identify and label themselves (Abes & Wallace, 2020). For some within the pan-disability community, this philosophy means breaking with the label of disability altogether in favor of an identity-based specific diagnosis (for example, the culturally Deaf) or lived experience (for example, neurodiversity). Regardless of the approach, a cultural definition of disability acknowledges that disability is a social identity that may be more, or less, salient to a person's sense of self. For many who view disability in cultural terms, it can be a deeply meaningful part of how they understand themselves in the world. It structures their lived experiences, perspectives, relationships, and interactions within social institutions.

Disability-as-culture also acknowledges the active knowledge production of disabled people and the values, norms, traditions, and creative traditions they share with one another (McRuer, 2018). For example, among those with hearing impairments, only a subset of deaf people identify as culturally Deaf, with the d/Deaf distinction conveying the active choice of Deaf persons to participate in distinct cultural processes. Those include: the creation of a distinct linguistic practice in American Sign Language (ASL); the creation of distinct Deaf artistic practices in areas like literature and cinema; the creation of substantially separate social institutions such as Deaf educational institutions; and the ongoing development of a Deaf politics (Padden & Humphries, 2006). Many of these same features are now shared in common with the community of autistic self-advocates who have worked to redefine autism. For instance, Kafai (2021) describes a move away from the focus on parental grief over not having a neurotypical child perpetuated by Autism Speaks to the consideration of neurodiversity as a routine feature of human diversity as described by the Autistic Self Advocacy Network. Still other groups—for example, disability cultural centers, are appearing with increasing frequency on college and university campuses. Often, these cultural centers take a pan-disability approach—arguing that all disabled people, regardless of diagnoses, share in common the experience of living in a world constructed largely for the non-disabled (Chiang, 2020).

Within communities that emphasize disability as a cultural identity, a primary goal is to create a sense of belonging and solidarity among those who have identities that can make them feel different or unwelcome (Jenks, 2019). Further, these cultural communities seek to use advocacy and activism to argue for a more accessible, inclusive world (Kafai, 2021). They do so in part by rejecting deficit perspectives that problematize disabled bodies and minds—arguing instead that disability is simply a form of human diversity. The psychiatric survivors movement, in particular, pushes back on the idea that mental health conditions require a "cure" (Cohen, 2005). They do so by suggesting that self-determination must remain a paramount goal and that involuntary treatment is a form of violence. Their goal is not to tell other disabled people what choices they should make regarding treatment but rather to advocate to the medical establishment that these choices should be their own.

Common Conceptual Models of Disability

In the preceding sections, Kimball and Friedensen (2017) sought to understand how and when disability is defined in the lives of disabled people. In contrast, Evans et al. (2017) have inventoried the *ways that society thinks about disability*. By exploring these ideas—and comparing them to issues of disability definition—it is possible to better understand how the idea of disability functions in our physical and social world. Thinking about models of disability has evolved over time. New models of disability do not replace old models. Instead, earlier models of disability continue to inform thinking about disability in tandem with whatever model is most common at any given time. By reviewing the historical evolution of models of disability, one can better appreciate the complex sets of ideas that inform current societal thinking.

Discussions of the history of disability models typically begins with the **moral model**, which was originally anchored in religion and which now has dimensions associated with economic productivity (Evans et al., 2017). According to the moral model, disability can be understood as a personal deficit—perhaps one associated with divine disfavor. For example, some religious traditions include texts wherein a protagonist is punished or experiences a test of faith by divinely sent disabling conditions (Schuelka, 2013). Or, the moral model can be reflected in a personal character flaw, as in the belief that a disabled person's inability to work might be malingering (Rose, 2017). Within a moral model of disability, the social stigmatization of a disabled person is understandable, and indeed even desirable. A non-disabled person has a vested interest in avoiding the moral condemnation experienced by the disabled and might even wonder why they must labor when the disabled person does not. Consequently, disability is viewed as a personal problem that the disabled person must solve or manage alone. The moral model fosters little social interest in supporting disabled persons.

With the advent of Enlightenment Era science in the 1600s and 1700s and modern medicine in the 1800s, the moral model began to give way to the **medical model**, which acknowledged the underlying physiological causes of disability (Evans et al., 2017). While moral models sought to cure a defective person's soul or character, in a medical model, the defect requiring correction was increasingly understood to be beyond a person's control. However, the medical model problematizes a person's body or mind as flawed or not normal. It does not acknowledge the broader context within which disability is experienced (Hayes & Hannold, 2007). Instead, the goal is to help return the disabled body or mind to a "normal" or healthy state as soon as possible (Beauchamp-Pryor, 2011).

The **rehabilitation model** grew out of the medical model in the late 1800s. It was the first major model of disability in widespread use that did not overtly suggest the need for a moral or medical cure (Evans et al., 2017). Instead, the rehabilitation model sought to address a functional limitation so that a disabled person might participate more fully in the activities of daily life (Imrie, 1997). A goal of rehabilitation sometimes could involve a return to full and typical functionality. For example, physical therapy following a spinal injury that does not result in paralysis can restore the ability to walk. The rehabilitation model could also involve the development of alternative capacities to approximate normative functioning. One example of an alternative capacity is the teaching of manualism (sign-language) or oralism (lip-reading and mimicked speech) in the education of deaf and hearing-impaired children (Edwards, 2012). Arguing for self-sufficiency, the rehabilitation movement strongly prioritizes the adaptive change of disabled people instead of changes in attitudes or accommodations in the broader society.

In many ways, the **social model** of disability can be understood as a reaction to that position, arguing that if a disabled person cannot participate fully in society, then society is at fault. The social model was the first approach to recognize that the experience of disability is influenced by societal barriers and exclusions (Evans et al., 2017). The social model makes clear that a person's functional impairments matter less in determining their experiences than the attitudes and behaviors of the people around them (Fine & Asch, 1988). In so doing, the social model shifted the primary perspective on disability away from a medical cure and toward intentional thinking about accessibility, inclusion, and systemic change. While a notable shift in approach relative to the models that preceded it, the social model still focused primarily on the individual.

The **minority group model**, sometimes referred to as the human diversity or socio-political model, was the first to recognize disabled people as a collective group. The minority group model suggested, for the first time, that disability should be considered as a social identity in the same way that people think about themselves in terms of their race, class, gender, sexuality, or other social identities (Evans et al., 2017). In so doing, the minority group model recognized that disabled people have long shared knowledge and created community with one another (Hartblay, 2020; Taylor, 2018). The minority group model did not appear until the 1960s and was not formalized until the 1970s as part of the emerging disability rights movement (Nielsen, 2012). In defining and helping to create disabled people as a collective with real political power, the minority model both catalyzed and reflected a growing community of disabled activists and advocates who worked in solidarity with those seeking racial and gender equity (Ferguson, 2012).

The minority group model anticipated a variety of **social justice model** approaches to disability. The social justice model explicitly argues that disability exists because **ableism** exists. Ableism refers to the normalization of non-disabled experiences and the active devaluation or discrimination of disabled people. It structures the way that physical and social spaces are organized (Evans et al., 2017). Ableism describes what happens when people without disabilities create a world that disabled people live in. That happens because many people without disabilities do not think about disability and also because they may prioritize their needs above those with disabilities. It affects the way that disabled people think about themselves and about others—with and without disabilities. Ableism is part of a complex web of power relations that affords power to those with some identities (majoritarian identities-such as non-disabled) and which creates the conditions for oppression for those with others (minoritized identities-such as disabled). The social justice model argues that disability justice is part of a broader struggle for a more just, equitable social world. It seeks to overturn an established set of social practices that work for a narrow few and disadvantage a greater many.

We conclude this section by pointing out that disability cannot be understood by using one model just as it cannot be defined in only one way. Every person experiences disability differently. As you will see in the forthcoming stories, the diversity of experience is shaped by a person's stage of life, identities, social roles, stature, and different environmental contexts they encounter. Disability is inherently complex and understanding it in a nuanced way requires a range of definitional tools and conceptual models. Mixing and matching these as the situation warrants is perhaps the best way of thinking about disability. No matter which definition or model resonates with you, the best approach is to listen to, and work with, disabled persons in ways that are inclusive to their unique experiences and needs.

Human Development and Identity

In this section, we review some literature related to adolescence and early adulthood as these were the points in their lives at which we interviewed most of our participants. Using selected insights from human development theory, we describe some of the changes in brain, body, relationships, and self-understanding that occur in early and later adolescence and early adulthood (Galván, 2013; 2018; Newman & Newman, 2018). At the same time that these developmental changes take place, young people are navigating changing contexts including middle and high school, college, work, and family settings as well as their position in society. We note the developmental work that occurs for most college-aged students as they come to understand their sense of self—including their disability identity—in more complex ways (Patton et al., 2016). One of the fundamental themes of this book is that every body and mind is different from every other body and mind. We urge you to keep this in mind as you think about the lived experiences of young people as they move through the stages of adolescence and early adulthood.

Adolescence, Early Adulthood, and Purpose

Erikson (1950/1963) provided the foundational understanding for how adolescence and early adulthood are viewed in the context of the lifespan. According to Erikson, a person's primary goal across the lifespan is to understand oneself in the context of caring relationships with others and meaningful work toward significant life goals. These relationships and goals may vary from person-to-person, but those who live fulfilling lives can typically identify decisions made with integrity toward these significant life commitments. For Damon (2008), these commitments are what give our lives purpose, and purpose is what gives our lives meaning. Purpose functions as a unifying principle by which we organize information about who we are. It helps us make decisions about those with whom to form and maintain relationships. It is a guiding principle that allows us to choose between one path and another, and it is an overarching belief structure that gives a stable and persistent sense of self. As in the case of many of our participants, individuals often change college majors and jobs. Yet, they can still hold steadfast in their commitment to a life of helping others. With major and job changes, they did not compromise the core of who they were. Rather, they found an unexpected pathway toward the realization of their purpose. How we make decisions about purpose is the result of developmental processes that influence our bodies, minds, understandings of self, and relationships to others.

Adolescence begins with puberty (Newman & Newman, 2018) which includes increased hormonal production, accompanied by rapid physical growth and dramatic changes to the brain. There is considerable variation in the onset of puberty. Although, for those assigned female at birth, it begins a year or so earlier than for those assigned male at birth. In addition to age of onset, pubertal changes show variations in the sequence of changes and the duration of puberty until a person reaches their adult height and body shape. Both early onset and delayed puberty have increased in recent years as the result of the increased prevalence of endocrine disrupting chemicals in our food and water supply, changes in overall levels of physical activity, and overall nutrition or malnutrition (Galván, 2017). Although puberty is typically associated with both observable physical changes (e.g., increased body hair, changes in body shape, acne) and temporary pubertal characteristics (e.g., challenges with emotional regulation, temporary changes in voice), the major physiological changes that occur typically include a rapid growth spurt, the maturation of the reproductive system, and changes in neuroarchitecture. These changes in neuroarchitecture catalyze the beginning of increasingly sophisticated understandings of the world, oneself, and others (Patton et al., 2016). As these shifts occur, the cognitive development and self-regulation of adolescents increases in tandem— eventually reaching adult levels in what is referred to as executive function including: attention, memory, metacognition, and capacity for abstract thought (Patton et al., 2016). New levels of executive function bring a greater ability to regulate impulses, and to make decisions by evaluating among alternatives with consideration for their consequences. These changes continue into the early twenties at least, and perhaps as late as the early thirties. One particularly important shift that occurs in late adolescence or early adulthood is the dramatic increase in the ability to think in contextual or relativistic ways (Baxter Magolda & King, 2007). These ways of thinking are essential to the ability to engage in perspective-taking—looking at problems from multiple points of view—which is essential for belonging in groups and the long-term maintenance of caring relationships.

Throughout the periods of adolescence and early adulthood, a number of important changes occur in understanding of self and others. Identity development involves understanding one's social identities, exploring various roles, and clarifying one's commitments to personal values and goals (Kett, 2003). During this time, young people typically develop a greater understanding of themselves that evolves and is continuously reconstructed as people's roles in society change and they encounter changing social demands. Adolescence and early adulthood are also critical time periods for refining and enacting a sense of purpose linked to a self-concept that describes who a person wants to be in the world—and perhaps even more importantly—who they do not want to be. The successful pursuit of goals and achievement of developmental milestones during this time creates confidence, while a lack of success can result in the foreclosure of developmental processes and an impediment in the ability to thrive (Archer & Waterman, 1990).

In the United States, the traditional markers between late adolescence and early adulthood are the arrival at the age of majority (age 18), the conclusion of public schooling (typically graduation from high school or the age at which you can legally leave high school), and entrance into the workforce (Arnett, 2007). Since World War II, increasing percentages of high school graduates have pursued higher education immediately upon high school graduation. For those who choose to enter post-secondary education, the environment provides young people with opportunities to consider career options, explore moral and ethical values, and encounter intellectual challenges that stimulate executive functioning. Meanwhile, over the past 25 years, the achievement of traditional markers of adulthood has been delayed (Kett, 2003). In the past, the decade of the 20s was expected to be a time for achieving financial independence, autonomy from parental control, and the establishment of commitments to work, intimacy and family formation (Newman & Newman, 2018). Some theorists, such as Arnett (2007), have argued that this shift has created a distinct developmental phase between adolescence and early adulthood called *emerging adulthood*. Whereas generations prior enjoyed comparatively high pay, comparatively low-cost housing, and a societal assumption of limited geographic mobility, the economic and social winds have shifted thereby delaying the achievement of many of these markers (Coté, 2014). The COVID-19 pandemic exacerbated, but did not cause, many of these pressures. As a result, and as you will witness in the forthcoming stories, many of our participants still want the same things that have traditionally been associated with adulthood—financial independence, a satisfying career, meaningful relationships, and affordable housing. However, as the literature suggests, the struggle to accomplish these goals seems harder to realize than ever before.

Our Prior Work on Disability, Purpose, and Identity

As we shared in the introductory chapter, this book is not our first attempt to make sense of our participants' experiences. To date, we have published twelve articles that characterize our participants' experiences relative to (and in some cases in contrast to) a scholarly consensus about disability in higher education. Reviewing the key findings from these studies will help to provide a holistic perspective on how disabled students experience ableism, navigate stigma and bullying, develop a sense of identity, and foster a sense of purpose. You will read about all of these phenomena through first person accounts in the forthcoming stories.

In Vaccaro et al. (2018), we proposed a model that describes how disabled college students developed a sense of purpose. It was an essential part of the way they "narrated the self." Purpose helps to mediate between the ways that the broader social world constructs ideas about disability and career and the story that disabled people tell about themselves. Within this framework, purpose is the lens by which a disabled college student can determine whether a major is a good fit based on interest, how supportive the learning environment is, and what they project their future career to look like. In Moore et al. (2020), we used this approach to show how different disabled college students make different decisions using these same building blocks. Specifically, aspiring teachers reported deciding to: persist toward their goal even while feeling unsupported, go in a different direction entirely, and/or figure out a new pathway toward their purpose.

Throughout the stories in this book, our participants talk about experiences with disability related stigma and discrimination. Disability stigma refers to the negative assumptions that people have about disability and disabled people (Evans et al., 2017; Fine & Asch, 1988). Stigma can be external—that is, directed at a disabled person by others—or internalized-that is, a set of negative beliefs about oneself (Silvan-Ferrero et al., 2020). Disability stigma is pervasive in society (Neilsen, 2012) and it leads people both to ignore the needs of disabled people and to act in ways hostile to their needs and interests (Dolmage, 2017). One example of this hostility is bullying, which disabled people experience at a much higher rate than their non-disabled peers (Rose et al., 2015). Just a few manifestations of bullying can include social exclusion, hurtful communications, physical attacks, and cyberbullying. Disabled people are also at higher risk for sexual violence and other violent crimes relative to their non-disabled peers (Basile et al., 2016). The literature about stigma and bullying suggests that these phenomena stem both from the devaluation of disabled lives and an underlying discomfort with the idea of disability (Watson & Larson, 2006). No matter the reasons why people hold prejudicial attitudes and behave in exclusionary ways—the impact is deeply harmful to disabled people. In our prior work, we delved into various forms of stigma and bullying as well as creative coping strategies disabled students used to combat all forms of exclusion in K-12 and college settings (Vaccaro et al., 2019). Some of the ways young people responded to bullying included: talking openly about disability and articulating their needs using available resources, practicing good self-care, working hard to succeed and challenging stereotypes, and viewing disability as a positive aspect of self.

From our participants we learned that disability was not the only identity that shaped their sense of self, outlook, interactions, and experiences in the world. In the introduction, we referenced intersectionality. The concept is rooted in a deep history of disability justice which was built upon wisdoms of Black, Indigenous, and brown communities (Acevedo, 2022; Berne, 2018; Crenshaw, 1989, 1991; Kafai, 2021; Mingus, 2011; Piepzna-Samarasinha, 2018; Wong, 2020). A comprehensive discussion of intersectionality is beyond the scope of this chapter. But it does warrant attention. At the most basic level, intersectionality refers to the ways systems of oppression are experienced as a result of social identity overlap and produce divergent experiences for individuals based on those disparate overlaps (Cooper, 2016). Examples of this complexity can be found in the forthcoming stories of Tippi, Yolanda, and Justice.

Throughout this book, the disability life stories illuminate just a few of the many ways that disabled people experience ableism as well as other forms of discrimination (e.g. racism, classism, sexism, heterosexism, religious oppression, etc.). The unique constellations of social identities—intersecting with disabilities—led to unique experiences and perspectives that shaped identity development. For example, in Vaccaro et al. (2019), we showed that social class helps to explain how disabled college students think about their disability and how it informs their purpose development. Students from less-privileged economic backgrounds typically reported having less time and space to think about disability-as-identity. Many participants prioritized career pathways that were connected with greater economic certainty. Meanwhile, their more well-to-do disabled peers reported fewer long-term financial concerns. They expressed confidence that parents or other family members would support them in difficult circumstances.

Elsewhere, we demonstrated that college-going disabled women struggled to distinguish between barriers and hostilities directed toward them as a result of their disability and their gender (Vaccaro et al., 2020). In their experiences, they were viewed as less-than by both ableist behavior and gender-based discrimination. For many, this construction led to the feeling that they had to prove themselves—even if this belief was itself rooted in ableism. In a separate study that centered on gender and sexuality (Kimball et al., 2018), we illustrated the complicated ways that disability, gender, and sexual oppression shaped the identities and daily realities of disabled youth.

All of this prior work has led us to this book. In the forthcoming chapters, you will read extended stories that cover all of these topics—disability, purpose, and identity—in much more depth.

Transitions and the Law

To fully appreciate the forthcoming disability life stories, a basic understanding of disability law is helpful. Under the Individuals with Disabilities Education Act (IDEA) and subsequent amendments (IDEAA), children with disabilities from birth through age 22 are legally protected and guaranteed services by any educational agency within the United States that receives federal funding. From birth through age 3, children with disabilities can be provided with early intervention services, which typically focus on helping a child meet developmental milestones. Early intervention services often occur within the home of the child. Early intervention typically supports children who have disabilities diagnosed at birth or shortly after birth and focuses on services for a child in their natural environment through an individualized family service plan (IFSP). Starting at age 3, children with disabilities who are found eligible for specialized instruction are entitled to an individualized education program (IEP), a legal document that details the accommodations, modifications, and legally binding services that are required to support a child with a disability. IDEAA requires that PreK-12 students who qualify to receive special education services free of charge, which may include speech and language therapy, physical therapy, occupational therapy, nursing, adaptive physical education, or instructional support. IDEAA requires caregiver/guardian input and permission for services to be implemented. A comprehensive review of the experiences of, and services for, disabled youth in elementary, middle and high school is beyond the scope of this chapter. Given the significant transitions that occur between high school and college—and that you'll read about in the forthcoming stories—we provide some legal and educational context for this transition next.

Under the Individuals with Disabilities Education Act and subsequent amendments (IDEAA), school districts must begin transition planning for students with individualized education program (IEP) plans by age 16 (McNicholas et al., 2018). Some state governments set the age, or grade level, lower and the individual needs of a student may also warrant an earlier start. Transition planning is a structured process designed to help a disabled student develop the skills needed for career, independent living, or future education. Based on the needs of a disabled student, a transition plan may include an extension of school services beyond typical age or completion criteria. By law, transition plans are supposed to be individualized and jointly established by the transitions team—including the student (Trainor et al., 2016).

The reality, however, is that transition planning sits within special education divisions that are typically understaffed and underfunded. Moreover, since transition planning takes place within school settings—not necessarily designed for that purpose—it is challenging to deliver life skills for independent living and gainful employment effectively (Grigal et al., 2018). Because of understaffing and underfunding, educators often have to focus limited resources on the needs of students who are not on a college-going track (Cobb & Alwell, 2009). As established above, there can be major disparities in the diagnosis of disability—and understaffing in schools can contribute to this problem. In some cases, these disparities result in material differences in the availability of diagnostic services to youth in a given school system or community. For example, a school district may not employ an educational psychologist. In other cases, however, the diagnosis gap is caused by what Leonardo and Broderick (2011) have called *smartness as ideological property*. Smartness as ideological property means that teachers and administrators have underlying assumptions about what a "good" student looks and acts like. That plays out in two ways: (1) it makes "smart" a more important identity than disabled for "good" students; and (2) it uses disability to excuse a lack of learning for "bad" students (Leonardo & Broderick, 2011). As Leonardo and Broderick (2011) have shown, these functions of smartness as ideological property connect ableism and racism in ways that make white students more likely to be identified as "smart" than racially-minoritized students.

In much the same way, twice-exceptional students—those with both a disability diagnosis and test scores that demonstrate giftedness have access to academic resources that other disabled students may not (Foley-Nicpon et al., 2103). They may also be cut off from needed disability support services because special education services are not associated with "smartness" (Reis et al., 2014), which can inhibit their ability to develop needed academic, social, and/or emotional skills. Indeed, one of the most pernicious effects of twice-exceptional discourses may be their capacity to normalize masking behaviors among disabled students such that latent disabilities may go undiagnosed for years as students try to demonstrate that they meet their schools' criteria for "good" students (Radulski, 2022). Even when identified and diagnosed, twice-exceptional students who perform well academically in high school may not be fully prepared for successfully transitioning into college, career, or life beyond high school.

Lack of coordination between school districts, families, services providers, and potential employers can also serve as a barrier to successful transition planning (Trainor et al., 2016). In an ideal world, transition services would have stronger linkages to higher education institutions given the age-typified behaviors of college search and college attendance (Trainor et al., 2016). Many colleges and universities fear being perceived as lowering standards by including students who would not traditionally go to college (Grigal et al., 2018). Others may be unaware of available resources, have concerns about necessary accommodations, or doubt whether faculty and staff are ready to meet the needs of disabled students (Trainor et al., 2016). As a result, while many students with disabilities do transition to college, they do so largely on their own and without the help of either PK-12 or higher education systems. When they transition to college, they face a complicated shift in the underlying logic of disability support. In PK-12 settings, most disabled students qualify for services under the IDEAA, which creates affirmative obligations on the behalf of PK-12 schools to identify and support disabled students. The IDEAA does so through six core principles, which include:

1 **Free and Appropriate Public Education (FAPE)**—FAPE establishes the legal right to an education in a public school setting tailored to the needs of the disabled student.
2 **Appropriate Evaluation**—When a student is identified as potentially having a disability, the school district is required to undertake the right comprehensive assessment at its own expense and to share the results with parents or guardians.
3 **Individualized Education Program (IEP)**—The IEP is an individualized plan developed collaboratively by a team that includes some combination of the student, parents or guardians, teachers, and specialists involved in a student's education.
4 **Least Restrictive Environment (LRE)**—LRE means that a disabled student must be educated alongside non-disabled peers to the maximum extent possible and must have comparable educational opportunities to the maximum extent possible.
5 **Parent and Student Participation**—This provision means that parents and students are equal participants in the development of the IEP.

6 **Procedural Safeguards**—The IDEAA provides procedural safeguards allowing parents to object to plans with which they disagree and requires school districts to regularly inform parents of their rights in the IEP process.

The net effect of the IDEAA is a system that requires school districts to act proactively to support disabled students. The process also incorporates parents/guardians of disabled students.

When shifting to higher education, the primary legal framework is the Americans with Disabilities Amendment Act (ADAA) along with Section 504 of the Rehabilitation Act, which we reviewed above in the section on legal definitions of disability. As a reminder, the ADAA is a reactive model that requires that disabled people seek accommodations under the law and that they sue if their rights are violated. This shift in logic can be quite confusing for many disabled students who had accommodations in high school. Even if they are legally entitled to accommodations in college, they must request them. If a student does not submit a formal request, the college is not legally required to provide these services. When disabled students try to succeed in college without needed accommodations, they often achieve lower grades and persist at much lower rates than would otherwise be predicted based on the strength of their academic records (Blasey et al., 2023; Mamboleo et al., 2020). Moreover, since higher education institutions are bound by the Family Educational Rights and Privacy Act (FERPA), rules that restrict access to student information, many parents who previously advocated effectively for their children in PK-12 settings, find themselves thwarted by college and university bureaucracies (Mamboleo et al., 2020). While FERPA waivers do exist, navigating them can be challenging.

The shift in onus from PreK-12 educational systems and families to college students themselves can be daunting for young people. As such, the development of self-advocacy and self-determination skills is critically important for disabled students. However, as noted above, transition processes may be ill-suited to teach these and other critically important life skills. As such, we have noted how important it is to actively foster the development of self-advocacy skills in children and youth (Daly-Cano et al., 2024). Young people need to hone these skills well before they transition into college and find themselves navigating new and unfamiliar systems.

The literature shows that collegiate disability services are both important and accessed too infrequently by students (Edwards et al., 2022; Lightner et al., 2012). Given the transition hurdles noted above, this comes as no surprise. Moreover, collegiate disability services offices are typically understaffed and many offices struggle to provide disability services at the start and end of semesters when the volume of requests for accommodations is at their highest (Lightner et al., 2012). Therefore, most colleges provide limited support services to disabled students. Colleges that can provide more extensive services often do so on a fee-for-services basis—which leads to greater disparities for families with and without economic resources.

As noted, college disability support services are provided in response to a request for accommodations (Mamboleo et al., 2020). These accommodations typically support student involvement in curricular or non-curricular learning spaces through one or more discreet strategies (Edwards et al., 2022). Ideally, the accommodations are tailored for a student's specific learning needs. Just a few of the many examples include: extended testing time; note taking; early access to materials; digital resources; and priority registration. Accommodations have positive effects on students' success outcomes (Blasey et al., 2023). But, there can be widespread confusion among students, faculty, and staff regarding their implementation (Edwards et al., 2022). This confusion may result in inconsistent utilization patterns by students. In fact, studies suggest that many disabled students pursue accommodations only after struggling, and some never utilize services for which they are eligible (Lightner et al., 2012).

One of the places that students struggle the most is in the classroom. Even with accommodations, many college courses are taught in ways that don't meet all learner needs. Yet, we know from universal design that the educational system can be accessible. Universal design approaches originated in architecture but have since expanded to focus on teaching, learning, and educational design (Peters, 2022; Rose, 2000). In higher education, universal design has become the overarching philosophy for a variety of approaches. For example, universal design for instruction (Burgstahler, 2009) and universal design for research (Williams & Moore, 2011) aim to reframe learning environments for access. The most common of these approaches is universal design for learning which rests on the philosophy that all learners benefit when the educational settings use:

1 Multiple means of representation to give learners various ways of acquiring information and knowledge;
2 Multiple means of expression to provide learners alternatives for demonstrating what they know; and
3 Multiple means of engagement to tap into learners' interests, challenge them appropriately, and motivate them to learn.

Implementations of universal design for learning environments have consistently demonstrated positive impacts on student success (Capp, 2017). Universal design approaches, under a variety of names, have been explicitly identified in relevant federal legislation (Rose, 2000), and multiple leading organizations have advocated for its widespread implementation. Nonetheless, recent reviews suggest universal design is relatively underutilized (Capp, 2017).

Disabled students who successfully navigate college face another transition into the workforce. Data show that disabled people have different career outcomes than their non-disabled peers (U.S. Bureau of Labor Statistics, 2024). Disabled people are more likely to be unemployed, underemployed, or employed in low wage jobs even when controlling for educational and professional factors (Wondemu et al., 2022). In some cases, disabled people may make adaptive choices recognizing how their needs and interests would (or would not) be supported in a particular pathway (Newman et al., 2019). In other cases, the inaccessibility of particular career pathways may force disabled employees out (Brown & Clark, 2017). Many disabled people do not access needed accommodations in the workplace—either due to the unwillingness of workplaces to provide them or an unwillingness to request them for fear of a negative response. Disabled people also experience less stability in the workplace—entering it and exiting more frequently than non-disabled peers (U.S. Bureau of Labor Statistics, 2024). This movement coupled with disability-related stigma, has a suppressive effect on career advancement and compensation structures. As you read the stories, you will see that our participants did experience many of these choices and challenges as they transitioned out of college and into the workforce.

The Role of Families

Families play important and evolving roles in the lives of people with disabilities. As such, we felt it was important to end this chapter with some additional information about families. Loved ones are critical in shaping disability identity and experience during childhood and beyond. For many participants in our study, their families were the first people to help them understand what it meant to be disabled. They were also early advocates on their behalf. The literature on disability is consistent: family matters (Friedensen et al., 2022). Yet, it is important to acknowledge that not all families are the same. They vary in their composition, their shared or diverging social identities, their economic resources, and their access to resources in the communities where they reside (Friedensen et al., 2022). Moreover, even families with similar attributes can vary tremendously in how they respond to a disability. Different disabilities can necessitate differing patterns of familial engagement (Rivera Drew, 2009). For example, insurance companies have advanced Applied Behavioral Analysis techniques as the covered modality for autism support. As a result, caregivers of autistic children have found themselves struggling to meet the extensive time requirements of this model and to identify needed providers (Wondemu et al., 2022). Simply put, the dispositions of families differ as does their capacity to meet the temporal, emotional, financial, and relational costs imposed by the need to navigate problematic healthcare and educational systems (Olsen et al., 2022).

Assuming that parents and families are able to successfully navigate the flawed system, they can fill vital roles in the lives of disabled persons. First, they typically provide the most direct physical and emotional support for disabled persons (Son et al., 2019). Although the specifics vary from disability to disability, parents and families often take on the roles of skilled professionals to provide disability support to their children, often without the pay, training, or infrastructure needed to make this sustainable (Rivera Drew, 2009). All the while, these same parents and family members also perform a critical role in advocating for a disabled child (Watson et al., 2011). They often perform investigative work to ensure access to needed resources. Families can also teach children to develop critical age-appropriate self-advocacy skills (Daly-Cano et al., 2024). These self-advocacy skills are particularly important in arguing for changes to inequitable or inaccessible educational systems (Kimball et al., 2016) as well as in pushing back against bullying or stigmatizing behaviors (Vaccaro et al., 2024). Finally, parents and families are among the most important contributors to the self-concepts of disabled persons (Rehm et al., 2013). As you review the stories, you'll see the powerful impact loved ones can have on a person's experiences during key developmental moments. After reading our participants' stories, and the specific and actionable advice they offer to families (see Chapter 18), we hope you heed their calls to action.

Conclusion

In this chapter, we examined prior research about several topics that you'll come across in the forthcoming stories. Our intention was not to comprehensively review all the literature about disability, education, family, career, or purpose development. That would be impossible in an entire book, never mind a short chapter. Instead, our goal was to introduce you to some key concepts, models, research, and laws that you'll read about in the 14 forthcoming disability life stories. Whether you were already familiar with some of these topics or not, we hope that you found the information illuminating and useful as you continue to read this book.

3 Overview of Our Research Project

In this chapter, we describe the research project that inspired this book. Given the broad intended audience for this volume, our goal is to make the details about our research process and products accessible to all readers. Therefore, we describe our decade-long project using everyday language. This chapter includes information about the 10-year research project, including the impetus for the study, interview process, and how we constructed the unfiltered disability stories. We also explain the ongoing consent processes we used to ensure that participants felt their life experiences and stories were curated and presented accurately.

Why this Study?

Over a decade ago, the idea for this book began to percolate. As a team of educators with and without disabilities, we were interested in conducting research that would lead to improved educational experiences for disabled students. We hoped our work would offer research-informed strategies that educators, parents, and service providers could use to foster inclusive, inspiring, and effective post-secondary experiences for disabled students. As parents, grandparents, and teachers ourselves, we also wanted to embark on a project that honored and documented the important developmental trajectories that young people experience as they move through early schooling, college, and the workforce.

As a team, we were committed to elevating the voices of disabled students instead of using our own voices to inspire positive change. Through countless team conversations, this research project began to coalesce. Soon after, we started the formal process of implementing a research study to document the experiences of disabled college students and to examine the process by which they developed a sense of purpose during and after college.

DOI: 10.4324/9781003495703-3

What Is Purpose?

In Chapter 2, we summarized some prior research on purpose development. We revisit the concept here since it was the impetus for our research project. In a broad sense, purpose is conceived as a higher order belief system that gives direction to one's life. Higher education experts contend that purpose development is the "increasing ability to be intentional, to assess interests and options, to clarify goals, to make plans, and to persist despite obstacles" (Chickering & Reisser, 1993, p. 209). When faced with adversity, a person's commitment to a sense of purpose allows them to survive and thrive (Frankl, 1959). Developing purpose during college is sometimes looked at narrowly as finding a vocation or career path. However, as a team of educators and psychologists, we take a more expansive view of the concept. And, our study participants talked about their pathways toward purpose in broad ways. Their perspectives align with literature suggesting that purpose can include "discovering what we love to do" and doing "what energizes and fulfills us" (Chickering & Reisser, 1993, p. 212). In the forthcoming chapters, the disability life stories illuminate varied perspectives on, and paths toward, purpose for disabled students as they transitioned from childhood into adolescence and then adulthood. While vocation and career pathways were certainly part of their quests for purpose, finding joy, being energized, feeling fulfillment, and loving what they did were also prominent narratives for these amazing young people.

Why Does Purpose Matter?

Doing what we love, feeling energized, and developing a sense of purpose are related to a plethora of life benefits. Empirical research shows that having a sense of purpose is connected to numerous positive developmental outcomes such as: self-efficacy (DeWitz et al., 2009), identity development (Welkener & Bowsher, 2012), hope (Burrow & Hill, 2011), resiliency (Masten & Reed, 2002), positive affect (Burrow & Hill, 2011), academic achievement (Pizzolato et al., 2011), civic development (Malin et al., 2015; Rockenbach et al., 2014), and life satisfaction (Bronk et al., 2009). These are benefits that we hope all college students (actually, all humans) experience. However, when we began our research, none of the scholarship about purpose systematically addressed this phenomenon for disabled students. This omission was troubling since we know that disabled students regularly have to confront stigmatizing attitudes, structural hurdles, and problematic support structures that may complicate their purpose development (Kimball et al., 2016). Because the college years can have a profound effect on the establishment of purpose (Chickering & Reisser, 1993; Nash & Murray, 2010), we were motivated to learn more about how disabled college students developed a sense of purpose during, and after, college. We were deeply interested in talking directly with college students to find out more about their perspectives on, and experiences with, purpose development.

Collecting Stories

We began our study by recruiting disabled college students on multiple college campuses in the United States. We posted recruitment flyers at numerous colleges. The flyers contained the following prose:

> Although students with disabilities are attending college at increasing rates, we know very little about how college students with disabilities develop their sense of purpose. This research study hopes to change this! Please join us on this adventure. We are looking for students with disabilities to talk with us about their goals, plans, and dreams for the future. Your participation will involve answering questions during private interviews.

To specifically reach disabled college students, we also enlisted recruitment support from disability services (DS) personnel at numerous college campuses. We contacted DS directors at eight schools where the research team had established professional contacts. We sent emails to DS directors introducing ourselves and asking them to share our recruitment materials with disabled students on their campuses. Those DS directors who agreed were provided this text of an email invitation for students on their campus.

Dear Student,
We are writing to invite you to participate in a research project that focuses on how students with disabilities develop a sense of life purpose. How did you decide on a major? What are your career aspirations? Have you ever felt encouraged or discouraged from your life dreams?

If you are interested in talking to someone about these and related questions, we invite you to consider participating in a research study that will explore if, and how, disability status/identity, self-determination, and the collegiate environment contribute to the development of a sense of purpose, including selection of a major and career plans.

The remainder of the invitation contained logistics and directions on how to participate in the study.

The recruitment materials also let potential participants know that our study was reviewed and approved by institutional review boards (IRB) on multiple campuses. One critical goal of an IRB is to ensure that research is conducted in an ethical manner, and that humans who participate in a study are treated ethically. Each campus IRB reviewed every aspect of our project to ensure that our plan aligned with the most updated standards for protecting the rights and safety of participants. Considering the disturbing history of abuse inflicted by researchers on disabled people (Nielsen, 2012), our team took great care in developing this study. We spent a lot of time considering inclusive language, developing thoughtful interview questions, and ensuring that the interview environment was not only safe, but also accessible for all study volunteers. In short, we made every effort to engage in a research project that not only met standards of *doing no harm*, but also afforded space for disabled people to have agency, feel heard, and get excited about the ways their story could help others.

Students began reaching out to volunteer for the study quite quickly. In fact, at one campus, within one hour of a Disability Services Director emailing the study invitation, we received 26 messages from students expressing interest in our study. Our team was both excited and humbled by the interest and willingness of students to share their experiences with us. The swift and positive response signaled to us that disabled students wanted to share their stories. Ultimately, 59 disabled college students eagerly participated in the study. These 59 students attended various types of campuses including public and private colleges, rural and urban campuses, small and large schools, as well as teaching and research-focused institutions.

As students volunteered for the study, we asked them to complete two forms. The first was a standard, IRB-approved, consent form where we described the study purpose and process—including the option to withdraw from the study at any time. The consent form also gave the research team permission to use study data to write publications. Once the consent form was signed, students were invited to complete a demographic form. To learn more about the participants, we asked them to share their age, gender, race, and sexuality. We then asked about their home state, major, and year in college (e.g., sophomore, senior). Given the focus of this study, we also asked the following disability related demographic questions:

- Please describe your disability.
- Do you have a documented disability?
- What specific accommodations do you receive on campus?

The first bullet shows how we invited students to use *their own words* to describe their disability instead of asking them to select from a predetermined list of diagnoses. Most participants used diagnostic terms to describe their disability. Yet, others created their own self-identities such as "anxiety and memory issues; Autistic and a pile of things you could argue either are a part of autism or not; and no use of right arm." As we noted in the introduction, words matter. Therefore, we honor student self-identifications throughout this text. You'll see the actual terms students used to describe their disability in Table 3.1. We also use student's own descriptors throughout the book. In some cases, the terminology used on the demographic form matches the more detailed descriptions offered during lengthy interviews. And, in other cases, the demographic terms

Table 3.1 Participant Demographics

Pseudonym	Self-Reported Disability	Age[1]	Gender	Race
Alice	Totally blind	33	Cisgender woman	White
Juno	Reading comprehension	31	Cisgender woman	Asian American/ Pacific Islander
Justice	I have Bipolar 1, PTSD, Fibromyalgia, and Non 24 Hour Sleep Wake Disorder (plus assorted smaller health problems)	30	Transgender, Non-Binary, Genderfluid (between three nonbinary genders)	White
Kalani	ADHD/Anxiety/Depression/ PTSD	29	Cisgender woman	White
Kennedy	Traumatic brain injury; preferred arm incapacitated	57	Cisgender man	White
Landers	Dyslexia	28	Cisgender man	White
Mercedes	Learning disability, memory and word finding difficulties. Difficulty with attention in a busy environment	26	Cisgender woman	White
Peter	Dislxik ... I mean, Dyslexic	28	Cisgender man	White
Poppy	100% deaf in the right ear.	29	Cisgender woman	White
Tippi	ADHD with anxiety and depression	26	Cisgender woman	Bi/Multi-Racial
Titus	I have learning disabilities that affect how I process information	35	Cisgender man	White
Willa	Legal blindness/visual impairment	30	Cisgender woman	White
Willow	Dyslexia, reading comprehension difficulties, ADD	27	Cisgender woman	White
Yolanda	Autistic; hypermobile	29	Transgender, Gender Queer, Non-Binary, Gendervague	White

[1] Reflects the participants' reported age at the time of the third interview.

listed in the table don't fully align with the complex descriptions students used during their first, second, and/or third interview. We encourage readers to view such differences, and/or changes in terminology, as a reflection of the complexity of disability, as well as a natural evolution of identity. The words we use to describe ourselves may naturally change over time—this is especially true for young people as they move from adolescence to adulthood. How we understand

and represent ourselves evolves as we grow and experience new settings. In our work, we made every effort to honor both the evolving as well as the core and unchanging aspects of self and identity that students conveyed to us over the course of a decade.

In addition to disability descriptions, we think it is important for readers to get a sense of the types of disabilities all 59 students in this project reported. Therefore, we organized students' terms into more formal categories so readers could see how the apparent and non-apparent disabilities of our total sample closely mirrored nation-wide student disability data at the time we began the study (Raue & Lewis, 2011). Participant disabilities could be categorized as follows: a specific learning disability 23 (39%); Attention Deficit Hyperactivity Disorder (ADHD) 16 (27%); mental health diagnosis 14 (24%); physical disability 9 (15%); Autism Spectrum Disorders 3 (5%); deafness 2 (3%); blindness 2 (3%); traumatic brain injury 2 (3%); or "other" health impairment 4 (7%). These percentages do not add to 100% because 42% of our sample self-identified as having more than one disability—which is a frequent phenomenon (Raue & Lewis, 2011; Zilvinskis, 2020).

Many of our participants wanted us to know (and convey to readers) that they are more than their disability. The forthcoming disability life stories illuminate these sentiments. To honor the complex and intersecting identities of our participants, we provide additional demographic details so readers get a sense of the diversity of our participants. In alignment with national statistics for college-going students, our sample was largely composed of women (National Center for Education Statistics, 2024). Forty-five of the 59 participants identified as women. Twelve self-identified as men. We also had two participants who identified beyond the gender binary and self-identified as transgender or gender-queer. The demographic form invited students to share their sexuality if they felt comfortable. Forty-five students identified as heterosexual, three as lesbian, one as bisexual, two as queer, and two as questioning their sexuality. Six students preferred not to answer this question.

We set out to understand the life stories and purpose development of disabled college students. So, we recruited study volunteers who were matriculated college students at the time of the first interview. That means our dataset was influenced by the demographics of the students who attended the four-year, predominantly white colleges where we conducted our study. Of the initial sample of 59 volunteers, forty-nine participants reported being White; five, biracial or multiracial; two, Asian American or Pacific Islander; two, Latina/o; and one, Black. Although these identities are comparable to the demographics of disabled students attending four-year colleges and universities in the United States (National Center for Education Statistics, 2024), it is not as racially diverse of a group as we would have liked. And, the stories found in this book only begin to scratch the surface of the complex racialized experiences of disabled people.

At the time of the initial interview, participants ranged in age from 18–50. As would be expected from a study of college students, our sample was not exclusively—but largely (80%)—traditional age collegians ranging in age from 18–22. At the time of the first interview, roughly half lived in campus housing, including campus residence halls and apartments. The other half lived off-campus. Most of these students resided in local apartments with peers; although a few participants lived at home with their family and commuted to class. The housing situations changed, as expected, once they left college. In the forthcoming stories, you'll hear about the quest for independent living, as well as the various living situations of participants.

The Interviews

Our research team was committed to learning, first hand, about the lived experiences of disabled college students. Therefore, we opted to conduct a qualitative study where we could engage in lengthy conversations with participants. Instead of focusing on surveys and numerical data, the goal of qualitative research methods is to capture the rich and complicated lived realities of human beings. To do this, qualitative researchers use a variety of data collection formats—such as interviews—to elicit people's perspectives, attitudes, and personal histories.

Given our interest in documenting rich and powerful student experiences, our research plan included multiple individual interviews over the course of a decade. We began by planning the study and obtaining approval from the institutional review boards (IRB) at multiple college campuses. The first interviews began shortly thereafter. Fifty-nine disabled college students completed the first interview. The second round of interviews happened between one and two years after the initial interview. Thirty four of the original 59 students participated in the second interview. The final interview was conducted roughly one decade after the first conversations. Our team was able to locate and talk with 22 of the initial participants.

Although we would have loved to follow all 59 students for a decade, it is quite common for the number of participants to decrease in longitudinal studies. Individuals change their contact information and sometimes their names. University email addresses stop working once students leave campus. As such, finding participants after almost a decade is challenging. Even when researchers are able to locate participants, sometimes they opt out of the study. Some did not have the interest, or time, to dedicate to the research project. As such, we respected the decision of some students to opt out of a second or third interview. For those 22 participants who stuck with us, we are deeply grateful. Their stories are a gift to us and to readers.

In this book, we present the stories from 14 of the 22 participants whom we followed over a decade. Why only 14? There are a few reasons. First, we had space constraints. Only so many stories fit within the pages of this book. Second, not all participants were comfortable with having their stories published widely in a book. We honored their wishes. Third, we chose diverse stories that offered powerful lessons. We hope that the diversity of life experiences shared in this book offer inspiration to all readers—knowing that some may resonate more than others with teachers, parents, allies, and disabled college students. Finally, we selected stories that illuminated both the extraordinary and ordinary lives of disabled people—highlighting this important dual reality across the chapters.

For accessibility reasons, we were committed to offering students the choice of format for the interview. Most opted for an in-person conversation for the initial interview because they were living on, or near, campus at the time. However, the interview mode increasingly moved to virtual formats (Zoom, Skype, Facetime) for subsequent interviews. This makes sense since students began to graduate or leave campus. The final interviews were all conducted via zoom largely out of convenience for participants who were living across the United States by that time.

It was important that students felt like they were having a conversation and were empowered to tell us as much (or as little) of their story as they wanted to. Thus, our research team employed semi-structured individual interviews to garner rich participant stories. This type of interview uses a series of questions and prompts as a guide. However, the interviewers did not ask all questions in the same order for everyone. Instead, our interview team listened and asked follow up questions to learn about the experiences that students wanted to share. The goal of this type of flexible interview format is to replicate the feel of a natural conversation.

The initial interview occurred during college. It was our first time talking to each participant. Therefore, many of the questions were designed to get to know how students made sense of their disability and other identities, how they experienced education systems, and what they had to say about their life goals, career aspirations, and sense of purpose at the time. Questions asked during the first interview included:

- What do you think when I say the word disability?
- Can you tell me about your disability?
- What does your disability mean to you? If, and how, does it shape your sense of self?
- Having a disability can be one aspect of someone's self-identity. Our race, ethnicity, gender, religion, social class, sexuality, and other social identities can also shape our sense of self. Can you talk a little bit about if, and how, any of these might shape your identity?
- Can you tell me about how your disability influenced your plans for college?
- While you were in high school, what advice did you receive about the ways your disability might affect your college experience?

- Tell me a little bit about what it is like to be a college student with a disability.
- Can you tell me a bit about why you chose your current major?
- Sometimes we are encouraged, or discouraged, from particular majors and/or careers. Can you tell me if this has happened to you?
- Can you give me an example of a time when you faced an obstacle and what you did in that situation?
- Following our dreams can sometimes be a challenge. How do you persevere despite life's hurdles?
- Are there any specific strategies you use to be successful in school, work, or relationships?
- Can you talk to me about the people, policies, and or programs at your school or in the community that you feel are supportive (or unsupportive) of your needs as a student with a disability?
- When you were little, what did you want to be?
- Can you tell me if, and how, your childhood dreams were shaped by your disability? Or, by people's perceptions of your capabilities and disability?
- Can you tell me how those childhood dreams relate to your present major and career goals?
- When you look into your future, where do you see yourself immediately after graduation? Where do you see yourself in five or ten years?
- If I asked you to tell me your life goals, what would those be?
- What would happiness look like to your future self?
- In addition to a career/job, what else would make your life complete and happy?
- Is there anything you would like to add to help us understand how you have incorporated your disability into decisions about your major, or your goals for the future?

During the second interview, we followed up on many of these topics, inviting students to tell us if, and how, their perspectives and experiences had evolved. Most participants were still in college at the time of this follow up interview. Questions asked during the second interview included:

- How have you been since we've last spoken?
- Last time we talked you lived (on campus/off campus). Where are you living now?
- Last time we talked, I asked you what your disability meant to you and whether or not it shaped your sense of self. Time has passed, can you tell me what it means to be a person with your disability today?
- Last time we met, you explained how [insert interview one responses] social identities influenced your sense of self. Can you talk a bit about how your race, ethnicity, gender, religion, social class, sexuality, and other social identities shape your sense of self today?

- Last time we talked, your major was ____. What is it today? Can you tell me about why it changed or remained the same?
- Last time we talked you saw yourself doing _____ after graduation. Have your post-graduation plans changed? Please explain.
- Tell me about some of the other things you are doing to plan for your career-like part time jobs, internships, research, volunteering, or connecting with professionals in your field. Can you tell me how these things are preparing you for your post-college life?
- What steps might you take to ensure you get a job you love in the future?
- What accommodations, if any, might you need in the workplace?
- How do you think your disability/diagnosis will be an asset in your career? Or a roadblock?
- What things, besides a job, would make your life meaningful or purposeful?
- Last time you talked about specific instances of encouragement and discouragement regarding your major, career, and life goals. Can you give me examples of encouragement or discouragement you received since we last spoke? How did you respond?

After the first interview, we were struck by how often college students reflected on their elementary, middle, or high school experiences. Even though our questions from the first interview largely focused on collegiate experiences (see above), early life experiences were clearly important to our participants. We learned how their childhood profoundly shaped their sense of self, educational experiences, and life trajectories. Therefore, we asked additional questions about pre-collegiate experiences during the second interview. Some of these questions included:

- Describe if (and how) you were included by peers when you were in PreK-12 school? What about here at college?
- What would you want every educator (kindergarten to college) to know about supporting a student with a disability similar to yours?
- What advice would you give to students with disabilities—those in college and those still in elementary, middle, or high school?

The third interview built upon the first two conversations to explore the ways in which our participants transitioned out of college and into adulthood. Interview questions we asked participants after a decade included:

- Tell me about how you've been since we last talked.
- In prior interviews, we talked about how you defined disability. Tell me how you'd define it today.
- How would you describe your current disability status?
- How important/salient is your disability in your everyday life? How, if at all, is the importance/salience different, or similar to, when you were in college?

- How, if at all, have the ways you view your disability changed since you left college?
- Please tell me about how your disability impacts your plans for the future and your thoughts about family.
- Tell me about the paid and unpaid positions you've held since college. How, if at all, do these jobs relate to your major? Were these the types of jobs you imagined when you were in college? Talk to me about the alignment and/or misalignment.
- In the jobs you have had since attending college, what, if any, roadblocks have you encountered? In your opinion, were any work-related challenges related to your disability or other identities? Tell me more.
- Tell me about your employment situation now. Does anyone know you have a disability? Can you talk a little bit about why you decided to disclose or not disclose?
- While you were in college, what information/advice, if any, did you receive about the ways your disability might affect your work experience?
- Can you talk to me about the people, policies, and/or programs that you feel are supportive of your needs as an employee with a disability?
- Where do you see yourself in 5 years? 10 years?
- During interview one we talked about your purpose as _____. When you think about your life's purpose now, how would you describe it?
- In our last interview we asked you about K-12 educational experiences that influenced your life. What advice would you give to your young self during your K-12 years?
- What advice would you give your 18/19/20 year old self going through college?
- Is there anything else that we haven't talked about that you'd like to share?

We conducted the third set of interviews as the world was attempting to move on from the COVID-19 pandemic. Given the significance of this historical moment in time, we asked a couple questions about the ways in which the pandemic impacted their lives. Those questions included:

- Talk to me about your job experiences—and how they were (and maybe continue to be) influenced by COVID-19.
- What impact has the COVID pandemic had on your life and/or your plans for the future?
- Have there been any particular ways that your disability has been a factor in how you coped with the pandemic?

We audio-recorded all three interviews and transcribed them verbatim. The interview transcripts yielded thousands of pages of transcripts. We've spent the last few years learning from the reflections, insights, struggles, and successes contained in these interview transcripts.

Constructing Stories from Interview Transcripts

The research team spent hundreds of hours reading, re-reading, and reflecting upon the interview transcripts. We documented consistent patterns that appeared in the student prose. Participants described experiences with a variety of topics including, but not limited to: disability, identity, schooling, coping, bullying, family, work, and purpose. Once we agreed upon important emergent and re-peating categories, we looked for patterns in the data to identify where those categories showed up in each interview. Categorizing the data led to a number of publications where we delved into important topics such as purpose develop-ment (Newman et al., 2019; Vaccaro et al., 2018, 2019a), identity development (Kimball et al., 2018; Vaccaro et al., 2019a, 2020), as well as student experi-ences with major selection, bullying, stereotyping, and coping (Moore et al., 2020; Vaccaro et al., 2019b, 2024). These topic-focused papers were written to help educators and campus staff learn about specific issues (e.g., coping, bul-lying) so that they could improve their practice. For our team, it was critically important that we share our work in ways that could lead to positive change in schools. And, given the popularity of those aforementioned research articles, we are confident that our work informs educational practice. We hope this book will continue to inform and improve experiences for disabled students for many years to come.

Yet, with their focus on specific topics and categories, those research articles could not fully do justice to the powerful, longitudinal life stories of our partici-pants. So, the team revisited the three interviews for each of the 22 participants. We re-read each person's 10-year story with a holistic (instead of a categorical or reductionist) lens. Through that process, we reengaged with the complex and evolving life stories we were gifted with. Inspired by these young people's tra-jectories, we decided to compose this book to share these moving stories with parents, educators, and service providers, as well as disabled people who hope-fully see some of their own stories reflected in these pages.

Producing each story in this book took time, careful curation, and constant checking to ensure that we were honoring the students' lived realities as told to us. We were committed to ensuring that readers would hear the voices of par-ticipants. Yet, we had the tough task of trimming the length without altering the essence of the story, or losing the student's voice. The three transcripts for each person were voluminous—sometimes close to 100 pages per person. Our team spent extensive time reviewing the transcripts to get a sense of the types of ex-periences that were most meaningful to each participant. We then extracted ver-batim quotes from those transcripts and organized them into a condensed story. Of course, we did have to make hard choices in how much detail to share as we streamlined hundreds of transcript pages into a fraction of that. As we made those choices, we constantly asked ourselves questions to keep the focus on the stories. What can readers learn from this amazing young person? What material are we using? What material are we excluding? How do we justify those decisions? How do we share both the struggles and successes, as well as the ordinary and extraordinary? Is this curated and condensed vignette an accurate portrayal of the story told to us?

We added our own prose only when necessary—for instance, to offer context or to provide transition sentences. To protect the identities of our participants, we also opted to remove or change the names of locations, workplaces, or other unique aspects of a story that could allow a participant to be identifiable. It is our duty to protect their anonymity. The end result is a set of 14 disability life stories composed of (almost exclusively) direct quotations from the participants. These are their words, their experiences, and their stories. We are simply story *re-tellers* who did our best to honor the stories conveyed to us.

Once the team finished each condensed story, we sent the chapter to the participant and asked for feedback. We wanted to know if we represented their story accurately. Was there anything that we got wrong and needed to change? We also asked one more time for permission to use their story in this book. After all, these are *their* life stories. We appreciate having the privilege of collecting, curating, and sharing them with readers like you. We hope that you are as moved as we are with their narratives of growth, resilience, and journeys toward life purpose.

Setting the Stage for the Stories

When planning research projects, scholars often find it helpful to use pre-existing theories or concepts to situate and/or frame their study. We're committed to keeping the research jargon in this chapter to a minimum. So, we won't delve into those kinds of research tools here. However, we do think it is helpful to describe some overarching concepts we kept at the forefront of our minds as we organized the research, conducted the study, and curated the stories. Three big-picture concepts shaped every aspect of our project: ableism, time, and context.

You might be wondering how three concepts are relevant to all 14 stories—especially since each story describes a person's unique journey. Indeed, none of the participants identified as having the same disability or constellation of co-occurring disabilities. Nor did they attend the same primary, secondary, or postsecondary schools. They had radically different home, school, and work experiences. And, they all developed a uniquely personal sense of self and purpose over the ten years we followed them. Yet, all of the stories are context-dependent and shaped by the realities of the ableist world we inhabit. Moreover, the stories are incredibly powerful in that they illuminate how humans grow and change over time. Therefore, we invite you to pay attention to the significance of ableism, time, and context as you engage with the life stories, individually and collectively.

Ableism

As we argued in the introduction and Chapter 2, the lives of disabled people are situated within an ableist world. Ableism includes both the normalization of non-disabled experiences and the devaluation of disabled ones. Ableism happens because many people without disabilities do not think about disability. And, as a result, they prioritize their needs above those with disabilities. The result is educational, employment, service and family environments, policies, and systems that are designed in ways that often disregard, ignore, segregate, and exclude disabled people. Ableism shapes what society views as normal or normative. Therefore, ableism can also influence the way that disabled people think about themselves and about others. You'll see all of these manifestations of ableism in the forthcoming stories.

Time

The powerful stories told by our participants remind us of the importance of considering someone's story over time. Over the course of a decade, the young people we talked to as college students developed into adults and took on professional, familial, and community roles. Their stories illuminate a trajectory of growth and change from childhood into adulthood. As we noted in Chapter 2, adolescence and early adulthood are times of great developmental growth and change. The forthcoming stories certainly depict immense personal and professional growth between childhood and early adulthood. Participant narratives reveal changes in perspective, experience, and identity over time. In the stories you will also see enduring values, passions, and core aspects of their personalities. But, even these unwavering aspects of their core selves did mature with time and experience. All of these chapters share a story of growth, maturation, and change over time.

Context

There is no singular experience of disability. That is, in part, due to the countless contexts that shape the lived realities of disabled people. In Chapter 2, we shared literature which illuminated the significance of environments in understanding disability. Just a few of the important contexts that influenced the lives of our participants included family, school, community, healthcare, and the workplace. In different contexts, disabled people may find joy, success, struggle, exclusion, and much more. For instance, some participants found incredible support in a home or activist setting while simultaneously experiencing bullying or exclusion in other settings (such as school or work). Even within a particular environmental context, disabled people can have radically different experiences as they interact with different people in different parts of that environment over time. For instance, participants who attended the same university experienced differing living situations, classes, and relationships where they encountered unique constellations of peers, teachers, policies, physical spaces, and support systems. To add to the complexity of context, as noted in Chapter 2, the legal context for disability, and the corresponding accommodation and support processes, changes dramatically from high school to higher education and employment settings.

As you delve into the following 14 chapters, we invite you to keep these overarching concepts—ableism, time, context—in mind. They provide an important backdrop to the extraordinary and ordinary lived realities you are about to read.

4   Meet Alice

Pronouns: She/her
Age: 33
Self-identified disability: Totally Blind
College major: English
Current living situation: Living with mother
Current job/position: Part time assistant helping blind people
Passions: Writing about people, journals, my faith, and music

Alice walks us through her educational experiences, including public elementary and middle school, her high school for the blind, the rollercoaster of college years, and post-college life. Throughout, her mother, faith, music, writing, and disability advocacy were strategies for success. Alice is determined to be an advocate for herself and for the disabled community, especially the blindness community. Not only does she use her voice, but she amplifies it to try to prevent harm to other disabled individuals. Alice's story illustrates the influence that negative interactions can have, but also the power of positive support and a sense of community. Through Alice's story, we gain insight into her perspective on disability and its place in the sense of self.

When asked to describe her disability, Alice explained:
I'm totally blind. I don't have any vision, but I can envision at the same time. If I explained my blindness to a child, I would tell them that my eyes are broken, that they don't work. Then, I'll explain that I basically use my hands to see. I use Braille and Windows, which allows blind or vision impaired people access to the computer. I was born blind. People always ask me "if you could see with surgery today, would you?" On one hand, it'd be cool because I could drive places and not have to rely on people. On the other hand, I'd be in my 30's and have to go back to kindergarten. For example, I'd have to learn how to read and

DOI: 10.4324/9781003495703-4

write. That would be kind of weird. I also have a mild learning disability that is a blessing and a curse because it's unspecified. It doesn't come out very often, so I can pretty much pass for not having one. I grew a lot in my time at college. I learned more about myself. I'm blind. It's just a part of me. It doesn't define me. It was one of the best things to come out of going to school.

Alice described the supportive and unsupportive people she encountered on her educational path and strategies she used to persevere.

When I was in second grade, a teacher told my mom that I wasn't going to go anywhere. I wasn't going to go to college or make something of myself. My mom was taken aback, but, at the same time, she knows me really well. She knows that I'll persevere and move forward.

I was thinking about how public school, and the adults in my life, for the most part, were terrible. In a meeting in middle school, I asked all the attendees, "What does accommodation mean to you?" I had them go around and answer. A lot of them were very condescending, kind of fake. When I was going to school, for most adults, work was about their paycheck. Adults that were so terrible to me really made me a better person. I had to grow up and say, "All right, I'm 12 but I'm actually like an adult of 25 or 30 something because you're not acting professional, but I am." I have my moments, definitely, where I get mad or frustrated.

I went to a school for the blind for high school. I went out of state for high school to prepare to go to college. It was one of the hardest sacrifices I ever made, but one of the most worthwhile. A couple of people who had been to college told me, "You're going to have a lot of really lonely days. You're going to have good days. You'll have to move forward." Where I went to high school, teachers and peers always said, "Oh, you'll be fine. You're a good person. People will like you."

But, college has been a rollercoaster. It has brought some of the greatest and lowest days of my entire life. When I decided to go to college, I majored in Journalism but later switched to English. I knew that some of the English professors were really great and really understanding about accommodations. English is a heavy major. Going to college is a lot of work. Some professors are more intense than others.

For me, it's really rare when I find nice people when I'm at school. When you're going through a lot of mistreatment and trying to go to school and maintain good grades, it's quite a heavy load. One professor was a tough grader. He's not the nicest person. That was really tricky. We just have to deal with mean people the best we can. We can try and kill them with kindness. I had a reader who quit mid-semester. I got so far behind, I didn't finish the semester until June. The work in this particular course was so much. The professor was good about giving me extensions. But he made this comment on my paper: "This is not sophisticated 400 level work." It was so mean. I'm a strong person, but I was just like, "Oh my gosh." I was trying so, so hard. I would think I got it and then I didn't. Usually, I can hold myself together if I'm in school. I was telling my reader about the feedback and I cried a little. My reader was really nice. She gave me a hug and she said, "Oh my gosh, it's okay. It'll be okay. That was really mean." It was nice that she reached out and was kind about it. The reality is that my university just doesn't deal with blindness very well. It really helps me appreciate the good people. I'm genuinely very surprised every time I come across them. It's so, so important to thank them—let them know that you appreciate them. There's a slim few who have gone above and beyond.

I remember talking with one professor before classes had started. He said, "Whatever helps you learn the best." He just really understood me. I have this distinct memory of doing a group project. He was always a step ahead ensuring I was included in the group. For me, I find that really rare. I just remember coming back from a class and in my inbox was this email to my group mates: "Hi. Can you guys make sure that Alice gets to the library and that somebody helps Alice find her van and this and that." All these things that I thought were above and beyond. I was like, "Wow, here I am with a few minutes before my next class thinking I don't have to draft this email and make sure people get it." It was already done. It was just something I never forgot.

My religion and philosophy professor was also super awesome. I think he should get professor of the year. He found a workaround. For my exams, he accommodated me by talking. We talked about material. He would ask me questions. Sometimes I would do different presentations on what we were learning. I also had this amazing English professor. She's the best honestly. She's a mentor for me. I still keep in touch. I actually spoke to one of her classes where they were talking about how reading out loud benefits everyone. It's good practice. She was able to take my disability and make it benefit students of all abilities.

Because educational institutions are largely designed for non-disabled, sighted people, Alice encountered many systemic hurdles that impacted her academic success and social connections.

In public school, I had so many gaps. I would always need to get things ahead of time, for example, my materials put into Braille. That was always really challenging. I didn't always have the right books at the beginning of the semester. Also, there was never enough time in the day for me to catch up, so I would miss recess a lot. My mom has been really great about advocating. My mom always said, "Remember she's a kid, she needs to play. She cannot be working all the time." On Wednesdays, I literally would go to school and have mobility after school to learn my way around. Then, I would have tech training—see somebody to help me with different skills—do homework, eat, and go to bed. I had the longest days.

Before each semester in college, Alice spent significant time learning to navigate campus.

Over the summer break, I'm there on campus doing mobility training—making sure I learn my way to classes. Then, I hope and pray that the location of my classes are not changed right before school starts, which has happened before. I have only one mobility instructor who I have to call and say, "Oh my gosh. This class is no longer in this building. They just changed it." I worked all summer to learn how to get around campus! I'm at a university where there is no assistance. It's really frightening to know that there are few people who are going to help. You kind of have to just jump in and figure it out, which is a good thing and also a little overwhelming.

Although disability services at college and in the community were available, they were not always helpful.

When I was in high school, people did tell me that college is really hard. People would say, "You've got to advocate. There will still be issues with services." I'm very open about the fact that I have not had the best experience with disability services on campus. Anything from just deciding how they're going to scan my books—like whether they're going to wait and do it a different way and not tell me. I was in a class that was very visual. I didn't have the book in Braille. I didn't have any graphs in a way that I understood them. I mentioned this to my professor and to disability services. They didn't know what to tell me. I just needed to figure it out. The head of disability services said my professor said I didn't need anything adapted. One of my readers would try to creatively come up with ways to help me understand concepts. My mom would come after work to school and read through some chapters for me, trying to break things down. If I came home on weekends, the same kind of thing. I got through it the best I could. I would go see the teaching assistant to help prepare for tests. She understood that I was at a real disadvantage. She tried to help me the best that she could.

I think community, state, and campus services for the blind want you to have a plan A, B, and C. Figure out if it's realistic for you or not. People might not support you, but you'll find a way to figure it out. That's kind of what I'm learning. If you're going to go to college, you have to have really good follow-up skills to manage readers and remind educators of your schedule. You get used to making calls and emails and being constantly on the go. I always tell people that for me, going to school is pretty much like working a full-time job and working double-time five days a week. It's like more power to you because you learn a lot, but it's a lot of work. It's very exhausting. I don't want to speak for all blind people—but it also took me a lot longer to get work completed. There was no time for anything. Most of my education has been that way.

At the time of the second interview, Alice was getting ready to graduate.

Thank God! I'm really proud of myself. I'm the first one to graduate from college in my family. It's funny because, for a long time, I haven't really felt like I belonged, even though I go here. I really struggled with "am I going to walk at graduation or am I going to just have it mailed to me?" Now I'm like, "No, I'm at the end. Woo hoo, I'm going to walk."

For Alice, ableist roadblocks served as an inspiration for activism.

I learned that I can use my blindness for the greater good. No matter where I'm at in life, I always make sure that I share my experiences. Talking about my disability kind of brings awareness to it. I'm all about changing the next generation for blind people. We also need to spend an equal amount of time talking about the few really good people that helped us and the ones that aren't that great. By being open, I helped a lot of college students learn. There is a real need to bridge the gap and help sighted young people learn that it's okay to be around somebody different. We're all a little different. I've had to pay it forward by sharing my successes and struggles. In most cases, college has been horrible. If somebody can have a better experience—that's really what it's all about. When you see change happen, that's when things start evolving.

Whenever I share my story, it gives me a platform. I used to speak to younger children, elementary through middle school. I speak a lot to college students. One of the things we talk about is person-first language. I say it's a fancy way of saying humans before disabilities. I can connect with people. I consider myself a pioneer in the community of people with my disability. It's funny, my family calls me a modern Helen Keller. She was very aware of people with disabilities, poverty, and unemployment. I just think it's so ridiculous that unemployment is so high for people who are blind. She helped start training programs. My friend is at a center for the blind that I went to as a kid. When I hear how she's treated it makes me so mad. I said, "Do you want to start a movement?" People have a hard time hearing the bad stuff because it makes them feel bad. It's hard for them to swallow what we've swallowed since we were young. You can say, "This is terrible!" But we all have a choice. You can either change it and help start something—help lay a new foundation, or you can just be like, "Well I'm sorry, that's sad."

After college, Alice continued her activism by supporting local political campaigns.

My friend ran for city council. We would phone bank and door knock. That was really interesting. I think campaigning is really important, no matter which side you're on, no matter what you believe. We need disabled people in politics. I think people think that blind people just don't care or don't debate like able bodied people do. That cannot be further from the truth. I wanted to go to a political rally. Somebody said, "I don't mean to hurt your feelings. But if we get separated, it could go really bad. Protests can turn really violent sometimes. You have to be careful. You have to be smart." You don't want to get hurt, but you want to advocate at the same time. It is hard to find a balance.

People are so surprised to see a blind person vote. I was so nervous about the election. Accessibility machines, like text to speech, are really tricky because sometimes they don't work. It's a machine that will read out your choices. I would get to a certain point and then it would stop. I advocated to disability law about that. Unfortunately, I didn't have a good enough case because when they checked everything, everything worked fine. So, that was disappointing. The other thing that's tricky is because of where I live they don't do training down here. I brought that up. They said, there's just not a market for it. So basically, they were like, "Good luck, it won't happen where you are." They just kind of give you a crash course. You're trying to listen to the machine and somebody else tells you what's going on. It was kind of overwhelming for me. So, next election I sent my ballot in by mail.

Alice reflected on the desire for social connection, the difficulties she experienced in forming relationships, and the importance of having caring, supportive people in her life.

I pray for the right people to connect with me. When people are really vulnerable, that's when you can relate the most to people. A lot of people in my age group really don't understand a lot of what blind people go through. They might try and then be like, "Whoa, this is too complicated. Well, good luck." Occasionally you get lucky. There's someone in your age group who takes the time and understands it and helps to tell your story. I'm always really thankful and appreciative for that. I think one of the worst feelings ever is to be in a place where there's so many people, but yet, you feel like you're the only one there. I wish I could say that I was involved with campus. I wasn't, partly because I was a really big outcast. It's really hard when people are afraid. A lot of people can't look past my cane. I think it's a choice when they choose to accept my blindness, include me, and decide to work with me. They're helping break the cycle in their own way. I signed up for a bunch of activities that I thought were really cool during my college orientation. But, I found that a lot of people weren't as welcoming when I attended club meetings.

Despite these challenges, Alice developed friendships online and with individuals from diverse backgrounds.

I literally have the most diverse group of friends ever. I love it. I wouldn't ask for any other group. I have a hard time with people my age unless they're different. I have friends that love to sing and that are gay, that are straight, that teach, that have disabilities, and that don't have disabilities. For me that's what makes my world go around. "Hey, we're all fighting for equality, it's just different." My personality, I really need balance in my life, so the diversity works well. I see the world of people differently because I have to rely on other people for everyday kinds of things.

When I have a hard time, I talk to a lot of people that have already been through what I'm going through. Just swapping stories and ideas, or just talking, helps. Support is key. I am a part of this online group. It's a social hangout. There's a lot of people on there from all over the world who are blind. People who went to school with me are on there. There's a really great guy who is blind, very successful, and one of the nicest people you'll ever meet. We've kept in touch. He is a leader in the blindness community. He is very busy, but he always makes time for me. I've always really appreciated that. He always told me that he would make time for me because he knew that I was going to be one who would make it. I'm really grateful for blind mentors, because it's really important to have people that have been in your shoes and remind you that things are going to pass. I'm able to communicate with other blind people online. Most recently, somebody found me. He is visually impaired. He's doing a research project on blind and visually impaired bloggers. He's from Egypt. That was a really unique conversation learning about differences in the ways international blind people are treated.

I have some sighted friends who are awesome. They live different lives. Some of them work. Some are married and have kids. Hopefully, I find *the* right person. I was with someone for quite a long time. You'll live and learn who's right for you and who's not. What happens, happens. Whether I have kids or not depends on a lot of factors.

Alice talked at length about her bedrocks of support, including faith leaders, family, friends, and even her reader.

My mom is pretty much my one main relationship, which is really awesome and really challenging. She's only one person. She's always been there for me and helped me to move forward. Thankfully I have my pastor and his wife, who have been really awesome. My pastor became like the dad that I never had and has taught me a lot. So, he's been really helpful. Writing, my faith, and music are a really big part of my life. I'm very interested in writing and learning about people. I write a lot in a journal because I'm a writer. Also, a big part of what gets me through everything I've been through is music. When I was at school, it was a big part of what would help me get through the day. My faith is really important to me. Praying was also a big part of how I got through school. My mom would pray with me about school a lot. The reader who impacted my life in a positive way, I believe was pure divine intervention. My university had decided that they were done looking for student readers on campus. Nobody was interested in working with me. So, I thought, "That's absurd! This is a college. College students need money." At church, we'd all been praying for a reader. Disability services just happened to look one more time and a young man came forward to work with me. Depending on your belief, you might think, "Oh that just happened." But I really believe that God sent him to help me through. It's a part of my testimony, so I'll share my story with whoever is listening. Anything can happen, we just have to pray about it.

There have been plenty of times when I have been at school where I'm wondering, "What am I doing?" I definitely have my days where I rely a lot on the few friends that I have, my family, or my mom. Everybody needs encouragement once in a while. Not that we want somebody to give us all the answers, but we're just kind of looking for reassurance.

Alice's dreams and plans about employment and a career have been evolving since high school. She has been frustrated by the quality of state services for the blind and lack of support for her future goals. But, she found people to mentor and encourage her.

I talk to my state services person who is assigned to support disabled individuals during the transition to post-secondary education. I'm asking, "You know what, I'm doing my part. This is your job to provide training on equipment. Why are you not supporting me?" I get annoyed about it because I'm an advocate for change. Honestly, a lot of people in my school life and state services just don't know how to communicate and it drives me nuts. State services outside of my university will help you when you're in school and when you're not, that's it. Depending on what kind of job you have, you don't get help from them. Also, if your grades aren't in a certain average and you fail, your services get taken. I think, "Okay, but you want me to make sure everything's perfect on paper but then not also help me learn this stuff." I'm supposed to not fail and do really well, but also get no help from you either? That's really hard to deal with sometimes. My state people were so unprofessional when my mom came to a meeting a couple years ago. When they found out I wanted to be self-employed they literally went, "Oh my god, what?" I was just like, "Cool. That was a nice reaction."

I wanted to go into broadcasting. I heard my broadcasting idol on the radio when I was seven. He just had the best personality and a really great sense of humor. I just fell in love with the idea. "Wow, you can play music, share events, and whatever is going on." He really planted a seed. I went to a station when I was in high school. I met with a really nice lady. She showed me around. That was really cool. After I graduated from high school, my school created an accessible broadcasting station for students. I'm told it was inspired by my love for broadcast journalism.

Alice elaborated on her post-graduation plans and dreams in her first and second interviews.

I think just making sure that I'm always happy and healthy. No matter what path I take, it's definitely doing something with writing about disabilities—whether it's starting a blog or writing about music that helps people with disabilities. My goal is definitely helping advocate for people with disabilities.

Eventually, I'd like to be self-employed. I'd like to start my own campaigns eventually and a foundation. I'd like to start my own YouTube channel and start raising awareness about disability advocacy. When I talk to people with disabilities about the specific details of a campaign I'd like to start, everybody tells me, "Wow, we really need somebody like you. Yes, that is exactly what we need." It's a really good affirmation for me.

After college, I got to be an advisor for my high school. They launched a program for late teens, mid to late 20s to help with different job search skills. It was about resumes and how to be an interviewee. That was interesting to be back. The pandemic changed the way work is done. You can work from anywhere. It's changed how we function really. It's helpful because it removes transportation barriers. There should be accessible transportation. Unfortunately, there's not; so, zoom helps us a lot. I was doing a lot of phone work. We were working with call center type work. We also tested a screen reader with certain websites. I got to learn Salesforce. That was pretty cool.

In the third interview, Alice noted that it had been a couple of years since the last time she had employment—noting obstacles related to bias, technology, and transportation. Despite challenges, Alice is hopeful that she can find a way to bring her passion for disability activism into career opportunities where she can educate others as a consultant and author.

I was so close to having a job part time. I brushed up on Excel. They hired a big company instead. I find that a lot of places don't really like to hire blind people because they think it's a burden. I can't pass for someone who's sighted because I have my cane. I was talking about this with somebody a while ago. You act differently around blind people than you do around sighted people, so, in that way I'm different.

If somebody were to offer me a job, I'm all for it. I would need a reader and technology that works. I have had my BrailleNote since 2009. I have a braille keyboard and an iPad. I'd really like to get a certification in technology. It is so ridiculous that blind people do not have freedom of choice of what screen reader they use. State services in various states are all about Dell computers. They have a contract with them. It's cheaper. But some computers don't always work well with accessibility features. It is so terrible that I don't have a choice for the type of computer I am given. Transportation is a big thing that comes to mind when looking for employment. I have to rely on cabs, family, or friends. I can't just get up and go places.

Nobody in college gave disability employment advice, but my high school did. I was told, "Understand that people are going to treat you differently. You deserve your accommodations. You can decide whether you want to disclose or not. You have to prove that you can do things." I learned to show them how these are the tools that I use to learn. This is how I won't be a burden to you.

I eventually would like to work for myself and with organizations that help disabled people. I have a book that's basically done. I just need to find a publisher. I've written a self-help book about things that I don't think are talked about enough. One of them is about how to take notes. One of them is about how to make friends, whether you're blind or sighted. I think that people think, "You're an outgoing person. It's a breeze to make friends." Thank you, but that's not true. So many people say there's no manual on how to raise a blind child. There's no manual on how to do blah with said blind person. I've heard that for years and thought, "Why don't I write one then?"

Professionally, I hope to continue to speak to people. I would like to start a podcast and hopefully my book will be out. I was talking to a class recently. The professor said, "Why don't you make this a course?" She had given me pointers, but I've expanded my talks quite a bit now with college students. I incorporate role playing exercises—that's really powerful. I started it over Zoom, but I recently started doing it in person. I'm with the nonprofit that does a lot of tech workshops. That's been really helpful. Definitely, I hope to continue to do more with that kind of work.

When asked "Do you think your disability will be an asset in your career or a roadblock?" Alice responded:

I think it can go either way. I've definitely had my share of roadblocks. I've also been blessed with really great people. I don't think we get to a point in life when it's like, "Roadblocks are over. Alright, sweet! Party!" I work hard. I try to do my best. I've learned what I can control. I can't control what other people do or say. It all depends, too, on the people that you work with. I bring an asset. They might think it's a roadblock with a lack of awareness. I try to focus on the positive end of it, like the few people who accept me and get to know me.

Reflection Questions

1 *Professionals with positions of power.* Alice shared experiences where professionals in positions of power were, at best, unhelpful and perhaps, at worst, detrimental to her educational journey. While it may be that these professionals had good intentions, the impact of those in power had negative results. Discuss the helpful and unhelpful actions of these professionals. How did negative interactions with teachers, professors, and other adults impact Alice? Can you identify a time when a person in power (e.g., teacher, doctor, employer) impacted your life, positively and/or negatively?

2 *Inspired to advocate.* Alice described how her experiences in school inspired her to become more socially active—both by supporting blind youth and through political campaigning. What factors do you suspect led her to being an advocate? What experiences in her disability story can you identify that led her to a life of activism? What life experiences might lead you to become an activist?

3 *Employment bias.* Like many other blind adults, Alice found it difficult to secure consistent employment since graduating college. In fact, the unemployment rate for disabled adults in the United States is nearly double that of people without a disability. Why do you think this is? What messages do these employment data send to the disabled community? How does ableism play a role in an employer hiring a disabled person? What can we do as professionals and as a society to challenge pervasive exclusion of disabled people in workplaces?

5 Meet Juno

Pronouns: She/her
Age: 31
Self-identified disability: Learning disability, reading comprehension
College major: Public health with a concentration on health policy management
Current living situation: A home with a husband and two children
Current job/position: Hospital administrator
Passions: Community health, psychology, gender equity, family

Juno identifies as a Chinese American and woman of color. She is committed to her education, public health, her husband, and two children. When we first met Juno, she was a graduate student striving to earn her master's degree in public health with a concentration in health policy management. Juno described how the salience of her disability varied over her lifetime. High school was the most complicated time of her life as a person with a learning disability. She explores the personal effects of academic tracking and social stigmas and how she wants to parent her own children. Juno's story is one of perseverance. It illuminates how major exploration, career moves, and family decisions can ultimately lead to the achievement of one's goal.

During the first interview, we asked Juno to start by telling us a little about herself. This is how she responded:

That's a very big question. I never bring up disability. I always say I'm Chinese. When people want to get to know me, I'll talk about things that are going on in my life, interests, or sports teams. I'm studying public health, I'm in health policy management. My thesis is on maternity leave.

As the conversations evolved, Juno shared her thoughts about the concept of disability, the nature of her own disability, and its impact on her self-concept.

DOI: 10.4324/9781003495703-5

Disabilities can be in different categories and levels. There's also a mindset. A learning disability is what I have. You're not as defined (as disabled) when it's not a physical disability. Mine is more of a learning and mental disability. It's kind of not something I really think about all the time. Most people would never know because a lot of people don't see my disability. I don't hide it. It's just part of me. It doesn't really come up very often. My disability is related to reading comprehension. I don't comprehend things as fast as most people. That's pretty much it. I've had it since elementary school. I've kind of grown from it. I don't think it affects my work right now. It did more when I was going through school.

I was diagnosed in the 3rd or 4th grade. My mom had to fight for them to test me for a disability. They wouldn't test me for some reason. She's the one who found it out, got me tested, and got all the accommodations. She was the one who went to all the teacher conferences. My dad supported me as well. I had to take extra classes to help with it, but I don't know if they really helped. They gave different strategies and tips on how to, not conquer it, but to help function a bit better. When I was in elementary school and middle school, I was with other disabled students. A lot of them needed an aide.

I went to a public high school. It was fine. They had different levels of classes, which kind of made me feel uncomfortable. All my friends were in the regular normal classes, honors classes, or taking AP classes. Whereas I was at the bottom of the food chain. They were reading Romeo and Juliet, and I was reading something easier than that. The teachers never really recommended me for regular classes. When I wanted a regular class, they said, "I don't think you're ready for it." It kind of discouraged me. I was like, "Well, why do you think I'm not ready for it?"

Despite discouragement, Juno did go to college. Once in college, she explored a variety of major and career options with some input from family.

I knew I wanted to go to college. That was my ultimate goal. At the time I didn't really care where I went to college. I didn't really know what I wanted to do because 18 is a hard age. I was really interested in psychology because I had taken some classes, but my parents were like, "You can't really do much with it. You would need to get a doctorate degree. That career path is so open. It's a hard field to get a job in right now." My parents were saying that I should stick with health—stick with something that has a career guarantee. It changed my pathway to what my major was.

Originally, in health, I wanted to be in nursing. But, it changed. I realized it wasn't a field I really was interested in. I couldn't really deal with death, dying, and sickness. It's really depressing. I knew I didn't want to do business because I don't really like that. I still don't like it. I didn't want to do anything math-based. Science-based was okay. English was off the table. I wanted to stay with health. The school I was in had nursing, physical therapy, nutrition, community health, and lab sciences. Community health sounded really interesting. It was something that I could still stay in the health field, but not have to deal with sick patients and blood. I picked that field. Towards junior and senior year, I got more into public health versus freshman and sophomore year when I was just kind of in general health courses. That time definitely shaped my career path and what I wanted to do in graduate school. I got my undergraduate degree in community health. I got a minor in psychology. After earning my undergraduate degree, I had two plans. Apply for grad school. If I didn't get in, I would get a job. My professor helped me a lot. He had a master's in public health, actually a doctorate. He helped me think about a master's in public health and where it could take me. I went to graduate school for public health.

Juno explained how having a disability impacted the way she thought about herself as a college student.

I don't really think about having a disability. I feel kind of awkward when I have to alert the professors at the beginning of the semester that I need extended time. If I know I don't need it, I won't use it. But, it's something to have. Other than that, I don't really feel like I have a disability. It's not as severe as I know other disabilities are. I feel like you're kind of slightly different because you get the extended time. The rest of the class wishes they had more time.

In college, Juno advocated for her learning needs. Although she did not always utilize disability services, she used other campus services and developed her own academic strategies to succeed.

The college was supportive of my needs. Everyone's been supportive. I really haven't found anyone who's been negative about disabilities or helping. I also advocated. My mom didn't advocate for me in college. It was all me. I made sure I had the paperwork that needed to be submitted to disability services to get access to extended time for tests. I submitted it to my professors. It was me going to my professors and saying, "I have this disability and need extended time." They were perfectly fine accommodating me. They never made a huge deal about it.

In college, I barely saw the disability people. My accommodations were just for extended time. Other than that, I was on the same playing field as anybody else. I just needed extended time. Towards the end of college, my disability paperwork expired. Then, it was getting a little bit more difficult, but I advocated for it, saying I had documentation since elementary school. I actually had someone who would review my papers, but then they stopped doing it. That was fine because there were other resources on campus: tutoring or a writing center. There are other resources that most of the other students use. I take advantage of those things. I go to office hours. Teaching Assistants just explain things in a different way than the professor explains things. It helps. I use calendars and reminders. I make lists of things that I have to do.

For reading, I use a Kindle. My mom got a Kindle. I took it, and that was it. I can look up words easier on that versus reading a regular book where I have to go out and actually look up the word. Other than that, one of my success strategies is just reading more, which I don't really get to read for fun much. I read more research papers.

Juno went on to graduate school. After hurdles in receiving accommodations, Juno actually found them to be less useful than expected. After learning to adjust to writing expectations, Juno found graduate school to be easier than prior schooling.

My mom looked to see if you can get disability services. I didn't know that you could get disability accommodations in graduate school. I also didn't know that you could get them in a workplace too! For graduate school it was a little bit more difficult just because I had to do the testing all over again to receive accommodations. They were able to accommodate extended time even in graduate school. I didn't really take many tests in grad school. Overall, my disability hasn't really impacted me as a graduate student. The only thing that it affects is more writing. My first year was a little bit harder because I had a hard time understanding what they wanted for writing. Other than that, it hasn't been bad because, in undergrad, I was used to it. Now it's just kind of normal, nothing really unusual. It was more papers, so I didn't really use extended time that much. Since I've grown older, I've read more, started to study, and been challenged more. So, graduate school has been a lot easier.

Juno talked about the journey from school into the workplace—including her decision not to disclose her disability to prospective employers and the lack of information she received as she transitioned into the work world.

I didn't get any advice or anything about how disability might affect my work life. I don't really think my experience as a disabled person changed much since graduating. I mean, I haven't forgotten about my disability. But, I'm not as defined by it as much anymore as I was in school. In school, especially middle school and high school, I was more defined by it versus college. In college classes, I was at the same level as everybody, regardless of a disability or not. Yes, I had accommodations for extended time, but other than that it was not obvious to others. Even now, through my work, I haven't said, "I have this learning disability. I need this accommodation." I don't even talk about it with an employer. I just never felt like it was necessary. It wasn't a huge disability where it would affect my work. I know that there are a lot of laws against discrimination, but I felt that it could affect me getting hired if I disclosed. I also wanted to be on the same level as everybody else and not have a stigma. It was more on myself being cautious or conscious about it. I never felt like I needed accommodations on the job.

Throughout her life, Juno was fortunate to find social support from her family and her boyfriend (whom she later married).

It was really my mom who was more of an advocate of me getting what I needed done. My dad and brother didn't really know much about it. It didn't affect my family dynamics. It was more in school where my disability mattered.

My dad passed away a couple of years ago. I was close to him. Both my parents lived in a different state. They're spread out. We do get together with my mom and brother for holidays when my brother can manage to get away from his work. My mom comes up every couple of months. As I get older, it's a little bit more difficult. Since the passing of my dad, my brother and I talk a little bit more. We still don't really talk that much, but that's always been the case. When we were younger, we fought like cats and dogs. My mom has always been supportive of things I've done. We talk once a week or so.

My husband—we met and dated through college and have been together since then. He didn't really know about my disability. Even when I told him about it, it didn't really change much.

Various sources of social support played an important role in her personal development. Describing how she responds to struggles or discouragement, Juno emphasized the importance of social support.

Sometimes, if it's really bad, I get really upset. Most of the time, I just talk it out with somebody, and that's about it. It goes away. I talk to my boyfriend and my parents and then with friends. I don't think my parents really understand what I'm discouraged about. When I was younger, we talked about it. Now it's different, just a different relationship. Last week, my advisor said I hadn't sent her my version of the proposal when I had. She wrote me an email saying I feel you're behind and explained it to me like I wouldn't turn it in on time. Of course, I returned it on time because it was more of a consequence for me. I kind of felt discouraged. I talked about it with my boyfriend and then my roommate.

Juno reflected on her personal growth, increasing independence, and evolving familial relationships through and after college. Looking back, she wished that her college had better prepared students for the fiscal decisions of adult life.

My college experience shaped me a lot—it helped me grow up. I was sheltered a lot, so I didn't get to experience as much in high school versus in college. College was the first time I was away from home. Granted, home was only 45 minutes away, but I wasn't going back home every day. I was living on my own and living with other girls versus my brother and parents. Living with different people was a different experience. I liked a lot of the independence. Later in college, I became an orientation leader and a tour guide. That helped with public speaking and getting me out of my shell. I wish I had broken out of my shell a little bit more in freshman year and sophomore year.

As I started having a family, it made me feel more adult-like. When I was living with my parents, it's kind of hard to comprehend, "Oh, I need to be able to pay for x, y, and z." I had to be able to afford rent and electricity and all that stuff. Now, owning a home with my husband and having a family, it's changed my thinking. I need money for all this! College had all these services, like career services which help with resume building and stuff like that. I don't think anything really helps you succeed unless you take advantage of it, or you're forced to take advantage of it, or you're forced to learn it. I wish they had taught about general life skills at college. There's never a course to learn how to do taxes or buy a house, or what to look for in a house. Basic financial stuff. After college, you have debt. What do you do?

In the first interview, Juno's career and life goals were beginning to be defined. She shared her interests in policy, passions about healthcare improvement, and an ultimate desire to work in healthcare management.

I am planning to get a job in the real world. That's my ultimate goal. I want to work on the policy side of things because it's very interesting to change, to make a bigger difference. Management is more a long-term goal. I need more experience in management and policy. I don't feel like I have enough experience in the management field because I went from undergraduate to graduate school. In five years, I hope to have a good position. Five years, what does that make me? Almost 30. I hope to be married by then. I hope to be well-established in my career, maybe have had two jobs—different jobs depending on if I'm happy with the first one. In 10 years, I hope to be in a management position. Having accomplishments—that would be nice. Being successful. Moving up in the pay grade, moving up in a company if I could. I'd like to be married and have kids. And, to retire at a reasonable age, before 80. Travel the world. There are still a lot of places I want to see.

A decade after our first conversation, Juno provided updates on her career path, including positions in healthcare management. Her current role seems to bring together many of her earlier interests and career goals, including psychology, policy, and management.

I have been working more toward growing my career since I graduated from graduate school. I actually took an extra year in graduate school to finish up my thesis. Since then, I've just been working. I haven't moved on from the hospital setting. I'm on my third job—those were just career path movements. They were all full-time. They all have benefits. When I was in graduate school, I thought that I would do more policy work. I did touch base on some policy at the hospital level in all my jobs. But after going through it, for the last six years, my roles have gotten away from policy and changed a bit more towards administration. My graduate degree is in public health and healthcare administration. I've stuck with those areas of administration in my last three jobs. Now, I work as an administrative manager for outpatient psychiatry and research. I'm kind of running the department and managing different things and calendars. My job role consists of the management and the research side of things. I didn't think I would go into research because I just never really had an interest in it. But there's more than I imagined to the role. It's research *and* outpatient *and* psychiatry. It's also working with research assistants. So, that is kind of my role. That's where I'm at.

Juno shared the ways her identity as a woman of color became salient as she moved into adulthood and became a wife and parent. Juno was committed to raising children in a way that emphasized all forms of inclusion.

I definitely have been more cognitive about being a woman of color, especially for jobs. That's definitely been more on my mind lately as a Chinese American and woman of color. I think that's more seeing the politics and what's out there. When Michelle Wu got voted in as Boston's mayor that was a huge milestone. First woman mayor. First woman of color. It's the first woman of color who is Asian. So, I definitely see that as a huge identity for myself.

So, my husband is white. I'm Chinese. Being married to a white person is a huge change for me. Being a biracial married couple is also huge. It's a little bit more common now. It's still hard. That's also another area that my kids will have to grow up with, being biracial, which is very difficult.

My husband and I are on the same page on how we want to raise our kids. I think it's also kind of how the world has changed, especially since when my parents were raising me. For instance, gendered things have come a long way—especially the different toys. So it's just kind of how the world is changing slowly. I made it known to my mother-in-law that I didn't want her to buy dolls because there are no dolls that will look like them. I didn't want my daughter to be raised saying, "Well, why isn't there a doll that looks like me?" That comes more from my own mom. She didn't really want me playing with Barbie dolls because a lot of them are white and blonde. She didn't want that to be what I associate with. There is a Chinese Barbie doll now, but my daughter just plays with a bunny. There's no gendered bunny. It's just a bunny. I have tried to develop that with her, not really doing racial or gendered things with her. Then, the same thing with my son. I won't genderize it. It's up to him to figure it out on his own. We talked about wanting our kids to be supported. If one is playing basketball, we would support them. If one wants to do gymnastics, we will support them. I'm not really big into gender-defined roles. Girls can play with cars. Boys can play with dolls. I don't think there's anything wrong with that. My daughter likes blue. Blue is considered a boy color. I didn't say, "You have to like blue." She just all of a sudden liked blue.

Juno talked about how the pandemic and her perspectives on technology, also shaped her parenting perspectives and hope for her children's futures.

The world is changing dramatically. I hope one day COVID will end. My kid won't have to wear a mask. I don't know about my son when he turns two if this whole mask thing will still be there. I just hope for a better future for them. We talk about being present in our kids' lives and having my son and my daughter be present in their own lives. I'm trying to not have TV as much with my kids. It's a little difficult. We don't have a tablet. I'm trying not to put a cell phone in front of her face as long as possible. I talked about it with my husband. We're both on the same page about it. I hope my kids have better careers than I do, they make more money than I do, and that their futures are going to be a lot different than how I was raised.

Juno's view on life purpose now combines practical monetary goals and a desire to find happiness as she balances her work and family life.

My goal? Not having a toddler anymore (laughs). Having teenagers or pre-teens is another level of stress. I want to be more successful in my career, grow more, and make more money. It's always been a goal, just to make more money. I think that's just a human nature thing just to have more money. In high school, my goals were very simple: college, graduate school, a house, and a job. I've hit all those kinds of simple goals. At this point, I haven't really set 10 year goals. I just want to grow in my career. I also want to be a good mom. That's been my main thing right now—being a good mom and good wife. And, working hard in my job and succeeding.

Reflection Questions

1 *Evolving career goals.* Juno shared her evolving career goals. Although her interests may have seemed like different pathways (psychology, health, policy, management), they ultimately coalesced into a management role that tapped into many of the interests and passions she had told us about a decade earlier. What intentional and serendipitous factors played a role in her journey? What can you learn from Juno about finding a rewarding and evolving career? How did her gradual clarification and revision of her career goals relate to her sense of purpose? What steps might you take to work toward a 10-year plan that brings together your interests, passions, and sense of purpose?

2 *Academic tracking.* Juno talked about the stress of being tracked into high school courses with low levels of academic expectation. She saw her friends taking "regular normal classes, honors classes, or AP classes." She described herself as "the bottom of the food chain" in terms of academic classes. Talk about Juno's academic and professional success—despite this tracking and discouragement. What might be some long-term implications of the academic tracking for disabled youth? What alternatives can you think of to avoid the social stigma associated with this type of tracking?

3 *Independence and preparation for adulthood.* Juno talked about how much she grew during college. She credits the leadership experiences and freedoms - in college to becoming a confident, independent adult. Yet, she also lamented the lack of formal college preparation for financially succeeding after college. What can we learn from Juno's collegiate experiences about preparing college students for the real world? In college, did you receive any education about financial planning? What kinds of experiences, programs, and services might colleges provide to foster confidence, increase knowledge, and build skills for success in post-college life?

4   *Identity and parenting.* Juno talked about the ways her race and gender shaped her experiences and worldview. She noted how important it is for children to see themselves reflected positively in the world—especially in toys and role models. Reflect upon the parenting choices made by Juno and her husband. Why is positive representation important for everyone? How, if at all, did you see yourself represented in toys, media, curriculum, and role models? What are some specific ways you can ensure that young people see themselves positively reflected in images within your spheres of influence (e.g., home, school, work environment, community)?

6 Meet Justice

Pronouns: They/them
Age: 30
Self-identified disability: Bipolar 1, PTSD, Fibromyalgia, and Non 24-Hour Sleep-Wake Disorder
College major: "I changed majors several times, but my major when I dropped out was biology."
Current job/position: Receiving Social Security income
Passions: Invertebrates, environmental education, art

Justice's story documents a lifetime of systemic hurdles in obtaining an official disability diagnosis and getting the support needed to thrive. Their family was willing to acknowledge Justice's physical symptoms, but resisted recognizing their mental health challenges. Consequently, Justice explains trying to succeed academically while not receiving accommodations, battling disease, and fighting for independence. Justice also experienced workplace discrimination while their undiagnosed and untreated disabilities worsened. Despite these hurdles, their commitment to their passions—invertebrates, environmental education, and art—remains consistent. Their main purpose in life—having meaningful relationships with friends and loved ones—also remains unchanged. Through Justice's voice, we gain a unique insight into what it is like to navigate life at the intersection of evolving disability symptoms and diagnoses while also exploring religious, gender, and sexual identities.

Justice defines disability broadly and then describes their own perspectives on the topic. Justice details challenges in getting a formal diagnosis, as well as difficulties managing fluctuations in symptoms.

Disability means a lot of different things to a lot of different people. If I were to give it a one-sentence definition, it would be something that—internal,

DOI: 10.4324/9781003495703-6

mental, or physical health-wise—interferes with someone's ability to interact with the world as it is currently set up.

I have some sort of chronic illness, which was almost definitely inherited from my mom, who has an actual diagnosed chronic illness. I have basically the same exact symptoms and a 50% inheritability rate. But, my doctors don't seem to believe that I actually have this chronic illness that I have all of the symptoms of, and have a 50% chance of inheriting. They won't test me for it. So, I don't actually have a diagnosis.

I feel like my entire life kind of fluctuates in cycles. Instead of just consistently being the same amount of sick all the time, sometimes I feel perfectly fine, and then other times I feel so sick that I can't get out of bed and go to class. So, a lot of times when I'm feeling fine, I convince myself that I'm not actually sick and that I was imagining it the whole time. So then I'll bite off more than I can chew, or the perfectly fine amount for me to chew while I'm healthy. Everything will feel great. And, I'll be like, "Yes, see, all I had to do was forget that I was sick, and I'm fine." And then a chronic illness flare will hit me. It's really discouraging because then I can't finish any of the projects that I started, including school projects. It's this process of constantly reminding myself when I'm not feeling well that I will feel better and be able to do these things. And, reminding myself when I am feeling better that I will not be feeling better forever. I can't just pretend that I don't have a disability because I feel good now and don't want to think about it.

I am taking advantage of the times when I'm not having too many hurdles. I cram as much as I possibly can into the times when my life is going fairly smoothly. So, I can coast for a while when I'm not feeling so well—without having everything fall apart. Because, if I'm not feeling well, and I'm in a good place, goal-wise, and academically, then I don't feel as bad about having to coast by. I can do the bare minimum for a couple weeks or a month or so until I feel well enough to get back on my feet. Then, I usually start feeling better a lot more quickly, because I gave myself the time to rest, because I had everything taken care of. If I'm on track with what the class wants me to be, instead of being a step ahead of things—then as soon as I stop feeling well, everything falls apart. And, I don't recover for the rest of the semester, because I don't have any chance to let myself recover. I'm trying to play catch up, and then I feel terrible. My grades feel terrible. Everything feels terrible. I just try to stay one or two steps ahead of everything when I'm feeling well so that I don't fall more than a step behind when I'm not.

In the first interview, Justice elaborated on their experiences with autoimmune symptoms prior to receiving a diagnosis.

Well, the first signs of it were actually when I was really, really little before my mom got diagnosed. We got a bunch of testing done at the doctor. They said, "We have no idea what's wrong, except that you seem allergic to everything we tested you for. You must have an immature immune system. Take Benadryl every day for the next few years until it goes away." Then, it seemed to go away around the time I also became allergic to Benadryl.

Around the time puberty happened, the weird pain came back. And so did a bunch of various assorted mental health issues. I thought that was weird because it's like, "I've never felt this way. This is a really frustrating way to exist. Could we get this checked out?" I talked to my doctor and she said, "Do yoga. It's a normal part of puberty." Does everybody feel this way? I just assumed that at puberty, everybody starts being in excruciating pain all the time. It didn't occur to me until like a decade later that people aren't in excruciating pain all the time. Then I hit, like, 20 years old, and it was still happening. It's like, "Are you guys sure this is puberty?" I didn't realize it until my mom started having a bunch of chronic illness symptoms herself, and said, "You should maybe get checked out for this because you have these symptoms too." None of them ended up going anywhere, but my illness kept getting progressively worse. Just this past year, she finally got an actual definitive diagnosis. I still can't find any doctors to test me for it. Kind of infuriating.

Justice cycled through various educational settings, never really finding the support that they needed to thrive from teachers or peers.

Nobody knew I was disabled in preschool through grade 12—other than one year when I was in a gifted class. I was mainstreamed by virtue of people not realizing that I could be anything else. I wasn't included very well. I can count on my fingers the number of friends I had throughout my entire childhood and adolescence. I got good grades, but I was not really functioning very well in school. Nobody would get me help because my grades were fine. Eventually I reached this point where it's like, I'm not doing well, but I need my grades to still be good. I would finally just get so frustrated that I would stop and be homeschooled for a year to a year and a half. I would get so lonely that I would go back to school. I'd realize that I still didn't have any friends at school. I just hopped back and forth between public school, private school, and homeschool because none of them were working for me.

Justice told us what it was like to be a college student with a disability. They experienced hurdles obtaining accommodations, but developed strategies to cope with lack of campus support.

It's a little bit like swimming upstream. Like, the system is really not set up for me. There are things like disability services. All of the times that I've tried to get help through disability services, it's ended up being so much extra effort. My disability gets in the way of getting accommodations for my disability because I don't have the energy to get accommodations. Getting accommodations takes more energy than just swimming through the class without them. To get more than a semester's worth of accommodations, I needed a proper official written diagnosis by the right professional. The doctor who had the ability to write an official diagnosis wouldn't give me more than a diagnostic impression. So, I wasn't able to get more than a semester of accommodations as a result.

Usually, it's easier for me to just come up with my own ways around things than to continue asking other people for help, even when, technically, the help should be provided. If, on the first try, I don't succeed, then I'll leave and come up with my own solution. People will ask, "Why didn't you just ask disability services? They'll give you these accommodations." I tried, but it didn't work. I came up with my own way. This is how I do it now. It takes me like three times as long as everybody else, but I figure it out.

In addition to chronic illness symptoms, Justice described themselves as having features of autism and mental illness. They experienced a lack of family support during the journey toward finding a diagnosis.

I've been having symptoms of autism since I was 2 or 3 years old. I just took them for granted as a normal part of existing. Until the past decade or so of my life, I just thought that's how everyone's life is. Everyone else must experience this also. In middle school, I started realizing that something huge is going on because I don't fit in. I feel anxious about everything.

My mom just refuses to believe that I'm mentally ill and thinks that all of my problems are just physical health problems. She has a history of a bunch of mental illnesses in her family. She, I guess, was afraid that she would pass them on to me. Like 9th grade, she took me to see a psychiatrist. She stopped letting me go immediately as soon as they suggested that I might be on the autism spectrum. Then, she refused to take me back to mental healthcare people for the rest of my time growing up. She explained to me why exactly they were absolutely incorrect. Being 13 years old, I was like, "Okay, sure. You're my mom. You're a mental health worker. Clearly, you know what you're talking about." I didn't question it again until I was 18. I remember at one point at the very beginning of college, I met some of my mom's coworkers. Afterward, she took me aside and said, "You need to stop flapping your hands in front of other people. My coworkers keep asking me if you're autistic." I'm like, "Well, of course I'm not. You told me I'm not." It didn't occur to me until years later that I might be.

Eventually, Justice took a leave of absence from the university. After experiencing new levels of independence while in college, Justice found it hard to adjust to living at home.

My brain has not been functioning well enough for me to do school and work at the same time. I can't work either. I really can't. I'm living at my mom's house because I can't do anything at all. I just got to a certain point in trauma recovery stuff. It just set off this chain reaction of mental health problems. I reached the point where I had to actually address it. Everything else fell apart subsequently. I just sit at home a lot. I don't really have any control over where I go. I wouldn't be able to afford a car even if I did have a driver's license. I'm in my twenties and have been living independently for the past four years. Suddenly, I don't have any independence at all. Maybe I should just accept that this is not going to get better and then make the best of my life with that knowledge instead of trying to force it to get better when it's not going to.

Finally, after years of attempting to receive a formal diagnosis, Justice received diagnoses from multiple doctors. They describe how these diagnoses impacted their evolving sense of self.

I've been diagnosed with bipolar one, PTSD, fibromyalgia, and Non-24-hour sleep-wake disorder. The different diagnoses came from different people. It took several years to accumulate all of those, which is very validating. It was nice when people actually believed me and looked into it like, "Oh, we should figure out what's going on here instead of just brushing it off as—It's just anxiety."

I was really in denial about a lot of my mental health stuff last year. Last year, I was in this place where I just was very convinced that everything was a physical chronic illness. It wasn't accompanied by any developmental disability or mental illness. This year, it's become really obvious that I was not correct. I grouped them into developmental disability things, mental illness things, and physical illness things. I think about them really differently. Sometimes, they are frustrating. Sometimes, I can use them to my advantage. I still think of them as disabilities, but they are also not things that I want to cure. I want to figure out how to exist in the world with them. Mental illnesses are what I actually think of as an illness that I want to get rid of. If they went away completely, I would be perfectly fine with that. They affect how my life operates a lot—always in a bad way, not necessarily in just how I function. When I'm having mental health problems, I don't feel like myself. Whereas when I'm having a hard time with developmental disability things, then I still feel like myself. I'm just frustrated with how I am—if that makes sense. The physical illness is not really as important to my sense of self. It's just something that's there. It doesn't really impact how I think about myself. It just adds another layer of difficulty to my life.

Over the course of three interviews, Justice shared their identity journey related to gender identity and sexuality. In the first interview, Justice identified as a transgender person and talked about how that identity intersected with chronic illness support.

Once I discovered that I could be trans, I thought about it and talked about it non-stop for a couple of years. I found out it was an option right at the beginning of college. Then, at the very beginning of my second year of college, I officially came out as trans. That's obviously been a fairly large part of shaping my identity.

I think about gender as a concept, but I don't think that much about my own gender because it matches how I feel. Now, I don't really have to think about it all that much. It's just kind of this thing that comes up occasionally. Like when I'm having a bad day—when I have to give myself my testosterone injection, my hands are cold, and I don't want to deal with the syringe. Things like that. But the rest of the time, it's just kind of on the back burner.

For gender, I think one of the hardest areas is that autoimmune illnesses are almost entirely a phenomenon that people with XX chromosomes get because there's a genetic component to them. In a lot of chronic illness support communities—for context, because I don't want to keep saying "chronic illness" because it's too many syllables—a lot of younger people with chronic illnesses refer to themselves as spoonies for reasons relating to a blog post that I won't get into. In a lot of the online spoonie communities, everyone is a girl. To the point where they can address a post as, "Hey ladies," and it's referring to like 95% of the community. The other 5% are almost entirely trans-guys and non-binary. I can count on one hand the number of cisgender guys I have met in my entire time associating with the chronic illness community online. Probably, I can count on both hands the number of guys in general, trans or cis, that I've encountered. So, it's really hard to get support and talk about the things I'm going through. They'll say, "Oh, well, here are some fun craft ideas to decorate your mobility aids." And I'll be like, "I don't want to tie pink ribbons on my cane!" It's tricky to relate to a lot of the conversations that happen.

During college, Justice encountered roadblocks when seeking health related services. The intersection of disability and gender identity shaped their provider's assumptions, which often led to inadequate healthcare.

The on-campus health services are kind of terrible. Like once or twice a semester, I'll go to ask about something chronic illness related because once or twice a semester I'll have a really bad chronic illness flare. It'll be interfering with my life. So, I'll go to health services and say, "Help, you're the only place I can get free healthcare, and this is destroying my life right now." Their reaction varies depending on which doctor I get. But, it's always roughly equally unhelpful. I've gotten people who thought I was asking for hormone replacement therapy, because I mentioned that I'm trans. It's like, no, I want help with this chronic illness. They say, "Are you sure it's not because of your hormones?" It's like, "No, this is still not about my hormones. I'm regretting even putting that on my medical records. This is about the fact that my joints are so swollen that I can't bend my fingers." I've gotten doctors who insisted that symptoms I've been feeling since I was in preschool are the result of anxiety that I didn't start feeling until middle school. Worst case scenario, they think they know what's going on, and whatever they think is going on isn't an actual problem. Best case scenario, they don't know what to do with me, so they give me a referral. I've had doctors refer me to other doctors who also had no idea what was going on. Although, to be fair, I had one doctor who actually acknowledged that something was wrong. It was just out of her zone of expertise, and gave me a referral, which was probably the only actually good protocol I've seen at health services in a year and a half.

By the second interview, Justice explains how their gender identity and labels depend on the social context.

I identify as non-binary right now. Sometimes, I call myself gender fluid, and sometimes, I call myself agender. I use he pronouns and masculine words when I'm with family and in certain other settings. In school and work settings, I tend to just let people assume I'm a guy. When I'm online, and in specifically safe spaces, then I go by they pronouns.

In the third interview, their gender becomes more nuanced and disclosure more context dependent. Justice shares their identity experiences, differentiated use of pronouns, and family relationships.

When I'm talking generally, I usually say non-binary because it confuses the least number of people—while still communicating that people should use neutral pronouns for me. Specifically, my actual gender is gender fluid. But my gender fluctuates between three genders based on the situation that I'm in. I'm not really sure why my identity changes from situation to situation. I just know that suddenly my brain is like, I am now loosely grouped with the women because I'm in a religious situation. Or, I'm loosely grouped with men when I'm with my brother. I don't know why this happens.

My ideal gender is nin-gender, which stands for neutral in nature, so just kind of nebulously neutral. That's kind of my default gender most of the time. Then, in a couple of other situations, but mostly around my family of origin, I identify as min-gender, which is masculine in nature, just sort of nebulously masculine. I use either he or they pronouns in that situation. The rest of the time I use only they pronouns, and then in spiritual situations and also sometimes when I'm like in LGBTQ specific spaces I identify as fin-gender, which is, you guessed it, feminine in nature, nebulously feminine. I do not use she pronouns—always they pronouns, unless I'm around my dad and brother. Essentially my dad, brother, and grandparents use he pronouns for me. They are not misgendering me; they're actually using the correct pronouns. My dad knows I'm trans. He knows that I'm a trans guy. I haven't talked to him about being nonbinary, because I prefer masculine pronouns with family anyway. He introduces me as his son to church and such. My mom knows all of the things. She's frank with pretty much anything.

Shifting from talking about gender to talking about sexuality, Justice described how their sexuality, gender, and disability identities were deeply intertwined.

I've come out as like every sexual orientation in existence at some point or another in my life, except as a gay. I figured out that I was not attracted to only one gender back before I identified as a guy. I got that out of the way before I transitioned. I never had the chance to identify as the G in the acronym. I'm also pansexual and panromantic. It's a lot easier to explain. It's just like, "Oh, I'm pan,"—which, in my case, I define as attraction, regardless of gender.

There's a lot of conversations in the community about how asexual people aren't asexual because of any sort of abuse in their past, or because of any sorts of diseases or disabilities. They really want to make sure they drive home the fact that it's a sexual orientation and not a side effect of something bad. But my figuring out that I identified as asexual was largely a result of me getting some space from being a sexual person, which was largely the result from an abusive relationship and a disability. The abusive relationship was largely abusive in relation to the disability. So, the abuse and the disability and the identifying as asexual and aromantic were all so closely tied together. Doesn't really matter what caused what. They're just kind of all in this glob of identities and feelings that can't really be separated.

In the third interview, Justice's sexuality becomes more detailed. Trying to find an authentic label was an ongoing process.

I have oddly specific labels. I'm aceflux, which basically means that I am sometimes more asexual than others. Part of the time, I am completely asexual, and I don't experience attraction at all. Other times I'm demisexual and experience attraction, but it doesn't come up until I've known someone for a while and gotten relatively familiar with, and close to, them. I am also some flavor of aromantic. I don't actually know what flavor of aromantic I am. I usually just refer to myself as demiromantic because that's the closest I have to an accurate label. Demiromantic means the ability to experience romantic attraction, but not until you become fairly familiar with someone, which is kind of what I experience. Romantic attraction is weird and confusing. I know that I feel it in some capacity. I just don't fully understand how, why, and under what circumstances.

Justice described many instances of workplace discrimination. During college, Justice was in AmeriCorps. Instead of having a fulfilling, career-building experience, it was a painful one.

In AmeriCorps, I got a lot of rather unwarranted advice about my disability and career path. So I did two years of AmeriCorps with different programs. In both of them, my supervisors gave me some advice about how I should pretend to not be disabled because being visibly disabled was bad publicity.

In the first program, my supervisor was overall a fairly reasonable person and a generally really good supervisor. But at one point, I had a panic attack at work and almost lost my job over it because it looked bad. That's not really a thing that I can control. And then the other one, my supervisor, was just generally really terrible about disabilities. We had a 14-person team, with three people who had noteworthy disabilities. By the end of the year, all three of us with disabilities had left. So I hung on until the last month, and then I got another job offer, and it was like, "Bye [laughs]."

During my second year, I disclosed to my boss that I was on the autism spectrum, and that I had an anxiety disorder. It never goes well when I tell my employers that I'm not neurotypical. This supervisor was just terrible. I was working in a school. She decided that she didn't feel comfortable with me working with kids or even being in the same building as them. I was officially banned from the school for the rest of the year. I wasn't allowed inside the doors except under very specific circumstances, like when the school was given 24 hours' notice, I would be there. This particular supervisor gave me all sorts of advice about how I should start looking for different career fields, instead of wanting to go into education. One of my official work projects, after I got moved away from direct work with children, was that I was supposed to brainstorm jobs where I wouldn't have to work with children. I had to give her the list. It was terrible. It was the worst job I have ever had.

Justice had a prescription related side effect at one job. Instead of being supportive and honoring their sense of agency, the supervisor involved the authorities, outed Justice to officers, and used the incident to pressure them to quit.

At some point around two-thirds through the year, I started an anxiety medication. I was having too many side effects to get through the rest of the day. I asked for permission to go home, and see my doctor about my dosage. I just need to call a friend to pick me up and take me to my doctor. It would not be good to be fumbling around, trying to run an after school program with 15 middle schoolers.

I tried to explain what was going on. I said, "I'm just too sedated to work today. I'm fine. It's a regular side effect that happens normally in a non-dangerous way. I know exactly what's happening." But, they took me to the nurse's office. The nurse said she was going to call 911. I explicitly asked her not to call 911 because that was unnecessary. I have a phobia of emergency services. Somewhere in the course of this, my supervisor told the police that I'm trans, and told the police that I'm on the autism spectrum. Basically what happened is that I got sent to the ER in an ambulance, that I got charged for and had to pay for. I spent the next several hours on suicide watch for absolutely no explicable reason. Really, all I needed to do was go to my doctor and discuss my dosage with him, and then not take that dosage again.

Anyway, I finally convinced the ER doctor to give me a note saying that I was fine. I could go back to work the next day. My boss informed me that she would be more comfortable if I did not come back to work the next day. It turns out that while all of this was happening, the entire school went on lockdown because of me. The principal was not comfortable with me setting foot in the school again. If I wanted to keep this job, I had to transfer to an office job. I spent the next third of the year with no job description, and them trying to do anything and everything they possibly could to get me to leave voluntarily. They realized that it was illegal to just fire me for being disabled. They just tried to treat me badly enough, that I would leave instead. I didn't. I'm sure that probably made their lives miserable.

In every interview, Justice expressed their passions for invertebrates and evolutionary biology.

Pretty much my entire existence revolves around invertebrates [laughs]. So I have a small group of really close friends who can tolerate me talking about invertebrates non-stop, all the time. When I was a year old my mom would go around the house swatting flies, and I would be like, "No, mom, don't swat the flies. I like flies." I'd pick up their dead bodies and drag them around to their funeral in my toy fire truck. I've kind of always been obsessed with invertebrates. I just kind of research invertebrates for fun and then info dump to anybody who will listen about it.

Despite taking a leave of absence from the university, Justice's engagement with art and environmental education was strong. It is through arts that Justice found connection and an outlet for activism by ensuring their writing and draw-ing represented characters from diverse backgrounds.

I'll make worksheet pages and coloring pages related to environmental edu-cation. I don't want to be an artist as a career. It's just an important thing that I do. I do art trades with other artists, have them draw my characters, and I will draw their characters for them. Part of it is a social thing. I do art as a way of communicating with other people. I write and I draw but I don't really do both of them together because I write and draw totally different things. So, when I'm on a drawing kick, I'm in some art role-play groups. I have friends who draw fantasy animals. Then, when I'm on a writing kick, I write fanfiction. Every few months a year, I'll flip back and forth between those. Most of what I do relates at least indirectly to one or the other of those hobbies.

What I consider activism is not in the form of being a part of a social activism community. It's more in the form of being mindful about things. I give repre-sentation in my character designs and things like that. It's just like self-activism instead of going to a protest. I don't have the energy to go to a protest. I can't really safely go to one anyways. Activism is important to me. I tried to make sure when I'm creating characters that I put thought and research into different pieces of their identity. I try to talk openly about identities that I have. I also try to be thoughtful and empathetic when talking about identities that I don't have.

Justice emphasized how having meaningful friends, social connections, out-lets for art, and a religious community would help make life meaningful.

Just friends, because otherwise I'm really lonely. Also, a religious commu-nity which goes hand in hand with friends. It's a very specific kind of friend group that I like. With friends, I want to relate to them on any level. They can be friends who share different brain things with me. It doesn't really matter all that much, what level I relate to them on, as long as I can relate to them a lot. Whereas a religious community, I want to be friends with them, but I want to be able to relate to them on that specific level.

I want to be a good, supportive friend and family member and to create things that mean something to people. Like writing stories and creating characters that people can relate to or that help people learn things about themselves or other people.

Between the second and third interview, they met their partner of four plus years. They talked about their household and some of the struggles they experi-enced financially.

We met while writing fanfiction on the Internet. We commented on each other's stories and then started talking. We're both disabled. So is his mom, who lives with us. It's just kind of like everyone is disabled, all the time, in our household. On one hand, it means that we get no chores done, ever. On the other hand, that means that nobody is judging anyone ever. So, it kind of evens out. We are very, very poor. We are supporting a three-person house-hold with two people with Social Security Income. We can't afford groceries very well. It's not very convenient. We've been stressed out about it nonstop for months.

Justice identified as Muslim and sought religious support communities. Justice found an online support group that was accessible to disabled people and supportive of both their religious and sexual identities.

I identify as Muslim. I've found a really nice spiritual community with fellow LGBTIQ Muslims. I went to a religious retreat. I made a lot of friends through that. I kept in contact with them. I would visit them for monthly meetings and during holidays over the course of the past several months.

I have a really hard time being active in in-person Muslim communities because they're frequently not accessible spaces for people with chronic pain. Getting out of my house is difficult because I'm terrified of leaving the house because of my PTSD. Like one of the few good things that has happened, socially, since the pandemic started is a bunch of places that had been hosting *not* online for ages were finally like, "Oh, maybe we should have an online presence, because people other than disabled people want to do things online now." Last Ramadan, a couple of LGBTQ and disabled Muslim groups and I got together and co-hosted a bunch of events scattered throughout the month over Zoom. We had everything from meditations together to sharing favorite core passages and pieces of Islamic poetry, and things like that. At one point we also had an arts and crafts Zoom.

People give Muslim spaces a bad rap and say that they're like actively homophobic and transphobic. I don't think that is as much the case. Many mainstream religious spaces don't know how to accommodate queer people. Some of them are like gender-gated spaces. There are many actual, real benefits, but accommodating non-binary people is not one of them.

There's a significant amount of overlap between the two communities, LGBTQ and Muslim. But, there's also groups that are specifically focused on one or the other. There's not a rule that you can only be part of one community. I did make some very good friends there. It helped me figure out my identity. And more than that, it gave me a chance to interact with other people who had similar identities.

Reflection Questions

1 *Hurdles and perseverance.* Identify experiences of hardship and perseverance in Justice's story and the varied contexts in which these occurred. How would you characterize Justice's strengths? What are some of the challenges Justice faces in medical and educational systems trying to get an accurate diagnosis and receive appropriate accommodations? How does Justice's family help and hinder?

2   *Missed educational support opportunities.* Justice talks of performing well academically in their schooling. Yet, they faced challenges making friends and experienced bouts of loneliness. What did the educators in Justice's life miss? What can professionals do to support students facing similar challenges? What are the risks of not supporting a student who is academically successful in school, but struggles with social-emotional well-being? How might these experiences have encouraged Justice to leave college? What interventions/strategies/supports in the K-12 and higher education context could have benefited Justice?

3   *Intersectionality of multiple minoritized identities.* Justice shared how their sexuality, religious beliefs, disability, and gender shaped their daily life. At one point they explained how their multiple identities "can't be separated." How does Justice's story help us understand the concept of intersectionality? How do your multiple and intersecting identities influence your life? Or the life of your students, peers, friends, etc.? How might this story generally, and with a focus on intersectionality in particular, inform the development of inclusive educational interventions and policy?

4   *Ableism and disability pride.* At one point, Justice says that their physical and developmental disabilities are "not things that I want to cure. I want to figure out how to exist in the world with them." What can we learn from this sentiment? What does it mean for disabled people to live in a world not designed for them? Discuss the ways that ableism shapes what Justice explains as "the world as it is currently set up." What can you do in your spheres of influence to design educational, familial and/or work spaces that are designed to include everyone?

7   Meet Kalani

Kalani's story illuminates her experiences coping with disability and bullying in school. We also learn about her commitment and efforts to succeed academically despite hurdles. Kalani shares her life dreams and passions for helping people. Her story shows an intentional scaffolding toward a nursing career and the impact disability had on her career trajectory. Kalani reminds us how important it is to follow one's passion and be open to different job roles in a professional field. Kalani is committed to raising a child who understands disability and who treats others with respect and kindness. Because her son was at home at the time of our third virtual interview, we had the pleasure of not only hearing about the purpose and joy she found in parenting, but we also got to witness it firsthand.

Kalani explained how her disabilities (ADHD, Anxiety, Depression, PTSD) and family structure led to her feeling "different, weird," and isolated during high school.

In high school I just didn't deal with stress in a positive way and I would freak out a lot. I would use choice words that obviously would not be classroom appropriate. I would just need to take space and obviously not be in the classroom because my behavior would affect myself and obviously everybody in the class. It was more when I felt like I was getting mad or anxious or whatever. I would be able to step out and usually go to the school therapist. Obviously

DOI: 10.4324/9781003495703-7

their goal was to get me back into the class before the end of the period, but that sometimes didn't always happen depending upon the situation. I would spend a lot of time in guidance, in the main office, in the principal's office, or in the therapist's office.

In high school I just didn't really have coping skills. I didn't really know how to deal with things. Because I was bullied so much when I was younger, I always felt like people were talking about me. I would call them out on it in the middle of class and not always think before I spoke. What was I bullied for? Everything. The fact that I live in a small town where it's generally the mom, the dad, and the 1.5 kids. My family didn't fit that profile because I am the youngest of seven. We're middle class, but a lot of people are from a higher class. I feel like I always had to prove myself to other people. So, it could be the fact that I didn't have friends, or the fact that I went to church, or the way I looked. I was different. I was weird.

Given her diagnosis and educational experiences, very few people (including herself) expected Kalani to attend college or succeed if she did.

I honestly never thought I was going to make it to college. A lot of people didn't expect me to succeed in college, if I did go. I didn't feel I could tell them I wanted to be a nurse. I have the ability to be one. I just never really felt my teachers saw potential in me. I was constantly compared to my older siblings who were smarter than me, better than me, and succeeded more. I didn't have my own identity. I don't think that they thought that I would end up making it with a bachelor's degree. They probably expected me to end up at a community college if I did go.

Despite her passion, drive, and experience as a CNA, Kalani was only tentatively admitted to college and not initially accepted into the nursing program. Yet she persisted, and was finally admitted.

I've always known I wanted to be a nurse. I became a certified nursing assistant (CNA) at 16. But, I didn't really get the support. I was in a group of 25 people and I was the youngest one going for my CNA. So, obviously I was getting put down there. But when I worked, something just felt right. It was what I was meant to do. Every time I've been in the hospital, or family has been in the hospital, I'm always like, "What does this equipment do? What medication is needed? Show me this. Show me that." I've always just been so fascinated by it. It's just a place where I feel comfortable. I don't normally feel comfortable in a lot of situations but I just feel this (healthcare) is right for me.

The transition to college was an adjustment. But, once Kalani had the right support systems, she began to thrive.

Freshman year, I was definitely struggling with just adjusting to a whole new life and all new expectations. I didn't really know who I was until I came to college because I never felt like I fit in anywhere. So, I didn't know what any of those things really meant and what it meant for me to be who I am. Then I got accepted to a summer bridge program. We're all so different. We all come from such different walks of life, but we're all a family. It just opened my eyes to realize I am me. This is where I'm meant to be. This is what I'm supposed to do. I learned healthy coping skills. I got set up with a therapist and I was put on medication that was working. When I came to college, I originally was not on Adderall. I was on my anti-depressant. Freshman year started to become difficult around mid-term semester. I was not having any accommodations at the time because I didn't know about them. After doing poorly throughout the beginning of the semester and then very poorly on the midterm exam, I called my mom and I said, "I don't know what to do at this point." I was living on campus. She said you should have somebody on campus that can help you with this. I ended up going through my advisor. She told me about how to get in contact with the disability services office. I initially set up an appointment, met with someone and then I had to get documentation from my doctors of my current medical diagnosis. Then, I was able to get accommodations. After that things slowly started to improve. Had it not been for getting into disability services and getting the accommodations I probably would not be where I am. I wouldn't be as successful as I am.

Because she was admitted to nursing through an alternate process, she encountered some faculty members who treated her as if she did not belong. However, she had other mentors who helped her succeed academically and personally.

This past semester I had a professor who definitely treated me differently because of my disability. I've also had a few in the past that have treated me differently. I feel like some people, once they find out you're in this alternate admission program, they look at you differently. So, I have to doubly prove myself to be like—I do deserve this seat in the College of Nursing. I have had a few faculty that do support me. Especially grade wise, I've struggled in a few classes. I approached faculty members and let them know what's going on. I let them know I'm struggling. Obviously they had to sign my disability services paperwork. I would say, "hey, I'm struggling. What more can I do?" And, they would help me out. They would see my passion and say, "I see that you are trying. You are meant to do this." My clinical nursing instructor knew the desire I had. She saw that I was comfortable with what I was doing. I try to remember those professors. My advisor, she has been phenomenal. I can't say enough good things about her. She has helped me on so many different levels in not just school but life issues. I can go to her if I'm having an issue with my boyfriend. I can go to her if I'm having an issue with the professor. I can go to her with anything. She's always had my back. She's definitely my main support when I'm on campus. If it wasn't for this advisor, I would not be where I am today.

Kalani experienced exclusion by peers because of her disability.

I feel like my disability defines me most when I'm in my clinical group because I'm not like them. I don't fit in with them so I'm "the weird girl." They don't say anything specifically, but obviously, I know I don't fit in with them.

It's a group of eight of us and I talk with all of them. I get along with them, but I don't get invited out with them. I normally find at least one person in the group that I can talk with. This semester, I have one girl I do talk with and we have classes together. We've had a class together in the past. She also has a documented disability. So, we take exams separately. We both know of each other's anxieties. She, too, was not invited out with the group. The six of them were all invited and the two of us were not. And, we knew, obviously, that we were not invited. She deals with it better than me. I take a lot of things personally because I feel like I'm the outcast and excluded because I'm not a person with a lot of friends. It does kind of hurt.

During and after college, Kalani continued to explore which type of healthcare setting would be the right fit. She spoke eloquently about how her disability impacted her educational and clinical experiences.

As much as I have a special love for geriatrics—because it's all I've done for almost eight years now—I definitely want to get into the hospital. I'm greatly enjoying maternity and psych which are the clinicals that I'm currently in. I'd consider working in either of those healthcare areas or the emergency room. I want to do something that will challenge my education and help me to grow. Getting good experience is my main goal, no matter which path I go down.

I have good days and bad days. Obviously, the bad days are a lot harder to cope with. I feel like everybody, obviously, has good days and bad days. But, with me, I just feel like my bad days are just really intensified. I have a harder time focusing. I have a harder time completing what I'm supposed to do. My mind wanders a lot more easily than it would on a normal day. I still don't think before I talk. The anxiety portion of my disability, it's both beneficial and bothersome at the same time. It is beneficial because it does give me a drive to keep working. It is bothersome because it stresses me out to the point where sometimes I procrastinate. But, I try to, when I'm in a work setting or clinical setting, use the anxiety to help me work through the challenges I'm facing on the floor. I use that anxiety as adrenaline and try to turn it into something positive. When it comes to the ADHD portion of my disability it's, again, both probably positive and negative. The positive for it would be that little bit of the hyper-activity portion which I use to stay on my feet and to stay on my toes during my shift. But, the negative is I sometimes can forget what I'm doing mid-task. Like, "Oh I forgot to grab a towel when I went out there. Instead I only grabbed one thing. So, I'll have to go back and grab something which can put me behind." But, the anxiety will probably contribute and get me back on track, especially at clinical. Sometimes I feel like they see me for having a disability because I can sometimes joke, like, "Oh you know, sorry I can't focus, it's my ADHD. I forgot to take my Adderall today." I try to use that anxiety as adrenaline and work through situations. But, it's definitely the ADHD that they see.

Despite hurdles, Kalani successfully earned her nursing degree. When asked what it felt like to be close to graduation, Kalani responded:

To finally actually have a dream come true. I mean, it also is kind of like an, "ha-ha! I-told-you-so! I could do it!" to all the people that doubted me. But when it comes to myself, it's definitely like I set my mind to something and I'm achieving it.

During interview one, Kalani ruminated about the things that would bring her joy and make her life feel complete.

In the future, hopefully I'll be working as a nurse. Hopefully, I'll have a house and be married to my boyfriend. Hopefully, I've started a family. I'd like to have a few kids. Saving someone's life! If I know I can truly, actually save someone's life and bring someone back? That would be pretty awesome!

During the final interview, Kalani reflected on those dreams and proudly explained how she achieved them. She also described the challenges of being a nurse during the COVID-19 pandemic.

Since my first interview, I've had a child. I finished college and became a nurse which is what I went to college for. I have a job. I have a house. I'm married, I'm pregnant right now. So, I'm just kind of living the American dream. I guess with disabilities, it's a modified dream. I still have the disabilities. But, they affect me differently because I'm at a different point in my life. I don't have to take tests. So, that's a huge thing! Test taking was such a huge, stressful part of college that triggered every anxiety I had. With being a mom, a wife, and a nurse, I still have responsibilities that I need to fulfill. But, it's different—so it triggers the anxiety differently. Not so much with the job that I have now—but with my last job, anxiety impacted my work constantly. I have a more laid back job now. I do pediatric home care. So, I'm only in charge of one patient. But, prior to that—before I was pregnant with my son and during my whole pregnancy, I was the supervisor for a second and third shift. The nurses were constantly getting locked in the hospital because of COVID. And, so the anxiety was unreal because I was constantly having everything put on me, having everything expected of me. And, essentially it was a race against the clock trying to get all these tasks done before the end of my shift. So, I guess I could relate that back to college when I was taking an exam and trying to finish. And, I think back to before I had the accommodations in school—just that constant anxiety of "oh my goodness, am I going to get everything done?"

Kalani's perspective on the ideal job evolved. Although some positions were not what she would have planned, she learned that sometimes the right fit for one's life situation are those that are unexpected.

After graduation, I didn't expect to stay in the nursing home where I was a CNA throughout college. I was hoping to get right into the hospital, eventually transition into labor and delivery, which is still my dream job as a nurse. And I didn't do any of that. I ended up just going full time and staying in geriatrics. I stayed in that line of work until my son was born. But, I switched since going back to work after he was born. I now do pediatric home care, which is again a field I never ever would have expected that I would have been in. But, I love it.

There's a lot less responsibility. Instead of anywhere between 25 and 75 patients I'm responsible for, it's one patient I'm responsible for. It's only one person I have to chart on. It's only one person's medication I have to keep track of. I stay in contact with a lot of people who work in the hospital and who work in the nursing homes. It's taken such a toll physically, mentally, emotionally on so many people.

Had you asked me this years ago if I ever expected to be doing home care in general, or pediatric home care, I would have said, "absolutely not." But, this opportunity came to me in the middle of the night. My son was probably about six months old and it's just where I'm meant to be right now. And, I tell my client all the time that mentally this is what I can handle. But, there are days where I'm like, "You know what? I don't feel like I'm being challenged enough. I don't feel like a real nurse. I just did all of the schooling. Is this really what I want to do?" But, then there are days where I'm like, "No, I'm still able to provide for my family." I'm able to come home every night, I don't have to worry about that stress of being locked in the hospital during COVID. Or, if the next registered nurse is going to come on duty. Overall, it's a lot more rewarding. And, knowing I get to come home to my son every night is the best, and my husband too.

During our last conversation, Kalani talked about her life purpose and how it centered around being a good mother. She was also deeply committed to role modeling asset-based understandings of disability in her family.

My purpose? Probably something to do with this little guy right here (referring to her son in the room). "What's mommy's life purpose? To be a good mommy!" My purpose is to try and be a respectful human and to raise a respectable human who respects himself and others. I'm not gonna bring my son up to know that having a disability, or seeing a therapist, makes you weak. It's not a punishment. My husband and I jokingly say, "Oh we're going to get him into therapy very, very early." And, that's totally fine. Like, it's a good thing we can all benefit from it. I'm very pro therapy. Mental health matters, and he's gonna know it. He's gonna know Mommy struggled, mommy still struggles.

Reflection Questions

1 *Pattern of exclusion.* During her early educational memories, as well as during college, Kalani felt left out by her peers and educators. What did you learn from Kalani's story? How did this exclusion impact Kalani? Why might a disabled student feel excluded in educational spaces? How can educators foster more inclusive and welcoming spaces for minoritized students?

2 *Crystallizing experiences.* At a young age, Kalani wanted to become a nurse. Even though she faced some discouraging setbacks when applying to nursing school, she points to instances that confirmed that nursing was the right path for her. For example, she describes how obtaining her Certified Nursing Assistant (CNA) license at age 16 helped confirm this dream. What other instances does Kalani share that sustained her pursuit of becoming a nurse? What instances in Kalani's story do you think had the most impact on her decisions to become a nurse? What experiences have inspired your own educational and career path? Consider the ways Kalani's life purposes remained consistent over time, but her ideas about the ideal job transformed as her life evolved. What can we learn from her career journey?

3 *Family and work matters.* From the first interview to the third, Kalani shared her dream of having a family. In what ways has her disability identity been impacted by having a child? How did Kalani's experiences shape the ways she thinks about purpose, parenting, and work-life balance? As a mother to a toddler, Kalani plans to talk to her son about disability in positive and asset-based ways. What is your reaction to her plan? How might you talk to young children about disability in a way that does not reinforce stigma or deficit notions?

8   Meet Kennedy

Pronouns: He/him
Age: 57
Self-identified disability: Traumatic brain injury
College major: Undergraduate; Computer Science; Graduate; Master's in Electrical Engineering
Current living situation: In process of moving into house with partner
Current job/position: Part-time computer programmer
Passions: Mechanics, motorcycles, electronics. To be productive, happy

Kennedy takes us through the often unpredictable journey of adjusting to life after acquiring a disability in a motorcycle accident. Kennedy offers a unique perspective, not only as a student with an acquired disability, but also as a nontraditional college student, returning to college in later adulthood. Due to the extent of his disability, Kennedy is often left wondering what difficulties can be attributed to his injury versus other factors such as age. He walks us through what he refers to as the "good and the bad," teaching a powerful lesson of persistence and inspiring us with his natural sense of curiosity.

Kennedy was a graduate student in electrical engineering when we met him in 2013. He was quick to share how, at 18 years old, a motorcycle accident impacted his educational journey. But, it never deterred him from his academic passions.

My background has been mostly math and science. I got interested in electronics at an early age. I was always taking things apart. I had a motorcycle accident about 20 years ago and I've been picking the pieces up ever since. I suffered a brain injury and lost the use of my right arm. I managed to complete a computer science degree just before I moved here. I've finally come to a point where I feel comfortable pursuing a master's in the electrical engineering program now, and I love it.

DOI: 10.4324/9781003495703-8

One of the things that I loved so much about being in school was that I knew that I was going to learn something—whether it was what I was looking for or not. I knew every day, I was going to be moving forward. But it also can easily be a bit overwhelming.

Kennedy shared how life changed for him after his accident and diagnosis of a Traumatic Brain Injury (TBI). Often speaking about "before" and "after" his accident, Kennedy offers ways he appreciates, and struggles with, the changes in his life following the TBI.

I mean early on, just relearning to do things like get dressed, driving a car, and driving a stick shift car brought a lot of joy. It kind of gave me the courage to try more things. On the bad side, definitely the standing out, kind of getting "the stare," even if unintentional. I mean I don't mind talking about it. I don't mind people asking about it, but I get self-conscious now. It's awkward. Somebody goes to shake your hand and a lot of times I put out my left hand and they take it back. That's just kind of awkward, but I would say there are some things that I can't do or I can't do anywhere near as well. That's always bothered me. I mean there's a mental part, too, because I had a brain injury as well. I found caps on mental abilities that did not seem to be there before.

One good thing that has come out of it is it has given me a higher tolerance for other pain. That's also not working so much to my advantage lately. But, for a long time, I could bash my hand on something and not really think about it. I'd see other people going "ow" a lot more than I was. They're like, "Oh, that had to hurt." Whereas I feel like, "No, that doesn't hurt. Nope, I got this other thing going on. No, actually, it doesn't hurt that much."

In the immediate aftermath of his injury, Kennedy spoke to the difficulty and frustration of not being able to jump right back into his undergraduate program.

I had just started. I took that year off, and I actually switched colleges and went full-time, which I believe was a mistake. I mean, I lived on campus, I did the whole full-time thing, and I don't think I was ready for that. And also, I was a math major at the time, so I signed up for all this calculus, which I wasn't ready to get back to either.

I think I convinced myself that I could pretty much pick up right where I left off in so many ways. Why should that be any different? But, it was a struggle. I ended up not being able to take the full course load. I tried different living arrangements, but eventually came back home and started taking courses from home. I started seeing a psychiatrist then too, trying to figure out what to do with my life. I think I was not finding what I needed. I don't want to say I was in denial. But, I did perceive, for a long time, that I didn't have a disability. I didn't think about it. There was much that I could still do. And, I expected to keep doing it, to keep going. I was definitely not prepared for the brick walls that awaited me.

Going back to school was… I think it was that I didn't realize how jumbled my brain still kind of was. And, there was nobody questioning it. So, I had impossible standards sometimes. But, I know that no one else told me to set those standards—no one else but myself. I mean, when I was first out of the hospital, I remember learning things like tying my shoes with one hand, and driving with one hand, even driving a manual transmission. That was a big deal. There were a lot of things that you don't think twice about—things you just do two-handed. Now, I'm having to think about doing things—and it's not just the difficulties of doing it or figuring it out—but it can be very time-consuming. It really slows you down. And, you don't feel like you fit in groups a lot more just because you don't feel in sync with people. Well, there is a lot of that.

As Kennedy has gotten older, he has found that his disability experience, including disability-related pain, is frequently changing.

It's more difficult to tell now what is disability and what's aging, I mean, or normal wear and tear. My right hand and most of my right arm is not usable. So I've been overdoing it with my left. As a result, I've got pretty early onset arthritis, tendinitis, carpal tunnel, you name it. That's taken a turn for the last month or so. I had physical therapy in the past. I've had some cortisone shots when it's gotten really bad. Mostly, I just depend on heat and topicals. Sometimes anti-inflammatories help, and sometimes they don't. This is one of those times where they don't seem to be helping.

The worst pain I suffer from is from pulling the nerves out of my right arm. I pulled them out of the spinal cord in the dorsal region. So, not only do they not grow back, but, you get a phantom limb pain through your entire arm. And, it constantly feels like it's under a vice. So, there's a 24-hour pain that has never gone away. And, there's also a fire-like pain that for the first year or so it would come and go. It would keep me up at night even. I would wake up to it. I began to control it a little better. I am learning not to do some things, like not to lean on it. I still have to watch out for that sometimes.

It's just kind of an overload. And, I actually tried an implant that is more commonly used for leg amputees or for spinal injuries. Not in the dorsal region, but I found someone here who was sort of playing around with it. I actually did the temporary implant for a stimulator that kind of worked to mask the pain. But, they had to turn it up so high that it would literally be shaking the whole top half of my body.

After returning to school, Kennedy had to consider the physical implications of his TBI and the impact on his cognition as well.

I think you get this sense of immortality when you're able to do so many things so well. When you can do everything that well, how hard could something be? Yet, I feel like I'm confronted with it more and more, at a higher frequency throughout the day. I think, "Oh darn, I wish I could have a second hand for this, or that," or, "I wish this didn't" or, "I wish that this simple conversation didn't feel like it was overloading me."

It put me way behind. I mean it really put [college] on hold to the point that I really wasn't sure what I was capable of in a lot of ways, and especially academically. I knew I had an interest in electronics. I went to junior college at the time and was kind of trying to get up to speed that way. I had originally started undergrad pretty strictly for mathematics, but by the time that I had finished the associate's degrees, that's when desktop computing really started taking off, and so I kind of fell into that. I worked at a university there and that enabled me to go back to school at night. Working in that environment and watching computing taking off is really what got me to give computer science a go.

I mean, I excelled at the math stuff, right. It just kind of came to me. That was, I think, more of where I didn't see the brick wall coming. Because, here I went in with straight as in math classes and then I'm here, and I can't. I'm practically flunking. I had to give up. And, it was kind of a roller coaster for me because when I went to electronics college I started to excel again in math.

Part of the struggle was definitely that I went into this full force, all at once. I was all in. And, no way could I handle trying to figure out the coursework, my way around this new environment, and living away from home. I missed things that might've helped. I have a tendency to get overwhelmed, which I think has gotten worse post-disability.

I was going to bed a lot with unsolved problems, and I couldn't stop thinking about them. At the time, especially in college, I was working full time and taking classes, and not getting enough sleep. I asked my primary doctor if they were going to help me get rest. So I was sleeping—kind of shift sleeping. And, literally, there were a few days where I would go to bed trying to think how I would write some code. And then I'd wake up and start writing where I left off. It was kind of creepy.

Coding sounds very difficult. It's still very difficult for me, not just because of the fast-paced atmosphere. I also don't feel like I have the deep attention span, a lot of the time, to figure things out or to go as far as I need to. I get frustrated. I mean, for something that I like so much, it's still not easy for me. I don't really ever feel like I mastered a lot of things. I don't feel like I take in material as well overall. I struggle sometimes with just about anything. Technical stuff or higher math used to come pretty easy for me. Another change is that I have a much harder time with exams now. That's been kind of rough for me. I mean, extra rough. Because I used to do very well with tests, I preferred them to writing a paper. Now it's kind of the opposite. I don't think my memory works anywhere near as well as it did—I didn't notice it right away, but within a few months, I started hitting brick walls. I felt like it was just the capacity to learn or to remember, and, while it was still good, it was definitely deficient. I literally went from not having trouble with most exams to having trouble with most exams.

Kennedy reflected on finding a career that suited his passions, but was also feasible given his TBI.

There certainly has been a lot of math in my major. Not quite as much, as I've been more selectively in computer engineering. It's a little less than straight electrical engineering. That was kind of a downside. I kind of had to make a decision, I think, not to take a lot of signals analysis classes. I really would like to, but I realized that I may not be able to handle it. Sometimes I wish I had attempted to go the full … I call it the full electrical engineering route. I mean, even though that is my degree, sort of, the track I went was actually in computer engineering. And, hence all the digital design work and barebones understanding of computing and processing. But I do feel like, had I been able to do the straight electrical engineering track, there might have been more doors open for me. And it was also kind of my first love. It was what I really wanted to do. But when I first started out at school, I had taken a course that was difficult for me. And, so I thought it would be a little less stressful to go to the computer track. In some ways, it was. But I mean, I still yearn for the *math-y* part. I wish I had. I was encouraged to take some electronics courses, which I did try to do, but towards the end, unfortunately, that was bad timing.

Despite the challenges that arose in returning to college, Kennedy persisted. He developed coping strategies that work for him. Kennedy explained how his mindset influenced how he dealt with self-doubt in school after his accident.

The first thing that comes to mind is just not giving up. I mean there were a lot of stops and starts even before that, and I think that became even more fre-quent and slower. I was taking classes all part-time, so it took several years. It became, "When is this going to be done?" kind of thinking.

I think that I already feel like I've gone from, "I'm not sure I can do this," to, "I do think I can do this!" The encouragement I've received along the way from faculty I've spoken to—not even those that have been my instructors—and working with Disability Services, it's been a tremendous help.

Here at my graduate school, I've asked for not only extra time, but also some-times a separate setting. That's helped somewhat, or at least lowered the anxiety. But one of the things, at least so far, that seems to be holding in graduate work is that there are a lot more projects and not so many exams, which is interesting. I was not really a project person. I was more of an exam person before. But, that seems to have kind of flip-flopped.

Last fall, I thought I had taken on a bit too much work and school. I went to my professor. I told him that I wasn't sure I was going to be able to do too well, or do the work. He immediately went, "Oh, yes you can." That helped me a lot, hearing that coming from him. More recently, I've gotten encouragement in the way of suggestions, just stuff to look at for this independent project. Yeah, that's been very encouraging. It's gotten me thinking about stuff that I thought of as kind of "off-limits." I mean just the stuff I'm working on now to the idea of pull-ing a whole thesis out of it. I feel like my professor kind of took me under his wing this semester and just started hurling ideas at me, until some stuck.

I've learned organization is very important. I've been finding more ways to chip away at things so that harder projects don't seem so insurmountable. Not just time management, but kind of work management, I suppose. Not giving up and doing the best I can. And, not being so critical. I mean, I think I've always been rather critical of myself. That's something I can't deny.

I've had so much encouragement along the way from family, teachers, and friends. That's gotten me upbeat quite a lot. I think accomplishment is something I get the most joy out of.

Kennedy shared how disability impacts his interpersonal relationships, especially with his fiancée.

I do feel like I struggle a lot with my fiancée. She likes to talk a lot and she likes to chat, and she likes to go over stuff more than once. Whereas I'm the kind of person where almost every word that comes out of somebody's mouth is more information. I mean, I can feel it by the word. And, I'm not sure how much of that is disability and how much of that is just me. I mean, she's starting to realize that that's happening and she's taking it a little easier on me. But, she gets kind of worked up, especially during the day because of her job. She's in a customer service position where she talks a lot and has to communicate a lot every day.

I'm sure it does impact my relationships in many ways that I may not even realize. But, I think one thing is that my fiancée tends to kind of mother me. I don't like that at all. I think she helps me more than I may need. That is something else that I deal with. Out in public, if you struggle with things, some people just kind of race in to help. That is something I think is pretty prevalent. But, you need to figure out how to do it yourself. I was always a pretty independent kind of person. And, I think that was destructive at the time, and it really bothered me. But it did help me see how other people struggle. Like someone in a wheelchair might be struggling to get through a doorway or something. And, I feel the same tendency to want to go help. And, now I kind of hold back on that and maybe ask, "Would you like help?" or just being there, things that I found help me.

Kennedy mentioned the support he received from his father and brother. He also described how the loss of both of his parents contributed to his self-esteem in the years following his accident.

Well, they were incredibly supportive. I have an older brother. Our parents let both of us be ourselves and just develop, kind of go our way whenever possible. Unfortunately, I lost my mother when I was 12, so I don't feel like I got to know her that well. My father did try to pick up the slack. I think that was a bit much for him, but I still feel he was very supportive. I mean he tried. I think I'd give an A+ for effort.

I'm still very hard on myself and I have difficulty looking at my successes alongside my failures. I think that comes, in part, from missing out on some of my support system. And, partly just thinking that I can go it alone when I probably can't or shouldn't. And, I get caught in the spiral of feeling bad about myself.

Kennedy shared how the COVID-19 pandemic increased tensions with family members and friends who downplayed the impact of the disease.

I can't stop thinking about the next variant or the next surge. Or, is it really safe to go out? But I feel kind of fortunate that I don't need to be out as much, so I don't feel like I need the socialization or just a different venue so much. And not to say I don't like it, I can't enjoy it, but I don't miss it as much as I thought I would. I think my disabilities sometimes make it harder for me to protect myself, even pre-pandemic. But I don't know if I mentioned it, but one of my outcomes was that I got a third-degree burn on my foot. And while it's in good shape functionally, it's very vulnerable, and it's kept me away from crowds ever since because I'm afraid I'm going to get stepped on. But it's something people don't see unless I'm barefoot. Then, they'll notice. I mean, it's that kind of stuff that I feel like I have to be on extra guard. And, I wonder if I'll ever feel less on guard.

I still get in arguments with my brother. When the pandemic started, he had a little bit of a different take. I mean he was in the camp of "it's no worse than the flu" kind of thing for several months. He actually remarried in September of 2020. That was kind of a scary time for me because I did not want to go at all. I didn't want us to go, my partner and I, but I felt like I had to. It was outside, which was good. Here we are. Nobody's vaccinated and there is a large gathering. I mean we were staying the weekend in their home. That was kind of nerve-racking. I was kind of angry with him for not putting that off, but it worked out. Nobody got sick.

Kennedy also talked about the support he received from his father and feeling a sense of increased connection with him in more ways than one.

I talked to my father a lot, and he was still very, very supportive. I used to make almost a daily thing out of it. I would take my dogs out for a walk and I would call him. He kind of had that student/teacher thing going on. And, I always felt like he said something that would make me think. Fortunately, I got to do the same for him a bit. I lost him, oh, just before I went back to school in 2012.

He kind of let me recover on my own. He didn't push me at all. I think some of his friends criticized him because it seemed like he wasn't pushing me. He insisted, "I'm letting Kennedy be Kennedy." There are some times that I wish I'd been pushed, I mean instead of me just trying to pick up right where I left off. I feel like it would have been more important for me to realize, "Hey, your life has changed. It's not going to be the same." But who knows?

Kennedy shared why he holds himself to higher standards, struggles with self-criticism, and is especially hard on himself even in the absence of external pressure. He elaborated on what supports help.

I want to say that I seek approval. But, I don't think I give myself enough of it. When my father was elated with my progress that really meant something to me. And actually, I don't think I mentioned this, but part of the reason that I came to grad school was to honor him. It wasn't just for myself. Academica was pretty important to him. He went on to get a PhD in psychology and he worked for the government mostly. He studied aging, did longitudinal studies, and some of the data he collected is actually still getting used. I used to love going to the office with him to see what new tests he devised to test subjects because, for me, they were like games. Yeah, that was a big part of my life, that connection with him, and I think I felt like I was extending it a bit somehow.

Reflection Questions

1 *Returning to school.* Students with disabilities often face challenges as they pursue higher education, including but not limited to managing their accommodations, learning their rights, and navigating complex social situations. What are some unique challenges that Kennedy faced as an older adult returning to education with an acquired disability? How might some campus resources or support programs be more, or less, helpful for older students? How can campuses create resources for older disabled students to meet their unique needs?

2 *Recognizing successes.* Throughout all three interviews Kennedy talked about coming to terms with his disability and holding himself to high standards post injury. He said, "I'm still very hard on myself, and I have difficulty looking at my successes alongside my failures." Talk about the ways these standards and self thoughts might help or hinder success. Think about your own life. Are there times when you focus on struggles instead of successes? What impact did this outlook have on you? What can friends, family, educators, service providers, and others do to help disabled people successfully navigate challenges, and also celebrate successes?

3 *Disability onset and worldview shifts.* Kennedy experienced a traumatic brain injury (TBI) which significantly impacted his life and worldview. He speaks of life before and after the accident. Kennedy's story reminds us that anyone can become disabled in their lifetime. How does this story differ from those of individuals who were born with a disability or diagnosed early in life? Do you notice any similarities between other participants whose stories included some reference to their life and worldview before and after a diagnosis? Have you ever experienced something in life that shifted how you experienced, or viewed, the world? What can be learned from situations that have a profound impact on one's life and worldview?

9　Meet Landers

Pronouns: He/him
Age: 28
Self-identified disability: Speech Apraxia and Dyslexia
College major: Human Development and Family Studies (HDF) with an Early Childhood focus, Graduate Teaching Certificate, English Language Learning (ELL) Certification
Current living situation: Living with mother and grandmother
Current job/position: Substitute kindergarten teacher and summer camp counselor
Passions: Working with young children, self-advocacy, and helping others

Landers rejects the notion that his dyslexia and speech apraxia had a negative effect on his life before, during, and after college. Although he might have to do things differently than others, he does not view himself through a deficit lens. When peers tried to bully him, he advocated for himself. His mother encouraged him to choose a degree that would allow him to find a job that would make him happy. After exploring a variety of career pathways, he realized his passion for fostering learning and development in young children. A combination of his passions, perseverance, and support guided his pathway toward teaching young children in daycare, elementary school, and community camp settings. Religion, race, and class shaped Lander's experiences and his perspectives as an educator who sees the value in teaching children to develop friendship across differences.

Landers reflected on his initial memories about being diagnosed with two disabilities.

My mom knew there was something wrong because when I was little, I just wasn't getting it. The teacher wanted to hold me back. My mom was like "He

DOI: 10.4324/9781003495703-9

doesn't have a behavior problem. I'm not holding him back." So, she's like there's something not clicking in there. She found a good doctor to help with getting me diagnosed.

Landers shared what his disability means in everyday life.

Disability means someone who has to try harder for something. For me, it's reading. Dyslexia for me is when I read, I get confused in the words. Then, I have to go back and read. I look at stuff differently than other people. My brother doesn't have any disability. If we have to read a chapter or something, it could take him half an hour. It could take me an hour or hour and a half. He doesn't really have to try as hard. But for me, if I have an assignment, I know I have to start two weeks beforehand. I make sure that there's no mistakes so I get a good grade. He'll do something the day before and be like, "Oh, here you go," and get a B. It's just the way it is. I just always just try harder. If I can't do something and I really tried, then I just can't succeed. I'm like, "Okay, then maybe this is not for me." But I always try my hardest until it just doesn't happen.

With my speech apraxia, I have to be more patient and think before I actually say something. Because if I don't, then I'm just gonna just talk. People won't understand what I'm saying 'cause I'm going too fast. My speech apraxia is just—it's just me stuttering. I'm having surgery to fix my mouth, so my apraxia should go away somewhat. Before, it was like I always stuttered. I spoke really fast before. No one really could understand me. No one really knew what I was saying.

I'm personally a shy kid to begin with. Because of my speech, I stutter a lot. But, it's changed now that I had surgery. They moved my whole jaw forward. They broke it and put screws in. When I saw the doctor, he showed me how my mouth is. I noticed how I didn't have that much room left in my mouth. I always, whenever I was doing homework, I'd keep my mouth open, and now I keep it shut. People have noticed how my face, how everything's changed. I notice in my mouth that I have more room for my tongue to produce more sounds. Now, my speech is a *lot* better than before. My mom says she's noticed. Before, I used to have to come out of my shell. Unless I was called on in the group, I'd be quiet, did my thing, and that was it. Other people said they notice how I haven't stuttered as much. I don't really worry as much about how I talk. I may stutter sometimes. That's just the way it is. I know it is a *lot* better than where I was before.

By the third interview, Landers reframed the way he thought about his disability as a combination of strengths. He also considered how his disability showed up in the kindergarten class he taught.

Disability is something that makes it harder for someone to do—makes it harder for them to do fast—like focusing in class or understanding something. For kids in my kindergarten classroom, it is not understanding stuff. They're five and six and if they continue to not understand material further along the road, it's gonna make it harder for them to learn. I learned how to handle it; I know my strengths and weaknesses. I know where they are, what to do when, and what not to do. It's kind of like thinking ahead.

Landers reflected on the ways other people viewed and bullied him for his apparent and less apparent disabilities.

Most people can just tell that I have a speech problem 'cause of the way I talk and how I stutter a lot. My words don't come out as fluidly. Other people looked at me different 'cause of my speech. Not the dyslexia 'cause I don't really talk about that. I don't really say, "Oh, I have dyslexia."

I usually ignore negative comments. It just depends on what they're saying. If they're making fun of my speech, I'm like, "Yeah, cut it out." If they continue, then I'll talk to 'em later. I'm like, "I think we should have a talk about this. It's not funny." When I was in sixth grade or seventh, I had a really big bully. He always made fun of my speech. I just got fed up. Finally, I thought, "It's been a month already, so it's time for it to end." I brought the teacher in. The teacher talked to him. I kept it inside, but my mom knew that there was something wrong. I felt depressed in how—everyone else doesn't have a speech problem, but I'm the only one that kinda does.

When I was in high school, some people said stuff. Some are kinda like, "You're just an idiot." They were just trying to be funny. I was like, "That's just not funny in any way." And my friend's like, "Yeah. I don't know what you're talking about." My friend got suspended for something like that 'cause some kid talked junk. He just couldn't take it. He started a huge fight around him and broke his nose. I usually just walk away and just say, "You know what? If you wanna continue, we can discuss later with a teacher." That usually makes 'em quiet. I just ignore people like that, unless they really start talking stuff. Usually, I just walk away or just ignore them.

Landers detailed the types of support he received during K-12 and college-level schooling.

I'm pretty sure when I was in second grade or first, my mom knew there was something wrong. She had me tested at the hospital. My mom always made sure I had the stuff I needed. For speech apraxia, I had a speech person help me.

I was diagnosed with dyslexia in elementary school. In second grade, my teacher was my tutor. She always helped all throughout elementary school and a little bit of middle school. I'd go visit her once or twice a week. She'd help me do all my stuff. All the teachers knew what I had. They would help me throughout the way and make sure I did well.

When I was in high school, I had a speech teacher help me. I had problems saying some words. She was like, "When you get older, you'll learn how to understand the words. In college you can continue to get speech help." When I was in high school, no one really took into account like, "Oh, this is what you should expect in college." I didn't have the best school counselor. I tried doing stuff on my own and didn't ask for help.

When I came into college, I said I didn't want disability services anymore, because I didn't really use it as much when I was in high school. I'd been getting good grades. Then, when I came to college, I realized that some of these classes are very difficult. I need more time to get some of the stuff done or I was not going to do well. At my first college, they said that my documentation was outdated. I had to get retested. My mom did all that for me. We got me tested. She got the paperwork so I could receive disability services in college.

The University Disability Services Office really helped because they make sure that your accommodations go through with professors. In the beginning, when I get my textbook on audio file, they make sure that it's at the speed I like. In college, I also used the extra time. I don't know how long it's going to take me to take a test. I don't want to get myself stressed out. My professors don't mind.

The University Disability Services Office had a thing there where they brought in all the other campus support offices so we could know about all the resources on campus. They talked about how they help you get ready for classroom success. Someone from the Tutoring and Writing Center came. So, after my class, I go see someone there. We talk about how my grades are, how I can improve stuff. I'm always at the writing center. If I have a paper, I always have someone look over my stuff. Writing tutors help me with ideas of how I should write stuff. He gives his input. I give my input. We make a solution.

In addition to making use of disability services and other support offices, Landers described the strategies he used to be successful in college.

College is harder—not a lot harder. It's a lot more time-consuming. Most of my classes have a lot of reading. I try to use software to read text to me. It depends on the class or the books. My dyslexia is just more making sure I've put enough time and effort into it. It affects me when I'm doing homework. I really need to focus. I always have someone look my drafts over 'cause I always have problems with some of my tenses and stuff like that.

We have to talk while doing the PowerPoint and I really don't like it. We are put in groups in class—so, hopefully I won't have to do the talking. When I have to do it, I study whatever I'm going to say. I make sure I write it down. I don't want to talk too fast. I don't want to stutter. When I'm not prepared to talk in class, I get all red and I get a little bit stressed out.

One of my strategies is time management. I taught myself how to make sure I have enough time to do things. I know tonight, instead of going back home, because I know I wouldn't get anything done, I'm going to go to the library to work and study until I feel accomplished. Sometimes I go on Spotify, listen to music, sit down, and read. Every weekend, I go to a cafe for three or four hours and do my homework and just read because I know that, *there* I can't get distracted. I can't leave. I have to stay there till I get everything done.

Last semester, I made the Dean's list in four classes! This shows I can still do everything like anyone else. It'll just take a little more time.

During the first two interviews, Landers talked about his evolving interests and career aspirations. He considered the ways his disability might influence his success in those career fields.

I always had different things I wanted to do for a career—it just depended on the time. In middle school, it was a forensic scientist. That always interested me. When I started looking at it, it was very hard, and I was like, "Oh, this is just not for me. I'll just watch the forensic TV shows." The forensic thing was a bit out of my league. I knew if I really wanted to, I coulda tried. Maybe the dyslexia did play a part in my decision 'cause it would've been a lot of reading, a lot of memorization. I really struggle with that.

When I was in high school, I was into technology. They had a career-in-tech thing. I really liked it. My aunt worked with computers and I liked what she did. She brought home equipment that I always got to play with. That was always fun, doing something with computers.

I went to an overnight camp. The director for the day camp and I started talking one day. I was about to become a freshman in college. She said to me, "You work really well with the kids. Maybe you want to work here? You should call my boss one day." I was like, "Yeah, why not?" That was the seed. At that time, I was working with computers. After two years of working with computers, I decided that I would rather work with kids and have more fun. When I actually started working with the kids, I thought, "I like this ten times more than computers. Oh, yeah! This is the thing I want to do." So, I decided to change my major to work with children.

My mom always said, "Do something that makes you feel happy." She works retail and she doesn't like it. So, when I was planning to go to college, her message was: "Do something that you enjoy because later in life, if you don't like it, then it's gonna be a hard time."

I really don't think my disabilities affect me that much. It depends on what I do. For work, maybe I'd need some reading accommodations because it takes me longer to read than usual. I never thought about my dyslexia with my choice to work with children. I know, to become a teacher, you do a lot of curriculum writing. But, If I want to do something, I would find a way to work around it. The only other disability concern related to teaching, would be my speech because my speech isn't perfect. I have to talk to parents all the time. Maybe when I'm talking to a parent, it could affect me because I have to make sure I speak slowly and they understand me.

When he was an undergraduate, Landers encountered a big roadblock in becoming a teacher. He could not pass the standardized text (Praxis) required to obtain a teaching license.

I was an elementary education major, but now I'm human development which will allow me to teach preschool through second grade. To be an elementary school teacher, you had to pass Praxis. Just dealing with them was such a big hassle to get accommodation for the test itself. You send your documentation to the Praxis. You give them your credit card information and then you have to fax stuff over. And all the phone calls you have to do! I kept calling. When I talked to a Praxis representative, I said "I'm going to make sure I have my accommodations for extra testing time." The guy said, "No, the extra half an hour is just for you to prepare before." So, I did all that work for nothing. I said, "I have an accommodation. I get this." He said, "They tell you online just to get there a half an hour earlier. There is no additional time." When I took the Praxis test, I was rushing through the end. I just couldn't get all the stuff done. My discouragement from the elementary education major was taking the Praxis. I just couldn't pass it after all my time studying. It was really hard for me to take it with my disability. I missed it by a couple points. I didn't even do the writing portion of the Praxis test. I would have to sit down for a month to work on that every single day. I just don't have that time now with school and everything.

Luckily, he learned he could obtain an undergraduate degree in human development with a focus on early childhood—which did not require a licensure test for employment.

So, I talked to my advisor. I told her I had a hard time doing Praxis. I asked, "What can we do? Is there any way I can still become a teacher?" I was just curious about it. She said, "You don't have to take the Praxis exam if you don't want to." I was like, "Okay, that's what's up!" I like working with early childhood more than older kids. I just thought instead of going through all that hassle of having to pass a standardized exam, why not just change my major? We went over a plan where I would graduate and be able to work with kids. That was the encouragement to change majors. After graduation, I would not be a teacher right away. But in early childhood, you don't really need your degree right away. You don't need a teaching certificate to work in most preschool settings. I plan to maybe work for a little bit. I will get my teaching certificate later, which is always good. There's a graduate school certificate program. Then, from there, I can go and maybe work at an elementary school.

During the third interview, Landers proudly shared that he did indeed go back to school to earn multiple graduate certificates and a teaching license. He passed two required standardized exams because he was afforded extended time due to COVID rules.

I went back after I graduated to get my teacher's certificate. When COVID hit in 2020, I unfortunately got laid off. We didn't open camp that summer. It is what it is. When I got laid off, I was like, "Perfect! I have to take another Praxis test!" This time, I did pass the first test. I passed very easily. The second one was very, very stressful. Since COVID, they extended the time. It worked out. The first time I took it, I was off by two points. The second time, I was off by one point. I finally passed by like a couple points. It took a couple times, but I finally did pass the test. It took three weeks for them to get the scores back. Every single day, I was just waiting for them to come out. Not the funnest time!

I'm also getting my master's degree in English Language Learning (ELL). I'm finishing up my thesis hopefully next year.

Landers completed internships and worked numerous summer and part time jobs with children. So, by the third interview he no longer had to imagine what it might be like to apply for jobs or succeed as a disabled educator.

I never thought about my disability, how it could impact going for a job interview. I know maybe my speaking might be an issue. But, I always remember to talk slowly. I always think about it for a second. I think about the question and then answer it to make sure I am saying everything and that they can understand me well.

When I'm at work, I don't feel like it affects me that much. I always have to think before I talk. But, in my part time jobs, I haven't really heard any concerns from them. They haven't really said, "Okay, what was that?" So, I thought, "Okay, then it must be fine." Plus, when I'm teaching preschool, I'm usually with the kids, playing with them. They're going to go play and build stuff and my disability won't matter.

Landers identified ways that his disability turned out to be an asset. He drew upon his talents to encourage children to learn and to help fellow teachers be more effective.

When I'm teaching preschool, they are so young that if I mess up words, they won't notice anything. The oldest kids are four years old. I don't have to worry. I always try to create a classroom environment where everyone makes mistakes and no one's perfect—even me. If I say a word wrong, they'll be like "Silly Mr. Landers." In kindergarten the vocabulary we're learning is very basic words. I'm not saying anything too hard. Sometimes I have to communicate with parents. I don't want to use the wrong word in writing or when talking. So, sometimes I'll send an email to my mom beforehand and ask her, "Does this make sense?"

When I was student teaching, I told my teacher about my disability. She wanted me to talk to all the teachers in the school. Did they have any questions they wanted to ask me as someone who has dyslexia? She thought maybe I could tell them what they should do with kids in their own classrooms. I told them my story. I told them what it's like for me. Sometimes I can't think of a word right away. I told the teachers that it is important to be patient.

Landers applied his passions, skills, and talents working with young children in his summer camp roles.

When I was at camp, I always helped out the counselors. When I became a counselor, I had different age groups. I had the youngest kids, who are second, third, and fourth graders. Other people can't deal with 'em. I was like, "Oh, they're easy. They talk. You might not know what they're talking about. You just play along with it. They're using their imagination. It's fun!" Summer is coming up. I'm going to become the head counselor, working with all the counselors. I'll be making sure the new ones know what they're doing. I'll help them out, because it's the first time they're doing it. My job will be to help with any problems they have with kids. I help run activities and make sure everything's going smoothly.

Landers gleaned satisfaction from seeing young children grow and develop.

I usually work with young toddlers and babies. I like those areas. Seeing kids develop. When I first started working four years ago, some of the kids I had were three months old. They couldn't do anything. They were sleeping the whole time. Now, four years later, they're in preschool walking and talking. Seeing them come from a little baby to someone tall—I enjoy watching them develop every day. One of the kids, a couple weeks ago, started to walk. He's advanced and does more and more. I like to see how they can grow in such a short time. I don't like people being negative or seeing people disappointed. I try to always make it so people succeed in what they're trying to do. I enjoy seeing a kid just doing something—like seeing them walk for the first time and seeing that big smile—seeing them succeed.

Landers talked about his strengths working with children and the strong reputation he had with colleagues who all knew about his disabilities.

I'm a friendly guy. I don't get mad or anything. I keep everything as a flow. With kids, if you're stressed, the kids can sense it. You have to be very, very mellow and very cheerful. If not, then the kids will notice. The teachers notice that too, so they're like, "Okay, he's very mellow around kids." One of the preschool rooms had 14 kids and there was only one teacher. So, I came in there to help. She texted me saying, "Oh, thank you for helping out yesterday, it was a very big thing." I was like, "Oh, it's not that big of a deal. That's what I'm here for. I'm here to help."

Everyone knows who I am. Everybody wants me to work with them because I'm very good at working with kids. I can be funny. During winter break, one of the teachers had a whole week off. And the teacher picked me out of everyone else to substitute for her class because she knew that I work well with the kids. I'm just really friendly with everyone. Everyone likes to work with me. They know me so well that they understand sometimes I say the wrong words. People understand that I'll blurt. I talk to them afterwards and say, "I'm sorry I did that." Sometimes I'll forget something or have a certain word in my head, I know I will forget it. Same thing with my speech. Most people understand I speak a little bit differently than everyone else. But they don't give me a hard time. I never really had a problem. Most people understand I'm different. I've also been there so long that everyone (my coworkers and supervisors) fully understand that too. I talk to them about my disabilities. With the staff, I make sure they know about my disabilities. I don't hold it back. I tell parents too because if their kids have a disability I can always be an advocate. I tell them what I grew up with and that I know that I can help them and their children.

I know other people have said there are not enough men in the helping professions. The school I am at now, there are, I think, three male teachers out of the whole school. I've definitely heard people say that it is definitely more helpful because there's not enough guys. People may not have father figures. I've kind of learned how to help. I've always been willing to help out with whatever I can do. One of the moms wanted someone to be in her child's life. The father was not around. So she asked me, "Can you babysit?" I said, "Of course I can." It is impactful.

By the third interview, Landers began taking on more responsibilities and leadership roles in formal and non-formal educational settings.

When I graduated, I worked at the Jewish Community Center as an early childhood teacher working with infants and toddlers. Over the summer, I worked at camp. I was the assistant director for two years. I oversaw recruitment of staffing and got camp ready for the summer. Last spring, I finished student teaching. I worked in the first-grade classroom. Now, I'm a full-time sub in a kindergarten classroom. I always have so much fun.

During the third interview, Landers also described how he learned to advocate for himself.

I try to be more of an advocate for myself. I think that is what I learned the most in the last five years. My patience has been tested. I learned how to be more patient and be more of an advocate for myself in the workplace. I learned how to stand up for myself.

Working at my summer camp, I wasn't the biggest fan of either bosses. They were like, "You have to call all these people, all the families." They wanted it done over the weekend! I was just like,

That sounds like a lot. That is 200 families. I'd need like a week and a half. No offense but I cannot call people all weekend. I have other stuff to do. I don't know what you want me to do. I can call a couple families a day.

I became more of an advocate for myself, making sure that they understood that I wasn't going to do what they said. I have to stand up for myself.

In addition to his disability, Landers talked about how other social identities, including social class, race, and religion impacted his life.

My mom didn't always have the most money. My mom and my dad divorced when I was in fifth grade. He gives my mom a hard time and gives me a hard time now when we try to get money for stuff that I need. That's why I kinda got the job, because I don't have to worry about asking anyone for money. I can do whatever I want now.

During and after college, Landers made the decision to work at a summer camp instead of a preschool classroom because of the difference in pay. He also reflected on how critical early childhood educators are to the developmental success of youth and how underpaid they are for this work.

When I was an early childhood teacher, I was making an hourly wage. It was not a lot of money. I was getting a college degree and if I went back there, I was not going to be making that much. It was one of the big reasons why I went to work in the camp world. The camp world was a lot more money. It was a solid job. I was surprised compared to what I would be making if I was working at a daycare. By learning more about social class, I definitely can see how it's very important. I see how it is a very impactful thing.

Early childhood workers in daycares are very underpaid. It is one of the most important jobs because they can see milestones. You notice. I remember this from one of my classes. What you do from ages 0–3 is the biggest thing you do compared to any other three years in life. When they're born, they need all the support that they can to learn to begin walking and talking by themselves.

During the last interview, Landers talked about the ways he was making sense of racial inequities as a white man and how he tried to weave in justice education with the young children with whom he interacted.

I look at what's going through the news with the Black Lives Matter movement and see what's happening. I also understand there's racial inequalities. If someone is a different color, it's like they're automatically treated differently, they're automatically outcasted. Where I work is a very diverse place. I teach everyone the same. I tell the kids everyone's born differently, but we're all friends. In kindergarten, they all tattle tale on each other and they all say, "I'm not your friend." I always say if they're not your friend, it's gonna be hard when you grow up and you want to be friends with someone. It is going to be hard to say that you don't want to be friends with everyone. That's more what I'm working with in kindergarten; I feel it is more the social stuff. It is making sure that they know how to make friends.

Landers described how religion, religious organizations, and connections with other Jewish people provided him invaluable social support and learning opportunities.

I'm Jewish. Religion definitely played a huge role in my life. Every time I see family it is during the Jewish holiday. For Passover we get all the family together. I see mostly my aunts and my uncles. It's always fun. On Christmas, I go get Chinese food and watch a movie. My other Jewish friends come over.

I think religion definitely plays a huge role—especially the social aspect. Most of my friends are Jewish. When I was in high school, I was in the Jewish youth group. That really helped 'cause I met a lot of people—a lot of good friends that I still talk to. It really helped me to be with so many people that share the same views. They're all Jewish. Everyone has their own views on stuff, but everyone knows that when it comes down to it, everyone shares the same religion; it just depends on how much you are into it. I went to Jewish overnight camp. Everyone there is very nice. It's all a bunch of Jewish kids doing athletic stuff and hanging out. I'm also part of the national Jewish fraternity in the United States. In college, most of the friends that I made were from my fraternity. I still talk to the people there. It taught me a lot. It helped me a lot, seeing other people's perspectives. My really good friend, he was reform. His fiancé is orthodox, so he became orthodox. I knew somewhat about it beforehand, but now he has helped me learn more.

I volunteer for a Jewish movement. I did that when I was in high school. I was like 19 or 20 when I became an advisor for my local chapter of the Jewish youth group. I still help with that. We do different events. We do conventions. It's always fun. They have a chapter board. They talk about different events that they want to do and how to get different members. It is always about improvement of the different fun events that they do. I work with teenagers and I always have fun doing something with them. It's been about eight or nine years. Most of the kids I've known since they were young. It's fun seeing them now all grown up. I always have a blast doing it.

When asked about life goals and the future, Landers talked about a variety of options which included continuing to learn, teaching children, and having a family.

For me, it's to continue learning and to have a job I really like and enjoy the pay. I'll be working with children every day. A relationship? That will come when it comes. But, I see myself possibly getting married and having children.

Reflection Questions

1 *Perseverance, adaptation and success.* Landers told us about changing his major because of standardized testing hurdles. Yet, he was able to adapt his undergraduate major to follow his joy and continue working with children. Landers was recognized for high grades by achieving the *Dean's List.* Then, he attended graduate school and earned a teaching license and English Language Degree. Have you ever had to change your plans or adapt to an unexpected hurdle? What was the outcome? What does Lander's story teach about perseverance, adaptability, and success?

2 *COVID-19.* The COVID-19 pandemic had devastating consequences for many people. However, a silver lining from the pandemic for Landers was the removal of testing time requirements for a standardized exam. What can we learn from this COVID-era change to offer extended standardized testing time? How might this, and other adaptations (e.g., remote learning, Zoom meetings) made during the COVID pandemic benefit disabled people? Consider ways you can make changes in your spheres of influence to foster environments that are more accessible for everyone.

3 *Jewish identity, support and opportunity.* Being Jewish was more than a religious perspective for Landers. Talk about how Judaism was a core

aspect of Lander's identity and social support system. What opportunities did the Jewish camp provide for his professional pathway? How can educators honor the religious and spiritual identities of students to help them find community and thrive? How can you support, and successfully work with, peers, students, and colleagues who have a different religious/spiritual identity or outlook than you do?

4 *Race, class, and disability.* Landers shared ways that social class and race influenced his life. Discuss the ways that these identities shaped his everyday experiences, and how they might shape your life or the lives of your students, colleagues, or loved ones. In Chapter 2, we noted the connection between social class and disability. How does social class show up in Landers' story? How does Landers draw upon his own experiences with race and class to teach children he works with?

10 Meet Mercedes

> **Pronouns:** She/her
> **Age:** 26
> **Self-identified disability:** Learning disability, memory and word finding difficulties. Difficulty with attention in a busy environment
> **College major:** Undergraduate: Nursing then Psychology. Graduate Degree: Occupational Therapy (OT)
> **Current living situation:** Living with family, soon to be married
> **Current job/position:** Occupational therapist, swimming instructor, researcher
> **Passions:** Working with children, swimming, and traveling

At first, Mercedes studied to become a nurse. But her learning disability made it difficult to learn and remember course concepts. After a disappointing lack of support at the first college she attended, Mercedes received helpful disability accommodations and support at her second university. She also learned a variety of learning and coping strategies which led to success in school and in life. She earned an undergraduate degree in psychology, then a master's degree in occupational therapy (OT). In the first interview Mercedes said, "I can't be a doctor. I don't have the memory to have all of that information." Yet, almost a decade later, she was in the final semester toward earning a doctoral degree in occupational therapy. She was also working in a pediatric outpatient center doing OT. Mercedes found a way to turn her passions for supporting disabled children and swimming into a thriving small business where she taught adapted swim lessons. She uses her professional and personal expertise to give back to the community by volunteering with multiple adaptive sports organizations, coaching soccer, and training other swim instructors to teach adaptive swimming lessons.

DOI: 10.4324/9781003495703-10

Mercedes described how she makes sense of her non-apparent disability compared to how others might view it.

To have a disability, to me, means that you're a little bit special. You have your weaknesses, but you also have your strengths. But, you have different weaknesses than most people. Most people don't have memory loss, but I do. But, most people don't also have the strengths that I have.

I think disability is something that you can overcome, but it makes things a little bit harder. So, I think that it is a bump in the road. It doesn't stop you from being able to do what you need to, but it makes it a little bit harder. You might have to try a little bit more and get some help along the way.

It's almost like mine isn't really a disability to others. You know? Everyone talks about extreme and physical disabilities. When you are talking about people with disabilities—it's like talking about someone who has Cerebral Palsy or is in a wheelchair. They're not talking about the kind of disabilities that are unseen or the invisible ones. My dad does not understand disability, he just doesn't get it. My mom is a nurse, and she has two brothers who are Paralympians, so she has a pretty good understanding. My mom was definitely a huge advocate for me, which I think is super important. But their understanding waxes and wanes depending on what's going on. It can be a challenge sometimes, but what family isn't a challenge?

In addition to her learning disability, Mercedes experienced mobility challenges due to an infection.

When I was a freshman in high school, I was hospitalized for a couple of months from an infection that caused nerve damage, which caused chronic pain. And, I was pretty much paralyzed and couldn't walk. Everyone said I had to get myself to walk. They told me every single day, "You have to get yourself to walk." I didn't want to do it because it hurt. And they were like, "You have to do it because if you don't walk now you never will." After being yelled at pretty much daily, I eventually had to push myself until eventually I walked. It was really hard. It was probably the worst experience of my entire life. But I did it. It was little steps at a time. It was like you have to be able to sit up in bed. Then the next day you have to be able to stand. Then the next day you have to be able to take two steps. And, then the next day you have to take three steps. It's a very, very long process and every single day you have to do more and more and more until you get to the outcome. So, you gotta break it down to manageable steps and rewards like walking down the hallway—then you can watch TV for an hour. If you want to get better, this is what you have to do. That's the only way you can get better.

Mercedes details her learning experiences and contrasts her inability to remember academic concepts with her amazing sense of direction and vivid recall.

I have a hard time remembering lots of information. I had a hard time with memory in high school specifically with physics, chemistry, and biology. I'm a very visual learner. Yeah, my memory is a little bit different. So, I'm not good at memorizing when it comes to academics, but I have a very photographic memory. I can picture things and events in my head. I can drive somewhere once and then drive as many times after without needing any directions. I can't exactly picture where things are, but I have a very vivid memory, especially if I'm driving. I have a unique sense of direction. I can get anywhere! I don't know how to explain that. It's an amazing sense of direction. But, I cannot remember a list of words.

I have a really bad anxiety when it comes to test taking and studying. I get very overwhelmed if I have a lot of work. I worry more about the work than sitting and doing the work. I think because I have memory issues, I have anxiety. So, I get very anxious about tests coming up because I know that I'm gonna have a hard time remembering things. So, then I worry about it. Anxiety shows up if I have a lot of assignments at once, or things like pop quizzes. I feel like right before I take that pop quiz I forget everything because I'm just so nervous about it. When it comes to actual tests, especially in a larger class where it's packed, I get really anxious and frustrated if the teacher isn't passing the exam out in time. The actual class itself, sitting in class, it doesn't bother me if it's big or small. But, with test taking I do much better in a smaller environment. The anxiety especially comes up if I have essays. Essays are huge for me. I have a hard time writing them. I worry about them while I write them. For essays I usually try to first make an outline instead of just going right into writing. I first try to get all my big ideas and write them down. I have very messy outlines.

Like making outlines, Mercedes learned and applied a variety of coping and learning strategies to reduce anxiety and thrive academically and personally.

I think my disability was there all along and then it became an issue in high school. In high school, in my sophomore year, I had a 504 Plan. Then, junior year, they changed it to an IEP. I was worried in high school about academic success, "What am I gonna do if I can't remember things?" At my high school, there's a tutoring center called the learning center where they helped me learn how to remember things and keep myself organized. That's where I took all my tests. They came up with ways for me to remember things, like grouping things together, and drawing pictures, and color coordinating. I still do these strategies on my own.

I have to write absolutely everything down. Actually, I'm a very organized person which is really good. I have anxiety and have to check something ten times to make sure that I'm going at the right time or place. Even this meeting, I had it written down like ten times. Routines help. I have the same morning routine, same night routine, same routine in the shower. If I don't do my routine, I'll forget my folders or I'll forget to put something in my backpack. Things like that.

Living with my disability, sometimes I'm frustrated with myself. It gets very frustrating. Sometimes I get mad at myself, that I can't remember stuff. Like, "Why can't I do this?" If I'm really frustrated with myself I kind of just stop what I'm doing and try to do something else. A lot of times if I'm doing homework, I'll just stop doing homework and go take a shower or go for a walk or something.

Exercising regularly had a huge impact on my ability to focus and engage. Everyone always pushed sports on me, or going to the gym. Yoga was kind of forced upon me for a while. When I was sick, I couldn't move and was super deconditioned. Gradually, I started to walk again. I started going for longer and longer walks. When I got to college, when my roommates were working out, I would go to the gym with them. Then it was, "Oh, this feels good. And oh, I'm losing weight–this is kind of nice!" I started just going regularly on my own. Once I got to college, it wasn't pushed on me anymore, and it was my choice. Exercise is fun and social. If I don't work out, I feel myself getting anxious, losing my attention, and getting really tired. So now, I do it.

Living with a roommate with my disability is really hard for me. I'm very sensitive to light and noise. When I'm studying I can't have any music on. It has to be silent. Too much light bothers me. I have really bad sleeping problems too. I'm a very sensitive sleeper. I am exhausted all the time because I don't sleep. If I have a roommate and they move, I wake up. And, I have a really hard time studying in my room if someone else is there. So, that's really hard for me. I get easily distracted and then my memory gets worse. So, I go to the library a lot—the quiet floor in the library, that's where I go.

Mercedes first selected a small private college campus—expecting to receive disability accommodations and support. She was disappointed by the limited disability services and lack of availability of professors. Ultimately, she transferred to a different college with a stronger disability services office.

I actually applied to 15 colleges. I had no idea what I wanted to do or where I wanted to go. We made sure that I only applied to colleges that had a disability program that was good. But, the private university, when I got there, I discovered that they only had one person who worked in disability services. And, they didn't really have a lot of resources or staff to help you out. I was really discouraged by the lack of support for disabled students. I didn't really get a lot of support there which made me really angry. I was very discouraged by that.

At that first campus, it was very inconvenient to take tests at the disability testing center. So, I didn't take tests there except for my finals and my midterms. It was such a hassle. Also, there was no help with strategies or anything like that. So, it was very discouraging and difficult, especially since I had a lot of support before that in high school. I stopped going to the disability services office at my first college. When I had a test, I would go straight to my professors. But, it was hard to actually see professors because a lot of times they worked at other schools too. So, they were only on campus for short periods of time.

Ultimately, she transferred to a different college with a stronger disability services office.

Now, at my public university, I use disability services. I have a case manager and she helps me. She showed me how to get a test done. I met with her to talk about finals and things like that. And also, on top of that, two of my professors do their own test taking for their disabled students. My math professor had us take tests with her the night before in a separate room. And then my psychology professor, anyone who wanted extra time went to a different location at the same time for their test and was proctored by a TA. I find it extremely helpful, especially because I don't have to go to disability services. It's not disability services who gave me the test, the professors gave me the test. It feels like I'm in my regular setting for test taking because it's a classroom setting—but it's much smaller and it's quieter. I can have my extended test taking time and my professor is there in case I have a question.

Throughout college, Mercedes identified teaching styles that helped her learn more successfully. Mercedes also began to branch out and grow in college, especially during her study abroad experience.

One professor, she gives a lot of examples. It's a huge lecture but she has people participate. She does a lot of hands-on activities. She'll have someone come up to the front of the room and she'll have a person act something out. She's very engaging in the classroom which is very interesting to me. It makes me more engaged. She tells lots of stories that relate to the topic. So, then I remember them better because I'm like oh, she's talking about that story. I also took a class on social problems. I really like that class because I feel like it's something that you learn and then you go out into the world and see it! So, you can relate to it. I'm very good at remembering things that I can relate to. I'll be like in the class and I'll learn something. And then, I'll be outside the class and then I'll see it, and I'll be like, "Oh wow! I learned that in class." Then, I remember the content easily and better.

I'm definitely more independent after studying abroad. I was able to explore and kind of go out on a limb in Australia. I worked at a hospital in Australia, went skydiving, and took random trips all over the continent. I think being free and enjoying life—and also, just being a little bit more go with the flow—had a huge impact on my development. I learned a lot in my classes, obviously. But, I think that I also just grew up in college. You know? You become an adult and you learn how to find, and figure out, your way. What I am doing now is trying to figure out what I'm gonna do. It's a huge learning experience for how to live on my own and pay for pretty much everything. I've just had that independent kind of soul, so I kind of want to take the reins.

Not only was Mercedes successful in earning her bachelor's degree. But, she went on to graduate school. The combination of smaller classes and a lifetime of developing successful learning skills fostered success and confidence in being open about her disability.

In grad school, the classes were a little bit smaller because I was in the Occupational Therapy department. I felt pretty open about my disability because I felt like it's an occupation that you kind of have to be understanding of people's disabilities. That is your job! I did feel open about it, but it was a little bit more eyes on me, because everyone knows that I had a disability. It was me and this one other girl who both had accommodations and everyone in the class knew it. They all knew that we were leaving to go take the test somewhere else. They all knew we had extended time. It didn't really bother me, but I'm sure it bothered other people, so it was a different experience.

I was pretty open about my disability in school. People would ask, "Why do you get extra time?" And I would explain, "You know, it's my brain, my brain doesn't work that way." I always have a feeling that people think it's unfair. "Why does she get that?" It's always in the back of your head, even if people aren't feeling that way.

Mercedes had many interests and considered numerous majors and careers.

I wanted to be an oceanographer. I love the ocean. I love swimming and I was in love with sea life and the water. This was about 6th grade. But, then I decided I didn't want to be an oceanographer because there's no money in it. From there, I wanted to be a lawyer. Then, I went to work with a lawyer one day who works in the courthouse in Boston and all she did was paperwork. So, I decided I don't want to be a lawyer anymore. I love kids. I have a huge family and I'm one of the oldest so I have a lot of experience with kids—and I was a camp counselor. I just love working with children. From there I had no idea what to do though.

In college, I just went into nursing thinking, "Oh this might be a great career." I went into nursing and then all I did was study. I did not go out. I did not have a social life. All I did was study all the time—and that was just to get a passing grade! I would study the content and then a couple weeks later I would have no recollection of what I studied two weeks before. So, I was like, "I don't think I could be a nurse because I don't know the bones. I know the bones, but in a month from now I'm not gonna know those bones!" So I always worry like, "Will I be able to get a job? Will I be able to do that job? Because I can't re-member what I learned a month ago. How am I supposed to remember that for a job?" So, that's what I get scared about because I know there's a lot of memory involved in being a nurse.

Ultimately, I was very discouraged because I was taking anatomy and physi-ology as well as chemistry—which I was not very strong in because there was a lot of memorization which was very difficult for me. It was a lot of information at once. It was too much memorization and I wasn't positive I wanted to be a nurse. Nursing is really hard for me. So, one semester, I decided that nursing was not the major for me.

I took psychology in high school and was so interested in it. My teacher made me love it. While I was at my first college, one of my friends was taking a psychology class and she was having a hard time. And, for some reason I knew everything. Like, I knew all of her work and how to help her be successful in the class! She would ask me, "What's the blah blah blah?" And I would know it! And I felt, "This is the first time that I actually understand something!" It was the first time I *knew* something confidently. When I initially came to this new university, I thought, I'll take a psychology class for general education credit. I'm in it. And, wow I'm doing great! This is actually something I know! I have 100 in the class right now. So, now I'm majoring in psychology. I think psychology is a better fit because I'm very interested in it. I love going to class. It's the one class that I love going to because I am actually focused the whole time. I'm very engaged because I find it very interesting. It's the only class that I will go back to my room and enjoyably read the text and do my homework *and* feel good about it.

Disability, lived experiences, and supportive healthcare professionals informed Mercedes' major and career choices.

I think my disability did affect my career goals because I was very worried about what jobs I could do that didn't involve a lot of memory. I was a freshman in high school when I was hospitalized. And as part of the hospitalization at children's hospital, they give you a psychologist to help you. And that person, to me, was a role model. She was so cool! Normally I would totally be against going to see a psychologist. Like, "No thank you, I'm not doing that!" But, she made me feel better. She was awesome. So, then I wanted to be like her.

After being hospitalized, that's when I saw an occupational therapist (OT) for the first time. I was rehabbed for months and months. I still have some nerve damage and I still have some chronic pain from it, especially in my back and my hips. And, I still have some neurological issues, but I'm used to it at this point. Because I went to occupational therapy when I was younger, I already knew what the field was. Then kind of along the way, I figured that that might be something that I want to do. I actually shadowed a bunch of occupational therapists and worked with an occupational therapist at the Autism Center that I was working at after college. Then I applied for graduate school at a prestigious university. And I got in and started a master's degree in OT!

I graduated with my undergraduate psychology degree. Then, I went and worked a year in ABA (Applied Behavioral Analysis) therapy. Then, I graduated with my master's degree in occupational therapy. I'll be done in May with my doctorate in Occupational Therapy.

Despite her confidence, success, and the strong influence disability played in her career choices, Mercedes does not always disclose her disability in work settings.

I work in an outpatient center in pediatrics. No one at work knows I have a disability. I think there's still a stigma and negativity about disabilities. I even work with kids with disabilities and I wonder if a parent would want me working with their child with a disability. I think there's definitely still a stigma out there. I don't want anyone thinking negatively about it, about me, or thinking that I'm not able to do my job.

Disclosing one's disability and trying to get accommodations for it? I think that it's a little bit harder in the real world (compared to college) because you don't want to be negatively viewed because of it. You don't want to make less money. You don't want to have a job you don't want.

There are other ways my disability impacts my work. I definitely have a lot of word finding problems and memory issues—especially when I'm trying to talk to someone about specific facts. I can see the word, but I can't remember the word. I have a challenging time talking with patients' families and explaining things because I just forget the healthcare words and the terminology. I can see it, I just can't bring the medical term out of my mouth. To deal with it, I end up saying, "Oh, I'm going to have to get back to you. I can't remember off the top of my head right now. But, I will look it up and get back to you." I do spend a lot of time sending emails to families with the specifics. It takes me a little bit longer to write up my notes because I have such a hard time spelling. I spend a lot of time Googling words and that makes me take a little longer to do my work. My disabilities definitely influence me every day because just doing daily things is a little bit harder. I have to be more cautious of what I'm doing and pay a little more attention than the average person.

In addition to her job in outpatient pediatric occupational therapy, Mercedes started her own business which was inspired by her passions for swimming and helping children with disabilities.

I love swimming. Along the way I started an adaptive swimming lesson business for children with disabilities. I always taught swimming lessons. Swimming was kind of my way to escape from everything that was going on. I have two uncles who are former Paralympians and so I always grew up around the Paralympics and around the sport. When you're in the pool, there's no gravity on you and you feel less pain in the pool. I started teaching lessons when I was 16. I started teaching at people's houses around the state. It's more accessible for families that have children with autism—the ability to have someone come to their house to teach at their own pool is huge. I actually go to people's houses and teach in their environment with their pool and their equipment. I have grown that business. This summer, I had 175 kids and three employees. So, yeah it's a pretty big business going on.

Through that business I kind of grew an online training program that teaches community based swim instructors how to adapt swimming lessons for people with disabilities. So, the training program would be for individuals at the YMCA, for example, how to adapt swimming lessons. There are all these children with disabilities out there who need to learn to swim. And, most centers don't have adaptive swimming lessons. Currently, there's no certification out there for it, or anything like that. So, I kind of teach how to adapt swimming lessons through the online training program. I give some examples and resources. The resources help swim instructors teach the lessons and feel more confident in taking on a kid with disabilities. After the training, they may not be the best instructor—they're not physical therapists or OT's—but it's better than nothing! I've been talking to some professors at my graduate school about the training program. I'm into research. So, having the program be clinically researched and backed by research, was important. I'm in the process of doing research on the training program. I am having community based swim instructors take the actual online training program and do pre and post quizzes to see their acquired knowledge. Down the line, I see myself having the research about this training program under my belt and getting that published.

Mercedes recognized social class differences in her small private and larger public colleges. Later in life, she learned how social class limited the health plan coverage, and in turn, the quality of care available to low income clients.

I'm like, high-middle class. My first private college had a lot of upper high class people. So, to me, it was a different lifestyle than what I had. I didn't have as much money as they did. It was just different. And, when I came to the public university, I felt like I fit in more economically. Because, here more of the students are paying for their own schooling, paying for their own food, all that stuff. Whereas, at the private college, their parents took care of everything and they got whatever they wanted. So, in different settings, I do think about my economic status.

Yeah, so it's interesting. For swimming lessons I work with a majority of very wealthy individuals. However, some of my clients want swim lessons, but they cannot afford it. So, I've been doing some fundraising to get some funds for that. And then in OT, I worked for a community based hospital and the majority of my patients are on state supported health plans. There are two different worlds in health access and care. When I work with those who have financial resources, I can ask parents to buy whatever equipment. You know? I can recommend anything under the sun for them! I can recommend all these helpful resources. When you're working in the OT world with those with less money, it is a little bit harder in the sense that you have limited resources and there's limited recommendations for care. For those on certain healthcare plans, I can only give out limited visits. There's a lot more limitations to what we can offer. And, I think coming from a middle class family, I don't really have a full understanding of it. So, I'm kind of learning as I go. But, access to money and resources definitely does have an impact on the care that I can provide.

Her passion for access and equity can also be seen in her commitment to making all sports accessible to disabled youth. Mercedes applies her expertise in OT to support youth in numerous community organizations.

I continue to do some work for adaptive sports New England and some of the other adaptive sports programs. I have done some adaptive skiing up at a local mountain. And, then through my swimming lessons I provide scholarships for kids with disabilities in the community. I also coach soccer. I got certified as a children's yoga instructor before the pandemic and then, once the pandemic hit, I started just doing online yoga classes for free.

Mercedes reflects on her future and the ongoing influence of disability in her life.

I am engaged and getting married in October. We've been together for eight years so he's known me for a long time. He knows all my inner workings, so I think that definitely makes a big difference. He also had accommodations in high school. His sister and his brother did too. They're all successful adults now. So, we talk about kind of just needing a little extra something. He knows that I can't always find the words that sometimes I need a little bit of time.

In the future, I see myself working in pediatrics and having kids of my own. I hope that the world is a little bit of a different place by the time I have kids. I think that kids don't always fit into this mold that everyone creates for them. Just because society says, "You have to be able to do X, Y, Z" doesn't mean that you really should have to do X, Y, Z. You can kind of have your own path. I mean when I was little, I hated coloring and drawing and all the spelling. And, all the teachers were worried about me. I still can't spell. But, I'm still successful. At the end of the day, I have other strengths. I think that people should love their child and help them be successful in what they *can* do, rather than focusing on what they cannot do.

When I talk with my kids one day about disability, I will definitely talk about invisible disabilities and physical disabilities at the same time. I think that having a background of OT and having an understanding of myself, it will be a little bit easier for me to talk about and give examples. I want my children to be involved in adaptive sports. I think that's very important.

Success to me is having a nice home and family and not worrying about money issues. I don't have to be ridiculously rich, I just don't want to have to worry about finances. I want to travel the world, especially Europe. And, I want to be successful and pretty much enjoy life. Success is being happy with where I am. It's really important to me that I like my job. Happiness? Well, I'm happy when I feel like I can take a breath and be like, "Ok, this is good."

Reflection Questions

1 *Perseverance and success.* In the first interview, Mercedes said, "I can't be a doctor." Yet, a decade later, she was about to become a doctor of occupational therapy. How might her story be a lesson to students who think they cannot be successful in a career related to their passions? What are your passions? How have you (or might you) follow those passions into a career where you can thrive?

2   *Finding joy in a side hustle and volunteering.* Mercedes turned her love for swimming into a growing small business teaching disabled children to swim. Then, she grew the organization to teach other swimming instructors how to best teach adaptive swimming. Although the business was not her full time job, what can Mercedes' story teach us about using our talents and living our passions in ways other than our primary job? Mercedes also volunteers for organizations that support disabled youth. What can Mercedes teach us about fostering our passions in, and beyond, a career?

3   *Making healthy choices.* Early in life, exercise, including yoga, was "pushed on" Mercedes and she resisted. Yet, in college, she learned to enjoy exercise. Mercedes also recognized the benefits that exercise had on her overall wellbeing. After college, she got certified to teach yoga to children. Do you know someone who feels pressured to do something and they resist? How can we encourage ourselves, or loved ones, to feel empowered to make healthy decisions in ways that don't feel "pushed on" us?

4   *College disability services.* Mercedes had a radically different experience with the disability services office at the two campuses she attended. Discuss those differences and the ways support (or lack thereof) impacted her success. How can students and parents determine if a college will provide the kinds of disability accommodations that they need? What kinds of questions should students and families ask during a campus visit to determine what types of support are available?

11 Meet Peter

Pronouns: He/him
Age: 28
Self-identified disability: Dislxik … I mean, Dyslexic.
College major: Public Health
Current living situation: Living on campus in an apartment provided by his employer
Current job/position: Non-profit Director and Campus Minister
Passions: Faith, bringing people together, fitness

Peter is a man of faith and a careful thinker. He grew up in a small town and was a student at public schools before transferring to a private boarding school for students with language-based learning disabilities. In each interview, Peter demonstrates his careful approach to decision-making. He identifies his options and tries to anticipate how his personal strengths and disabilities may play out. Peter applauds the specific services of his private school and the importance of his faith community. As someone with dyslexia, he weighed whether or not a career in the military was the right move for him personally. Peter remains committed to his faith, his goals, and finding (or building) a community wherever his adventures take him.

Peter shares his early passions and memories of figuring out what he wanted to do when he grew up.

In first grade, we made time capsules. I really like my teacher for doing this. As much as I hated the first grade, this is actually really cool. We wrote what we wanted to be when we grew up and what we wanted to do after high school. I scribbled in my little squiggly handwriting and wrote, "I wanna be a scientist." I put it in the tube. I didn't open it until I graduated high school—which was kind of cool. I think that's the earliest I can remember wanting to do it as a career was the first grade.

DOI: 10.4324/9781003495703-11

Growing up, I definitely struggled with literature and reading. One of the skills I developed was mathematics. I like math. I did really well with that in middle school and throughout high school. I really like science because the labs—the applied stuff—you get to see it. I didn't really know what exactly scientists were or what different fields were, but growing up, I wanted to do something with science.

Also, growing up, I wanted to be in the military throughout middle and high school. When I got to high school, I figured I wanted to be in the Navy, so I joined a junior military group called the Naval Sea Cadet Core. I traveled to and from military bases during my vacations. When I wasn't living at school. I was living on the military base. I did that when I was 16. I did that for two years. I was really leaning toward joining the Navy. But, I figured coming to college—this was the right time to do it. I can always pursue my career in the military afterward.

Peter described his experiences with dyslexia in elementary school before he was diagnosed.

In first grade, I was kind of a weird kid. I had a bunch of food allergies, couldn't read, and probably was not the most popular kid. I didn't like school because I wasn't good at it. My diagnosis is with writing and reading. With me, it's typically with spelling—which I'm continually struggling with. I was actually caught late with it. A lot of people are caught early—around 1st or 2nd grade. But, in my case, I didn't figure out that I was dyslexic until I was in the 5th grade. At that point, I couldn't read or write at all. In fifth grade, I had a teacher writing all my assignments in class. Instead of being the teacher's pet, the teacher was my pet and would follow me around. Nobody wants to hang out with that kid, or act like a friend, when the teacher is always there. I would say my social life sucked through elementary school.

Peter appreciated the unwavering support provided by his parents.

When I was a kid (after being diagnosed with dyslexia), they both looked up lots of successful and famous dyslexics and would use them to teach me that I could be successful too. Since I was diagnosed with dyslexia in 5th grade my Dad inspired me to give a talk to my class about it. This was during my time in public school. My Dad helped me make the presentation and taught me how to do public speaking. He even came and gave the presentation with me in front of all my classmates. I was bullied a lot back then, so this meant the world to me. Support like this from my parents, as well as going to a private school with other dyslexics that I could be friends with, gave me the confidence to be proud of my identity as a dyslexic. My mom also drove me to school every day for the first year of private school which was over an hour's drive one way. She also fought for me at every IEP meeting and never gave up on me living a normal life.

A key memory is the interaction his parents had with his school, which led to their decision to move Peter to a different school.

There were legal issues between my parents and the public school. The school did not want to let me go, but then they also told my parents that I wasn't going to graduate. I found out later that the school system told my mom, "Peter is never going to read, and that's okay because there are places for people like that in the world." I was not present at that team meeting. I think a lot of it was controlled by my parents. That went on for a couple of months before I was pulled out. By the time I figured out, "Oh, this means I have to change school systems." That meant going to school two hours away instead of right down the street. I think the impact on me was that my environment completely changed.

Having dyslexia made me feel different. If you can't read or write, something has got to be wrong. I assumed I was just not that bright. It's kind of a horrible thing to learn. It's a self-fulfilling prophecy of people always telling you something, and eventually, it will come true.

I remember I was the only person with dyslexia in my public high school. It was weird. Everyone teaches you it's ok. But, if you have dyslexia, it was a bad thing. I was actually happy to find out I had a dyslexia diagnosis because it was an explanation for why things weren't working out. Before I was diagnosed, I took my differences as an intelligence difference, which definitely impacted me negatively. Instead of feeling like an outcast, it's just more fear. Fear that the teacher is going to call on me. A fear that a task is going to come up that I can't do, which is going to be socially unacceptable.

I got pulled out of the public school system. But, I couldn't get into a good private school until the next year. So, for 6th grade I got thrown into the one school that would accept me. It was small, like eight people per grade. So you had eight people in all your classes. There were a lot of behavioral issues and a lot of attention issues. It just didn't really match up with my dyslexia. It was a difficult experience.

In the transition to the private high school, Peter gradually came to understand that dyslexia is a learning difference that comes with strengths as well as challenges.

Going to the private school, I remember somebody new said, "Hey what's your disability?" I said, "I'm dyslexic." He was like, "No way! Me too!" It definitely became a proud identifying factor of who we were. Being diagnosed with dyslexia, a lot of people talk about that as a tragic moment, like being diagnosed with some horrible illness. But my first question was, "What is dyslexia?" They explained, "This is why you can't read." My first response was, "So I'm not stupid?" I was just so happy and relieved. This is something that, even if it's not treatable, it's identifiable.

Being dyslexic is definitely an identity of mine. It's definitely something I'm proud of. It's not something I'm ashamed of. So, I would say it's an identity for me. I like meeting people on campus. Once in a while, I find out someone is dyslexic, I'm like, "Ahhhhh, we have a connection. That's really cool." Even today, if someone says, "My brother has dyslexia," I say, "That's so awesome! We should talk!" It's almost a uniting fact of common ground. Then, I realized that not every dyslexic feels that way. I think it's very particular to my experience. Not everybody was friends in that private dyslexic school, but the one thing was nobody ever made fun of you for being dyslexic. It was a small school, but it was big enough to have cliques. There were about 300 people, 100 boarding students. It was enough that you had the skater kids, the sports kids, the geeks, but at the same time, it was small enough that everybody knew everybody.

Today, I see dyslexia as a learning difference, not necessarily as a disability. I think in certain environments, it is a disability. But in other situations, it's an ability. For instance, with dyslexia, I definitely have a better kinesthetic sense. I feel like if I was put into a trade like woodworking or carpentry, in those types of environments, considering my ancestors were masons, this would be a great gift. Now, in today's culture, or in the environments that I'm looking at, it would be a disability. Especially if you're going through courses that will not accommodate you, then it is a disability. Nevertheless, if we get the same assignment doing some research together, I think it doesn't necessarily have to hinder me as long as I have the freedom to do that assignment differently or use technology to overcome it.

Peter's private high school provided important new opportunities to explain dyslexia to others.

I was a student advocate. I actually gave speeches (on dyslexia) at colleges while in high school. We went to people who wanted to go into the special education field. We talked to them about what dyslexia was. It was actually cool. We got to talk at Harvard once, so that was nice. I printed two sheets of paper. One had words misspelled and vowels mixed up with the spelling. If you looked at it hard enough, you could figure it out. But it kind of took you a while. People would be like, "In-the-case-of-four-four." They read like that, like stuttering. Then we gave them another sheet that was perfectly fine. It was a Wikipedia page that we printed. The papers all looked the same. We mixed them up and handed them out. We'd call on people, "Excuse me sir, can you read line one?" He just struggled. Some people would just look and say, "I can't read this." We'd say, "Excuse me, next one, can you read it?" She'd just read it flat out. We saw some people's faces just like, "What?" They were just completely shocked and wondered, "How is everybody else doing this?" Some people caught on to it right away. They realized the papers were different. It's kind of funny when you're tricking people. But we did that to give them a sense of—this is what it feels like when you call on somebody to read and they can't perform.

Peter's high school prepared him to advocate for himself and to think about college.

One program my high school did to help us prepare for college was to have graduates come and talk to us about do's and don'ts. That was helpful to hear from the students 'cause, I mean, some of your teachers haven't been to college for a while. Things do change. So, it's good to hear it from your peers, too. When I applied to college, I brought my documentation and did all that. My family was also really supportive. My mom helped me through a lot of that.

At my high school, you had a case manager who worked really closely with you. She talked about what you need in school. You also had a tutorial teacher who worked with you one-on-one with reading and whatnot. My case manager was always a familiar face, a very kind person. She was always there at IEP meetings. If I ever felt like I didn't know what to say or I didn't know what the other person was saying, she would fill me in on things. I felt like that was a nice transition of "This is your life. You are in control of it." But there weren't a whole lot of decisions to make. Then, when it came to college, my parents still helped me out with filing what tests I took to prove that I was dyslexic and was officially diagnosed with it. Collecting all that information and passing it on to my college was sort of an instance of passing the baton of responsibility from my parents to me.

I think a lot of it, too, is not just being responsible for self-advocating, but being more active. The school educated me on being dyslexic and how to advocate and talk to a professor about it. I even feel like I was over-prepared, but I feel like I haven't had to use a lot of it. With the disability services here, if a professor says, "What disability do you have?" I can just say, "Go talk to the campus disability office." I don't even have to deal with it. Nevertheless, I feel like I have the skills to discuss it if I want to.

Peter talked about what he was thinking as he considered his next steps after high school. This includes his awareness of how dyslexia might figure into his plans.

I actually thought about going into the military and the job market. I looked at all of my options. One was to go into the military. One option was going to the civilian world to get a job. One was to go to college. Honestly, I felt that being dyslexic, if I was ever gonna go to college, now would be the time to do it. I knew taking a couple of years off would definitely hinder my ability to pick up a running start at college.

In hindsight, I actually think it would be helpful to go out into the workforce first—to know that when I'm going through grad school, I have a purpose, I have a goal. I have background experience. Right now, I find myself thinking, why am I in college? Why am I taking this class? Especially the general education requirements and stuff like that. I think it's good to have that goal, purpose, and drive. I don't think learning ever stops as long as you stay in a community that promotes your development. I think that momentum can keep going on after school.

There was this issue with disability services at college. Instead of just going to the office and telling them when your exams are and scheduling them in person, they put the scheduling system online. I went to them to schedule in person, and they said, "Oh, you can just do it online." I totally get that it saves them so much time. It is a good system. But I went home, and it wasn't working on my computer. I thought, "Ahhh this is so frustrating!" So, I was like, I'm gonna write my paper. I'll come back to this. I totally forgot to go back to it. Actually, I went back to do it and realized I had missed the deadline for registering. I didn't have the accommodations in place to take it. So, I didn't take the test at the disability center, which was kind of stressful because it was finals—kind of a big deal. I had to talk to my professors to see if they could accommodate me. They were all really helpful. They definitely went out of their way to help me.

After a bumpy start in college, Peter got some good advice that helped him plan for his major.

I came into college undeclared. I actually wanted to do kinesiology, but I didn't start on the kinesiology track. Unfortunately, I'm not that great at math anymore, at least not calculus. I got a D in calculus which is one of the requirements to get into kinesiology. So, I retook it, studied really hard, took it with a better teacher, focused a lot that semester on just calculus, and ended up getting a C⁻ instead of a D⁺. It was an improvement, but not the improvement I needed. Plus, I was already behind on classes for the kinesiology major, so I would have had to tack on another year. I mean, I like school, but I don't like it *that* much. So, I realized kinesiology was probably not working out for me.

I talked to the Dean of Students about how to possibly drop out with an Associate's Degree or transfer somewhere to get my associate's degree because I figured leaving college with debt and no degree would be pretty bad. Turns out, I really didn't have a whole lot of great options for leaving. I talked to one of the deans of the undeclared department. She's really helpful. She mentioned that kinesiology is in the public health department and that public health is kind of a broader umbrella type of field. The other thing was I wanted my minor in psychology because it's a low course load and a lot of my psychology classes would count towards my major in public health. That definitely helped me make my decision—so I wouldn't have to add on extra years.

Now, I'm doing public health and psychology. I've been taking most of my public health courses this year. One of the courses is epidemiology, and I absolutely love it. It does have a lot of hardcore study designs. That's where all my psychology background in research comes in handy. You can do research with public health. I really like that aspect. Where I'm going to go with that major, I don't know. Usually, they want you to get your doctorate or at least a master's. I'm kind of done with school, so we will see what happens.

Beginning with his early high school experiences with the Naval Sea Cadet Core, Peter gave a lot of thought to a career in the military. Even after having positive military experiences, he decided to pursue what he describes as "the civilian sector." A significant factor in Peter's thinking is his perception that dyslexia was not a good fit for military service.

I did a bunch of advanced training every year, like recruit training boot camp. Basically, it is to get us a taste of: "Hey, if you want to go this route, this is how you have to practice and what life is going to be like." Then I went to rescue summer school. That was really cool. I realized that it was focused on helping people. I was always focused on helping people. I knew I didn't want to be just a trigger puller. If I could get a job where I didn't have to carry a gun, I would be very happy. I have total respect for people who want to join the infantry or to be a Navy Seal. I just know that's what I didn't want to do.

As part of this military experience, Peter had a mentor who introduced him to the role of military chaplain.

I was talking to this Master Sergeant, and he was saying, "I hope everyone knows how important the chaplaincy core is." From his perspective, a lot of guys don't go to therapy because their records can be opened by superiors. They don't have the same privacy rights as civilians have, which makes sense. The chaplain is somebody who sits behind the safety line on the base. When you talk to a chaplain, that's between you, them, and God. Nobody gets access to that conversation. Those guys roll out with us. The sergeant tells me, "Yeah, when we needed to talk about the guys we lost. We wanted the chaplain who was in the truck with them. You know?" He (the sergeant) preferred to talk with Chaplains. That really hit me, knowing that confidentiality was so important and that they're on the front lines with you.

Peter weighed the pros and cons of a career in the military. Eventually he decided that a civilian path was better for him.

The army is not really where I wanna go after college. So, I'm leaning towards becoming a civilian, which means I'd have to drop being a cadet after this semester. If I drop, I would definitely be sleeping more. So, I think it would take a lot of stress out of my life. I think my grades would definitely go up because, you know, sleeping helps pretty much everything in your life. But I would miss it. It's weird to compare it to a frat 'cause we're not a partying group, but it really is that for me. It's like a family. It's a really good, supportive group. Not everybody there wants to go into the military. Some people already know that they won't. So, it's not as tight as a military group would be. But, as far as college is concerned, it is a family.

They offered me a military contract. It was pretty awesome. A lot of people weren't offered that, and they had to leave. But I just didn't feel like it was the right decision to make at the time, so I left. I feel a lot safer about being dyslexic going into the civilian sector versus the military. A lot of the military reports are on paper. There's a big thing if you're doing watch logs and you mess something up. You have to blot out that whole line and rewrite it. If you mess up too many lines, you have to rewrite that page. A lot of times, if you make enough mistakes, they'll make you rewrite the whole book. It's just one of those things where what you write down on a watch becomes a legal document, so it's very serious. You can't request accommodations in the military. I wouldn't. I don't think a disability will affect me as much as a civilian.

Dyslexia influenced many of Peter's life choices. Yet, technology and other strategies have made it possible to succeed and thrive.

Being dyslexic definitely shaped my life choices as to what I thought I could do or what risks I was willing to take. I think our society is so based on reading that it is a disability. I understand that it's not just a disability, but I think that it's shaped my decisions. Dyslexia played a huge factor in whether or not I joined the military. So, it fueled me to go to college instead of joining the military. It's also shaped my life in terms of social anxiety and my past experiences of getting bullied in school.

I think the hardest thing now is personal paperwork. It totally makes my blood pressure spike. It shouldn't. I know what I'm doing. But just doing legal paperwork is really stressful because I know it's something I can mess up. But I think I'm very fortunate to say that I don't think it hinders what I do for a living. I don't think it hinders my dating relationship. I don't think it hinders any of my personal stuff. It's still causing stress at times, but when I was in fifth grade, I did not expect to have a device (cell phone) in my pocket that I could speak into that typed messages for me.

Technology has gotten to the point where it definitely helps me out. My phone has spellcheck! I remember the days when it didn't. I definitely have people who call me out for spelling errors. I've come to terms with it. I know that I'm constantly getting better, but it definitely can take down your confidence. One of the biggest things I've learned, especially through college and after college, is that normal people make spelling mistakes. When I was in the school for dyslexics, I saw people misspelled basic stuff. I'm like, "Oh! They're fine. Nobody actually cares that much."

The calendar on my phone is actually the only reason I showed up today for this interview. I forget things, especially when they are 2–3 weeks away. So I'll put things in my phone to remind me at this time. It's nice to have a smartphone that I can put things in my calendar. I also use sticky notes a lot. I have a kitchen table where I do my homework. I have half of it filled with sticky notes of due dates. It's a better reminder to physically write things down. I like that tangible, external reward of being able to crinkle up that note and toss it into the can.

For me, this is a good time to be alive. I hated my college experience. It is not uplifting or encouraging. The whole concept of "you're not ready for the real world." It's very arbitrary, depending on your views of the real world. I feel a lot of it is meaningless. Everything changes. Nothing is stable. I mean, specifically for me, my friend group has changed about every year. Your living situation changes every year, if not every three months. Your classes change every three months. Your schedule changes every three months and is not consistent from one day to the next. One day, I have to wake up at five o'clock. The next day I have to wake up at noon. Every week, your assignments have a different due date. It's hard to predict an all-nighter. It's that type of inconsistency and not necessarily doing the things you want to do. I'd say the biggest impact it has on my life is just writing papers and doing homework, which takes two to three times as long as everybody else.

Peter's faith is a core aspect of his identity. He found a strong sense of community in church groups and with peers who shared his religious beliefs.

I'm a Christian. That is a huge identifier for me. Obviously, that's what I do for a living now. But, even before then, when I was in high school, I was the only kid who went to church. I'm sure there were other Christians in high school. But, of all the boarding students, I was the only one who requested that the school drive me to church.

I am very religious. I am a 7th Day Adventist Christian. I think that has a large impact on my life. It's definitely the center of my life. A lot of my friends I've met through the church. We believe the 7th day as being the Sabbath. So, from Friday sundown to Saturday sundown, we don't work. This means we don't make others work. So, I don't really go to the movies on Friday nights. I don't tend to go out partying. I also don't drink for that reason. When they hear I don't drink for religious reasons, people are like, "Oh, then I'm not gonna invite you to this party." Don't get me wrong, I love being around drunk people. I think they're really entertaining. They're fun people—some are anyway. But, I don't push my beliefs on anyone. All my friends know that. They're really comfortable with that. My beliefs are the center of my life. So, the people who care, your good friends, will not make it an issue. Coming into college and trying to make friends for the first time is kind of difficult with some people. But I'd say most people are accepting of it.

I love my church group. During finals week prayer requests, we're all talking about what we're studying. We usually eat together afterwards. It's just nice to have people your age that have the same background. Being religious definitely gives me confidence just 'cause I pray a lot. I pray before all my meals. Some of my friends think it's weird to close your eyes and pray. No one has ever given me any reason not to. A lot of people actually come up to me and say that they're glad that people are still doing that. But, I personally like it just knowing that I have a close connection with God. That just keeps me confident and helps me deal with my stress. I have a support group, too. I've been through some rough times. I have people in my church community who are there for me.

Faith is something that I take seriously in my day-to-day life. I would say more so now. If you stay with anything long enough, you tend to grow with it. By teaching or explaining what you believe, oftentimes you learn a lot from just teaching. I'm able to not just live it, but also to help others, and be there for others. To grow in that community definitely grows within yourself.

Peter's approach to work after graduating from college illustrates the way he thinks through decisions, reflecting on his strengths and sense of purpose, and also being open to opportunities that come his way.

In 2016, I was thinking about that military career and applying for things like the Centers for Disease Control (CDC), Veterans Affairs, or other different programs. Even public health positions are civilian contractors for the army, which I had no idea existed. So, I was applying for a bunch of stuff. I don't plan on requesting accommodations. I'd like to just get to the point where I can overcome them, which I feel like, for the most part, I have. I guess it depends on what field I end up in. If I ended up in research, there's not a whole lot they can do to accommodate that. If I went to grad school, I definitely would like to have those accommodations. In terms of the workforce, I would rather find a system that can compensate for my disability.

Trump takes office in 2017. Politics aside, he put the hiring freeze down which impacted public health sector job opportunities. All the applications have to have background checks. That goes into effect for a couple of months. So, by the time I'm starting to get a lot of rejections, it's like six months in. And, of course, the whole time I'm freaking out. I definitely was desperate. I was worried about dead space in my resume. So, I found a free clinic down the road. I told them I have a degree in public health and just wanted to volunteer because I love what those guys do. Even if it's just sweeping the floors, I was happy to help out. I thought this was something I could talk about in my resume or an interview about how I've contributed. But, they didn't take volunteers. I was pretty desperate for six months because that's when your college loan payments started. I was still with my parents. I didn't even have a volunteer job. One of my friends messaged me to tell me about this job I should apply for. It was an assistant chaplain position at a university. I'd be assisting the school chaplain. It was great. You would think that I would have loved to apply. But, I was like, nope. I've been warned that if you do what you love for a living, you will learn to not love it. I didn't want to have to beg for my salary. That's what public servant ministers do. I don't want to do Bible studies for a living. That's not my thing. So, I did not want to do it. Then, on the last day that they were accepting applications, I just applied. I figured maybe it's just practice or whatever. A few days later the head chaplain calls my phone and says, "Hey, you have the position! We'll see you on July 17." I did not know if I wanted it. But, I took a good hard look in the mirror. I was like I have no way to pay off my student debt. It's the best thing I've got. So, I took a one-year position. I thought, "Okay, so what's the worst thing that can happen?" Funny story, I got my license the day before I had to drive down to [southern state]. So, my first drive without my parents or my brother was to the south. I was nervous. I was supposed to be there for a year and then leave it to do whatever else. About a month in, my director told me that she was looking to be a pastor down in Georgia, and she might be leaving. Then a month or two later, she got the job. Then, a few weeks later, she left! So, I was there for only about three months and then she was gone.

Six months later, they still hadn't hired anyone. I took all the board members out to lunch, one on one. I just said,

> Hey, I'm doing the job for the meantime. I want to make sure that I'm steering this ministry in the direction you guys want to go. So, what's your vision? What do you want? What do you really hope to see a year from now?

I just talked to them and got to know what they were looking for. They got to know me. I showed them I'm going to hold it together for now. People told me, "You're a great pastor. You should be in charge of people. One of them told me, "Apply for the job permanently." I thought, "I'm not qualified." My boss had two master's degrees and then worked in ministries for eight years. I don't have a degree in theology. But, I took the permanent job temporarily. They back-paid me for the whole calendar year so that was really sweet. I did not expect that. It's my fifth year here.

I would not have imagined it. But, now that I'm here, I feel like what I studied in school and what I'm doing matches up perfectly. I'm super happy being here. We were going through a global pandemic and I have my degree in public health. So, we had the right policy on our COVID-19 response. That's been a blessing. Also, studying psychology, I think the people that I work with do have a lot of theological questions. There are different types of chaplaincy; there are hospital chaplains, military chaplains, FBI chaplains, police chaplains, public university chaplains, and even private school chaplains as well. But actually working with higher education, you run into a lot of philosophical, tight-ended theology-based questions. A lot of it is understanding how science fits with religion and belief. Having my background in science, I think, uniquely helps me relate and respond to that. I could have studied theology my whole life, but then I would not know that much about public campus life or how to really use science or its limitations. I'm not a psychologist or anything, but I do think that my psychology background has really helped me understand why people make decisions about what they do.

You know, people often think that campus ministers are constantly being wrestled off campus. That's not the case here; they appreciate us. We're all just here to get college students to the end, to graduation. That's why we're here. Campus ministers are also able to help address social issues—not at a policy level, but like a programming level. You know? I think that really ties into what I studied in public health and psychology. It is such a privilege.

On campus, there's a giant boulder that people paint. And, every once in a while, they'll be like a swastika that goes up or some anti-semitic that goes up. When stuff like that happens, the campus will ask, "Can you do something to unify the campus?" And, I was already planning it! I can grab people really quickly who can talk to other leaders of other minority organizations. We can connect and tell them, "Hey, you guys have been in this fight for a long time. How can we help you?" We're here to help people bond and support each other in a peaceful way. One of the things I love about the Church is we're a super diverse church. As a campus Ministers Council, we try to do something to show whatever racism has been done or whatever heinous acts, we say, "This is not what our community stands for. This is not what we're going to support. We're not just going to stand back and watch it." It's great that there are people of all backgrounds supporting anti-racism. But it is especially powerful when it's white people that are standing up and saying, "Hey I'm not okay with that." I just love being able to have that community on campus, impacting not just individuals.

Peter shares thoughts about his future. He is open to new possibilities that reflect his sense of purpose. He does not yet have a crystallized direction; but he is hopeful that his faith will lead him in a positive direction.

Because I work with college students that are going to graduate school, I get to see graduate students all the time, freaking out over life. So, I'm not eager to run back to a master's program. I'm trying to figure out the best path because there are some master's degrees in pastoral ministry, which is not exactly what I want to do, but it still qualifies me for chaplaincy. Chaplains aren't just mental health responders. They're not just like social workers. They do theological assistance as well. I really benefit from that. I want something that does both. I knew one guy who got his master's split—half of it was for social work and then half of it was for a master's of divinity. So, if he decided not to be a pastor and just quit his job, he could open up his own counseling business because he's licensed. That sounds amazing.

I want to have a stable career. I feel like that's something I'm leaning towards now. The last time we met (prior interview) that would not have been a goal of mine at all. I would like to be married, have a family, and career—stable. There's the other side where there's benefits to not having that. Not having a family. The freedom to just travel.

I am in a long-distance relationship with my girlfriend who is living in another state. She's from Canada. So, potentially, 10 years from now, I could be living in Canada. This is hard to visualize, but it's a real possibility. I could also be going back to school. You never know! So, I think those are possible outcomes. I love the fact that my girlfriend understands dyslexia. She loves reading. She's read *The Hobbit*, the *Harry Potter* books, and *Lord of the Rings* books multiple times. She just loves reading so she's totally down for reading a book to me.

I think you can have meaning when it's not defined by yourself, there is joy in that. You can have joy and happiness. I think happiness is connected to your circumstances; joy is independent of your circumstances. You can have all of these. Wherever I go, if God is leading me to it, it'll be better than where I am right now. I look forward to that, even though I don't know what that is.

Reflection Questions

1   *Diagnosis, identity and confidence.* Before being diagnosed, Peter described feeling ashamed and outcasted. He believed his lack of success was due to lack of intelligence. Once he was diagnosed with dyslexia, he felt relieved, even exclaiming, "So, I'm not stupid?" Discuss this part of Peter's story. Then, consider his rumination that not everyone is happy about a diagnosis or proud to have a disabled identity. Discuss

the different strategies peers, family members, and educators can use to effectively engage with youth whose identities vary widely, and may change over time.

2 *Technology.* Peter talked about the ways technology (e.g., spellcheck, calendar) has improved his life. He also explained how, when he was young, he could not have imagined the ways technology could improve his life. Discuss the ways technology can be used to help students and employees succeed. Imagine the future. What kinds of technologies can you imagine that could make your life easier? Or the lives of your students, coworkers or loved ones?

3 *Decision making & finding purpose.* Peter was at multiple crossroads where he had to make significant decisions (e.g., major, jobs, moving). How would you characterize Peter's approach to decision-making? What can we learn from his strategies and outlook? Peter allowed himself to be open to possibilities that he had never considered. How did that openness shape the trajectory of his post-collegiate life? Talk about a time when you were open (or not open) to unexpected possibilities. Reflect on the ways you have thought about the future. How comfortable are you with the idea of being open to an uncharted future?

4 *Happiness and joy.* Reflect on Peter's quote, "happiness is connected to your circumstances; joy is independent of your circumstances." What does this quote mean to you? What circumstances in your life foster or inhibit happiness? How might you change, resist, or work around circumstances that inhibit your happiness? Or the happiness of those around you? What brings joy to your life?

12 Meet Poppy

Pronouns: She/her
Age: 29
Self-Identified disability: Deaf in right ear
College major: Psychology
Current living situation: Renting a room
Current job/position: Medical Scribe, EMT
Passions: Finding Zen, pets, educating others, and having people in your
    life that matter

Poppy expresses a strong faith in herself. She is comfortable self-advocating and disclosing that she is deaf in one ear. In each interview, she was vulnerable when explaining how her disability had been used against her. Nonetheless, she consistently demonstrated grace and confidence in self-advocacy. She is also persistent in bringing disability awareness to others. Although her disability may not be apparent to others, she feels there is nothing invisible about her disability. Poppy is a hard worker; holding multiple jobs during and after college, sometimes simultaneously. When searching for her purpose, she always knew that she wanted to make a difference, which led her to explore multiple career options.

Poppy grew up learning to adapt to a world (and social situations) where hearing is the norm.

I've been completely deaf in my right ear for as long as I can remember. Being completely deaf in my right ear basically means two things; I cannot tune in to or out of any sound, which can be incredibly irritating. I cannot sound-locate. I always joke around whenever people hear sounds, and they snap their heads at them. I'm always like, "Oh my God! What magical power do you have?" I just will never understand it. My disability is definitely present basically every moment of every day. I feel that being deaf in my right

DOI: 10.4324/9781003495703-12

ear makes me experience the world in a different way. Your right ear is said to link more to language because the language part of your brain is in this hemisphere. Your left ear is more for melodies and sound. I'm always humming, singing, doing something. In conversations, I pick apart someone's tone more than I do what they're saying.

I break it down from the root of the word: dis and ability. It's an impaired function of someone's ability to be a normal human being, *whatever that means*. It's funny because I'm disabled, people look at me, and they can't always tell. Since graduating, I got a tattoo on the back of my ear—a little mute symbol. I felt so obligated to be able to prove my disability. I look like a normal human being, so I literally marked my own body. The deaf community—it's a community that I am very proud of.

Poppy described how she interacts with, and educates, people—including family and strangers.

My family loves telling me what I can and can't do—specifically what I can and can't hear. They always do that—like when I ask, "Where are you?" They respond, "I'm over here." For the love of God, you haven't lived with me long enough to know that that doesn't help me. I don't know where *here* is. I will *never* know where *here* is. Stop answering with that! It's way more frustrating with family. I try to cut some slack to everyone else, especially new people. Why would you necessarily remember that I am deaf? It's not like you encounter someone who is deaf in one ear every day. Even if you do, a lot of people don't feel the need to explain it. But, my family, "How long have you lived with me? How long have you known that I am deaf?"

In general, in social situations, there's just a lot of background noise that every other person can tune out. And, I just can't. That is a very big thing, but it is also continuously explained to people. I've actually had one kid who was blatantly—95% sure he was either incredibly hammered or on drugs because he was incredibly hostile. I told him that I'm deaf in one ear and to stop talking into my right ear. He just said "ok" and talked into my right ear again. I was like, "I just said that I'm deaf in that ear. Stop." He turned around and started accusing me of lying. I was just like, "Who do you think you are? Why would I lie about that? I'm just trying to be here for this concert. You're in my way. Leave me alone." I'm sure I may have just laughed and walked away at that point. I was just like, "You're ridiculous. You're hostile."

I just watch people. I try to learn their norms and mannerisms. Once you get that baseline, you can pick up other cues and see how the other person is feeling, which can give you some hints into the context of what's going on. If you miss a couple of words, you can figure it out. I have to plan things very wisely. If I want to show up the best, whether for work or life, I need to think about the environment I'm about to be in. Where to sit or stand is a huge issue because you want to angle yourself right for the speaker. You might want to be open to other people talking as well. The way in which to navigate that is always an issue. If

someone walks on my right side and tries to talk to me, I get physically uncomfortable. I want to scrunch up and get away. I don't anticipate that ever changing.
If I'm really comfortable, I'll just grab the person's arm and yank them to my
left side. If I'm not totally comfortable, I try to do a weird little half-step and go
to the right, like square dancing. If I don't feel comfortable at all, I stay there, try
not to twitch, and walk with my ear sideways.

Poppy navigates uncomfortable situations with a smile and a laugh.

A nice smile puts everyone at ease. I swear my laugh is my saving grace
every time. Even that activates the serotonin, dopamine, and all that lovely stuff
and generally makes you happy. That's pretty much my go to. I smile a lot of
the time. Then, I'll kind of just take a moment and try to be like, "Alright, what
just happened? What is this situation? Let me reassess for a second and then try
tackling it."

In general, I smile and try to explain myself if it seems like a situation where
the person is willing to hear anything I have to say. To be perfectly dramatic, I
want to say I'm the unsung hero. It's one of those disabilities that flies under a
lot of people's radar. I like to try to make them think about invisible disabilities.
They don't necessarily recognize how much I am struggling with mine, even
when I'm in the process of explaining it. For the most part, I try to laugh it off
and explain it a bit. Most people are very open to that and understanding. But,
they will forget often. They generally are apologetic.

It's funny how sometimes I'll think that I've explained my disability to them.
Then, as time goes on, it becomes apparent that it didn't quite get communicated. I need to break it down a little bit more. I say, "I can't sound locate" or "I
can't tune out a sound." That's all I need to say for them to understand exactly
what that means. Some people do that smile-and-nod thing but do not know
what I'm talking about.

*In addition to educating (and re-educating) people about her disability,
Poppy also encountered well meaning individuals who tried to compare their
situation to hers. These conversations were quite frustrating.*

Many people will say, "Oh yeah, I'm hard of hearing too." If I know they're
not hard of hearing, it makes me mad. They'll be, "Me too, I understand." I'm
like, "No, you don't." It's 100% different to be at 80% of hearing capability in
both ears than to have no capability in one ear. Especially when I say I am deaf
in my right ear. It's like a small pet peeve of mine when people say, "You're
completely—you can't hear at all?" Yes, that is what being deaf means. 100% no
hearing in that ear. Having people try to relate can be very difficult when I know
they're not. I appreciate the empathy, but the understanding is not there. Don't
say it when you don't have it.

*Poppy's initial diagnosis and early school experiences with her mother re-
veal her mom's role as a quiet advocate behind the scenes.*

They found out that I'm deaf after the age of 5, which is unfortunate because,
if I had found out just a couple of months earlier, I could have gotten some

scholarships and more support. I didn't realize it initially, but I found that when I was diagnosed as being deaf in one ear, my doctors printed out these resource guides for my mom to hand to my teachers. Even though I was always in the classroom with my peers, the guidelines pretty much always had me on the right side of the room. It was recommended that she try to ensure they (teachers, peers) were looking at me when speaking to make sure that I heard and understood them.

Once the school found out that a student who was deaf in one ear was coming into the school, they compiled information, sent it out, and let the teachers know—even the ones who may or may not be directly interacting with me. As much as I can explain it firsthand, it was also helpful for educators to have a foundation for what I'm talking about. I don't know how long my mom passed them to my teachers. But, I did know at some point, it would become my responsibility to let teachers and peers know, or to make sure that they understood my needs. She did initially get the ball rolling. She would ensure that people were relatively aware whenever I was in a group activity. Early on, I didn't realize that she was giving the information packet to my teachers. That is the way that my mother has always been; she is quiet and works behind the scenes.

Poppy recounted childhood stories of classmates who were unsympathetic or taunted her.

One kid would come up and whisper in my ear. I don't even know what he would say. Why does it need to be my deaf ear? Why are you that close to me? Most of the time, things like that didn't bother me. It was always that one kid that took it too far. There is one very specific person who didn't understand the word stop. He did use my disability against me.

It can also be hard to socialize in a large or small group when it's very loud. That is absolutely a struggle. I remember vividly one day in art, someone had twisted the volume knob all the way up when it was off. Then, it was turned on, and it just blasted. I was in front of the speakers. I remember having a complete mental breakdown, thinking "I'm going to become deaf in both ears." I was so scared that I was going to lose my hearing. I remember the girl, who was the one who had turned on the power, was like, "Seriously, why are you even crying? This is the stupidest thing ever. You can't become deaf from that one instance." She was not sympathetic at all.

From early life experiences, Poppy learned to self-advocate. When she got to college, she used those skills to educate peers and advocate for her needs with most instructors.

The children's hospital gave me a lot of tools to communicate. I think that college allowed me to advocate for myself more adequately and efficiently. For the most part, I pretty much explained it to everyone in my residence hall a couple of times, and would remind them whenever they needed reminding. Everyone was open, understanding, and willing for me to throw them on my left side. I've actually had the same roommate since I got to college. She's actually from my hometown. She already knew where I was coming from and what my deal was. It worked out really well.

It was kind of difficult trying to figure out how to initially let professors know and what to do. That was probably the biggest change because all my high school teachers pretty much knew. I would just go up to them and tell them I need to sit on the right side of the room. I personally am not super close with any of my college professors, but a couple of them were like, "Hey, if you need anything, let me know. If you're uncomfortable with your seat, I can make sure that we change that." For the most part, those are in small classes under 30. Bigger classes above 80, professors don't really give a shit.

Like many disabled students, Poppy tried to first succeed in college without utilizing the disability services that she was legally due.

Initially, I didn't seek out the advisory programs in terms of my disability or use the campus resources as much as I wish I had. Then, my sister was like, "Hey, hit up disability services." The disability services office is awesome. From there, I got an email at the beginning of the semester. I set up a meeting to go see them. They kind of helped me out. They showed me different recording things that I could use and note-taking that I could do. The smart pen records. If you tap near the notes, it'll record that part of the lecture or play back that part of the lecture. I decided not to use the recording in class because, while it's awesome that it's offered to me, I like challenging myself a lot. I'm a bit anxious, so I like putting myself in slightly uncomfortable situations to try to find new ways to deal with them. I make sure I get to class early, sit on the right side of the room, do my thing, and try to go with it.

Despite her attempts at self-advocacy, Poppy experienced a number of collegiate hurdles including staff turnover in the disability services office and peers who were unaware of her disability or who would forget.

The disability service office staff were actually really good. They do a lot of really cool things. But it's almost like you need to go out of your way and hunt them down to get started. It's a revolving door—the number of emails that I get about, "Oh hey, this person just got into the office. That person is now leaving the office." It was confusing because when I first started, they kept switching over disability services staff. I was supposed to be assigned to one person. Then, the next month that person will have left their position. I would get a new person. That's one thing that sucks and that they don't do well—change.

I'm a psychology major. When you're in a classroom setting with the same people several times a week, I sit in my same seat. I stay in my seat. We're all creatures of habit. Once I get to my seat and sit down, there's this habit-forming area where you don't need to talk very much. Most of the time, it's lecture structured. Granted, you always got that one person who didn't repeat the question that was asked and would just answer it. I'm like, "Well, I have no idea what's going on. Great!" That has been amplified because that's just my life all the time. People are talking, and I have no idea what's going on. Sometimes I'll just space out, especially if I'm in a situation that's out of my control. Ideally, I have access to another student who can get some extra credit or service hours for being a note-taker. To my understanding, if they cannot find a student, the professor or the TA should do that. The number of times that I have not gotten the notes that I need is kind of obscene. And I mean, I tell myself, like even now, I'm like yeah, I really need to email that professor and be like, "Hey bro? What is the deal? Because I need these notes! That's part of my accommodation. Like you're getting in the way of that. And, it's your job to make sure your note taker is doing their job." But, I would not say that. A lot of the time, I just struggle through. Part of that is me challenging myself. But, part of that is definitely not wanting to deal with the anxiety of telling people, "Hey, you're not doing your job."

The college experience is more than classroom learning. Poppy told us about navigating the collegiate scene as a deaf person.

Once you turn 21, you can go out to bars. It wasn't terrible in college. But it was a good test run. Those bars and restaurants are so loud. I remember being at a bar in college. My friends said, "You are screaming at us!" I'm trying to scream over the volume, to the point where I'm going to lose my voice. Then, I suffer the next day. I don't want to do that. To me, it sounds like I'm talking at the same level, so they held their hand up for me. They had me lower my voice and told me when I was at room level.

It's also kind of unfortunate in social situations because it's really loud with a TV blasting and many different conversations going on at one point in time. It's a struggle. It can be kind of frustrating. A lot of the time, people forget that I'm even deaf in one ear. I'm trying to interact with them but they'll keep whispering into my right ear. I have to repeatedly be like, "No, I can't hear you. I need you to…" I've started learning how to read lips to compensate, which has worked well. I still have a lot of room for improvement.

Whenever I think of myself in a social situation, it's not just, "Oh, I'm going to this social situation." It is, "Alright I need to consider how much noise is gonna be at play, how I'm gonna situate myself." In terms of my disability, it plays a role in everything. It makes me really anxious to think, "Well, what if it goes wrong? What if they don't care? Are they willing to do those very minimal steps to meet me halfway?" I think about all of those challenges. I like trying to be very open and conscientious of who I am, especially in relation to my peers because of my disability. I've become more observant, especially in interpersonal and intergroup relationships. My senior year, I took a psychology class called "Close Relationships," which I really enjoyed. It gave a lot of advice on interpersonal relationships, which helps in the workplace and outside of it. That one gave me a lot of tools for understanding and approaching certain situations.

Poppy reflected on the growth she experienced during the college years. Those experiences fostered new skills and prepared her for post-collegiate life.

College was an amazing test run for my disability in the real world. I learned how to better define, explain, and show my disability. I want to keep exploring, advocating, educating, and giving whatever information I have, in case it helps someone else.

I put so much energy into trying to incorporate what I learned in school into my workplace and my everyday mindset. I rely quite a bit on self-advocacy. There are resources available. What they are, I'm vaguely aware of. I don't know that I would ever consider a hearing aid. Surgery, maybe, if it got bad enough. Since college, while I feel more confident with the skills and tools that I have picked up, I am also more aware and realistic about my limitations.

College continued to push me mentally, physically, and socially in terms of my labels and in terms of my lack of labels. This growth and development just seem to be a nonstop trend. College gave me tools to fan that fire. It also gave me the understanding and desire to continue gaining education. I don't ever consider my education stopped. I've had such amazing teachers throughout my life which really blew my mind and gave me a passion for learning. College only kept that going. After college, I've had EMT basic education, firefighter education, and a doctor who is mentoring me on the side.

Beginning in childhood, Poppy's career aspirations were shaped by her disability.

When I was young, my parents asked, "What do you want to be when you grow up?" I wanted to be a policewoman or some sort of military person— mostly a policewoman. That dream was crushed. I grew up diagonally across the street from a safety police officer who was really chill. I thought it was cool that police and military personnel would keep people safe and enforce the laws. I think my dad was also a police officer at one point in his life. But, I don't think I found that out until later on. I was crushed when I realized that I can't sound locate. So, if there's ever a gunshot or anything that goes off, I would be like, "Whoa, hang on, bad guy. I need a moment to kind of spin in circles and find you." I would be a sitting duck. Just the number of things that could go wrong and the number of things that require sound locating would not be realistic. But if I were a police officer, I would definitely not want a desk job. Because what are you gonna do? Do a bunch of data entry and filing? Not gonna lie, what I want to do is be out in the field interacting with people and doing things. I don't want a desk job. Well, I'm probably gonna get one anyway.

Poppy expressed her interest in psychology and understood that this career path required a graduate degree. Yet, she had little guidance about how to plan for graduate school.

I want to become a therapist, some sort of clinician. My high school didn't offer any courses in psychology, which was kind of interesting. It almost gave me the impression that it wasn't a real option and that I couldn't really do anything with it. But, I've always been interested in people, and as I've said, I've learned to be more observant to help myself adapt. It just never occurred to me that I could do something with it until I got into college.

Social psychology is more about viewing group relations, interpersonal relationships, and how people interact. Clinical psychology is like abnormal psych: depression, anxiety, schizophrenia, and any of those types of disorders. I also want to incorporate social and combine them. But, I get confused about grad school. I wish that someone would give me a timeline—the number of years in grad school. Do you have to technically do a residency? I'd be in residency or working in a practice under people, ideally with the mindset of potentially getting my own practice. My timeline is very sketchy. I have my backup plans in terms of what I want to do if my career plan doesn't work out, like teaching and waitressing.

After undergraduate school and while preparing to apply to graduate school, Poppy explored her options and considered psychology-related career paths.

I've pretty much been waitressing. I saved looking at grad schools as my winter task. I need to find car insurance first. Then grad school, getting a GRE prep book and getting the application taken care of. That is soon to come. I started to take an interest in psychology in the military—how unique the military mindset is. This is not only for the actual military members but also for their family and social spheres. In my freshman or sophomore year, I took a course that was called "Children in Military Families." It was very much up my alley. That sunk in the idea that "that's what I want to do." Right now, I want to get a PhD in regards to combat-related PTSD. My thought is that I will start with therapy because that's what I want to do. If I have a PhD, I know I can create my own practice. Because, especially in combat-related PTSD, there is a higher burnout rate among therapists. PhD would also allow me to think about education and becoming a psychology teacher in later years.

By the third interview, Poppy had decided that graduate school was not for her. She was exploring other interests and options.

I originally planned on taking a year off and then trying to go to graduate school. Unfortunately, after learning certain things, I think that a PhD might not be how I wanted to go. I did my undergraduate thesis. While there was an interesting combination between me and the professor I was working for, it didn't come together the way that I wanted it to. So, I wasn't sure that I wanted to be writing 60-page papers for the next however many years of my life.

The volume thing did create a lot of apprehension about going to a potentially loud work environment. I had always been a server and bartender. I wanted to get out of that because, with my hearing, it's not always the best situation. I've been getting more into the medical field. So, out of boredom, curiosity, and trying to find a new purpose, I took an EMT class and ended up really liking it. I became a paid EMT. Fire and EMT are very large communities, that's where my brain was first reaching. We're always trying to provide details for sports games and education classes. I also gained an interest in firefighting. During the pandemic, I got my state firefighter certifications. Ideally, I would like to continue EMT and firefighting. I find it very fulfilling.

When I was debating on nursing school, physician assistant school, medical school, and paramedic school, I started being a medical scribe, which is now my full-time job. It is super exciting. I originally was looking for the ER. I was worried that that might be too much because too many people can be talking at once. I can't tune in to or out of sound. Again, I have to be more selective. But I'm working with a cardiology doctor, who works more one-on-one with patients. He's just an amazing mentor, so I'm learning a lot there. I want to learn things. I want to be challenged. I've already been. The cardiologist I work for gets consulted on acute care and emergency visits. It's not always the heart that's involved. Sometimes he's trying to balance GI problems and kidney problems. He's doing the balancing act the whole way. I love constantly being given a new puzzle.

A love of internal medicine is obviously a gift that my mentor has bestowed upon me. It would be a waste not to pursue that. It is interesting. Now that I work for the doctor, I go to a different end of the hospital. I'm making friends there. I'm coming into a hospital family. But, ultimately, I like to keep myself open in regard to my plans. If my mother has taught me anything, it is that life does not necessarily go how you expect it to go.

Poppy encountered roadblocks that required her to practice self-advocacy in the workplace.

I try to let my employers and co-workers know as soon as my needs come to my mind. Everybody, unfortunately, I have to remind them that I am disabled all of the time. Some coworkers are much better about it. I would just hope that every time one of my coworkers gets called out for forgetting that I'm deaf, it kind of opens their eyes to the fact that not everybody is visibly disabled. Sometimes it will be like, "Hi, I'm Poppy. I'm deaf in my right ear." Some people are like, "Oh my God. Why are you telling me that? I'm just trying to meet you." I really try to do it anyway. Then, when they give me that look of confusion, it gives me the opportunity to be like, "Hey, you look confused. Let me explain this." I address it right away. If I'm going into a new environment, my employer or co-worker will better understand if I ever need anything. I know I've had several co-workers, or even employers, be like, "If you need anything, let me know." I feel like by starting the conversation, we can bring our ideas to the table. It usually solves most of my problems. My disability gives me a unique outlook on what people are saying and how people are saying it. I had to do a lot of self-advocating across the board. There was a willingness and reciprocation of "This is what I need. Can you give it to me?"

Poppy focused on self-care and self-love in her personal and professional life. It is both the little and big things that make her happy as she works toward finding her life purpose.

We all have trials and tribulations. Those challenges make me reassess my purpose in what kind of mindset I want to start each day with.

Friends, social interactions, ideally pets, or access to other people's pets—that is definitely happiness. It's all around finding that Zen, having people in your life that matter, and doing things that make a difference. I'm an intern for Big Brothers and Big Sisters. I'm also trying to learn everything that I possibly can—being open to all these different options. It is being aware of what's going on, about the different possibilities and directions you can go toward. I'm just trying to soak up as much as I possibly can.

Nurturing, relationships, and work—those are the three things that make my life meaningful. When I was younger, I came up with a little kitschy mantra: to love and be loved. That's still accurate. The definition, however, has gradually changed—where it used to be I expected to love outwardly and get love from the exterior. Now, more of that mantra has been focused on, yes, I can love other people. But, I can't expect them to love me back in the way I need. Granted, learning communication skills has helped. But, I'm really trying to focus a little bit more inward. What does Poppy need? What are more advantageous coping skills, methods of self-love, and self-care? I need to renew and prioritize myself—and try to focus on my health. I've been thinking about the yoga mindset. It's very much about centering myself and having that purpose. Be relaxed. Be healthy. The other day, I asked my manager, for example, to go outside for silence for a couple seconds.

My spiritualism has shifted more toward myself currently, and not so much toward my career. I'm trying to work on nurturing things, which seems to be the theme right now. Not only do I feel purposeful in making sure my boyfriend's dog has a good life, she also helps me have a healthier life. Helping others obviously goes into loving. Love is more than just romantic love. I entertain myself. I have an herb garden going. Love, as much as it can be an exterior loop, can also be a little bit of an interior loop. I'm just trying to work on building that interior loop. I think that shows.

Over time, Poppy shared her hopes for the future, romantic relationships, and her evolving sexuality—which influenced her life plans. While in college, Poppy explained:

I really want the simple things. I like staying open to everything. I definitely want a dog and cats. I want a nice, comfortable, and roomy house.

Ideally, I would like to be married and have a family. In 10 years, I'd like to be in some sort of relationship. But, I'm not that kind of person that's like, "I need to be married by the age of 35 or I'm gonna die." As far as I can tell, I'm heterosexual. I've always been with men. I think that I will always be with a man. But if a woman walked into my life and she was everything that I wanted, I wouldn't be like, "You got the wrong anatomy. So you can leave." That's something that I think about, especially with the whole lack of understanding as a society. It's not just black and white. There's a lot of gray. There's a spectrum. All of those constantly play into who I am and how I see myself.

After finishing school, Poppy had been in a number of relationships and began to describe her identity and romantic interests in new ways.

I don't know if I've ever thought about what genetic traits I would pass on to a child. That would require me finding somebody that I even wanted to have a child with in the first place! I thought about it vaguely in that way. But first things first.

I have been in two and a half relationships since we last talked. The first one was the one who lost his mind at the beginning of the COVID pandemic. The second one was fine enough, but unenthusiastic. The third one is actually one of the people at the restaurant who regularly advocated for me when my back was turned. It was really nice for someone to just be able to think of someone else and remember their disability and limitations. He gets a little irritable sometimes. So, I've been working on finding romantic support.

In terms of a relationship, we talked about trying to find someone more supportive than I have had in the past. It's funny because I basically put everything on a spectrum. I really hate labels. If I were to label myself, I'm a cis woman, queer, and disabled. That whole combination. We're in the middle of gay pride month. We just had our pride parade. I'm definitely part of the pride community. In the restaurant, I feel comfortable being who I am. But, like in hospital work, EMS work, or as a firefighter—unless you ask me directly, I ain't telling you about my sexuality.

Poppy reflected quite a bit on the intersection of gender and disability, noting the lack of safety she felt as a disabled woman.

My single parent mother raised me. The way that I view the world in terms of my gender is a bit different. I certainly think about how the day-to-day life of a woman is not similar to the day-to-day life of a man. I wouldn't leave the house, or even walk from my job to my car, without my pepper spray or pocket knife. I do get those common reminders of I'm in the victim class. When I waitressed, I had lots of cash. I couldn't walk to my car with headphones because if someone approached me from behind, I wouldn't be able to hear them. If I hear someone approaching, I won't be able to pinpoint where they're coming from as quickly. When parking at night, I stick to more open areas where I'm more familiar with better lighting. I know none of my guy coworkers ever worried about that.

In addition to lack of safety, Poppy described prejudice and discrimination she experienced as a woman. But, over time, Poppy grew more confident in standing up for herself and other women.

At the end of the night during one of my restaurant serving shifts, the new owner asked for opinions. I shared my disagreement with one of his thoughts. He ended up calling me out. He basically belittled me and talked to me like I was a child. He doesn't like women who dissent.

When I became a firefighter, I went up to a table of my regulars (where I was waitressing). I'm sharing with them that I'm becoming a firefighter. It was before I even had my certifications. One of the guys literally goes, "Well, I hope you don't ever have to save my house from burning down because it would probably burn to the ground." Being a female firefighter is a big offense to some men.

By the third interview, Poppy had grown more confident in standing up for herself and other women.

I'm definitely part of the women's community. Whether that be making friends in the girl's bathroom, giving good advice, giving rides home, making sure they're safe, or what have you. I like to be that loud-mouthed, smart ass. I will put you in your place if you step out of line. I will keep people and other women safe. I've been fighting for it! Part of me feels obligated to educate. Being a woman, I'm ready to tackle discrimination, educate others, and fight.

Reflection Questions

1 *Evolving life plans.* In what instances did Poppy change her life plans? What factors influenced important life decisions in her career trajectory and personal development? How did her passions, interests, and disability influence her decisions? How do some of her core values, such as keeping people safe and helping others, provide a consistent foundation for her career explorations?

2 *Self-advocacy and challenging oneself.* Like many college students, Poppy did not utilize disability services when she first arrived on campus. This choice was in part due to her desire to challenge herself and succeed without support. Ruminate on the notion of challenging oneself. How can this mindset help one grow? At what point might decisions to challenge oneself, and not utilize support, become a detriment to success? What can K-12 and higher educators do to prepare and support college students who qualify for accommodations but wish to "try" college without them? How would you start a conversation with a disabled college student who was deciding whether or not to utilize accommodations on campus?

3 *Beyond disability.* Poppy discussed numerous aspects of her identity. Consider the ways disability, gender, and sexuality influenced Poppy's life experiences and sense of self. What did you learn from her story about the ways various identities intersect to shape someone's lived experiences? Poppy's story highlights the ways in which our sense of self can evolve over time—especially during the transition from adolescence to adulthood. What can you draw from Poppy's story to

support youth exploring various aspects of their identities? Identify three things you can say or do to ensure that youth feel supported as they explore their identities?

4 *Safety.* Poppy uses the phrase "victim class" to reference the ways her disability and gender intersect to inhibit her safety and opportunities. What can you learn from Poppy's story about the intersection of gender and disability? What terms might you use to describe these phenomena? How might you work within your sphere of influence to foster safety and equity for disabled women?

13　Meet Tippi

Pronouns: She/her
Age: 26
Self-identified disability: Attention-Deficit/Hyperactivity Disorder (ADHD), Anxiety, Depression
College major: Animal science with a concentration in management
Current living situation: Living with a partner
Current job/position: Assistant trainer of marine mammals
Passions: Working with animals, animal conservation, advocacy, building community partnerships, sustainable living

Tippi has a passion for conservation efforts and working with animals. By the third interview, she was doing important work at an aquarium. Tippi is frank about disability-related struggles, fear of failure, and unsupportive work environments. Her story is also one of an advocate for justice who stands up for the rights of all disenfranchised people impacted by inequitable workplaces. Her reflections show how people's perceptions about someone's capabilities can have a lasting impact on one's sense of self and confidence. But, Tippi also shares how a combination of perseverance and support can build confidence and foster a pathway toward a fulfilling life of purpose.

Tippi shared her perspectives about the concept of disability generally and her disability in particular.

I don't take disability as a bad thing like some people do. I take it as I just need extra help or a different type of help than what other people need. I learn differently. I have to adapt. I need help trying to figure out how other people learn and how to get the most out of my experience with my disability. I feel like it almost gives me a reason to want to work harder, to prove myself. A lot of people get drowned in their disability. I'm super careful about it. I don't want

DOI: 10.4324/9781003495703-13

anyone to be like "Oh, well she has ADHD." I'm not letting anyone blame my success, or failure, on my disability. I'm not letting anyone blame my grades on my disability. People all the time get straight A's and have disabilities.

While some see their identity as defined by disability, Tippi had a different view.

It's more like just a part. It definitely has its challenges, it's just … it's not *who* I am. It's something that I sort of have to deal with. I'm not me *because* I have ADHD. Or, I'm not me *because* I have anxiety or depression. It's something separate that bothers me or impacts me on occasion—more than it's shaped who I am as a person. The medicine for anxiety helps a lot and also gives me the perspective that it's a chemical imbalance. The depression isn't you. It wasn't something that was wrong with me, because medicine could fix it.

Nothing needs to be going wrong in my life; I'll still have depression and anxiety. It's not something that I can just get over. But I have learned how to cope with it. I get overwhelmed very easily. I get panic attacks. Anything can trigger them, especially school. It's just like the worst thing in the world. Depression has crippling effects. In the times where it doesn't, I do as much as I can. Get as much done. Prove yourself as much as you can. Show yourself how good you are at things.

In reflecting on childhood, Tippi described how others' perceptions of disability, especially in school, impacted her sense of self and views about the opportunities available to her.

I don't want my disability to define me. When I was younger, I definitely thought it defined me because it was constant attention. I constantly had disability teachers coming into my classroom, helping me, sort of singling me out in front of everyone. The kids would be doing something and I would be there with the disability person, having them take papers upon papers out of my desk, having everyone stare at me. I'm just like, "Oh my God, please let me die." That kind of attention made me feel like, "Something is wrong with you. Something is wrong with you, so you need a special teacher. You can't take this class because you have a disability. You have an Individualized Education Plan (IEP), you can't take honors classes." Basically, I was never given opportunities because of my disabilities. I'm like, "It's holding me back more than anything." The help was holding me back. These experiences definitely give me the lens that I want to prove myself. I work harder because I don't want my disability being blamed because I failed.

Tippi received support from loved ones, especially her immediate family. Throughout her life, this support fueled her confidence and desire to succeed despite hurdles.

They have been super inspirational. It's nice to have them be supportive no matter what I decide to do. They're not pushing me toward something. Knowing that I can do anything is a nice feeling. They are constantly telling me, "Don't let it get you down. You're no different than anyone else." My mom is a very unique woman. She has been so supportive of me, so excited, and proud of me for what I'm doing. She wants the best for me. It was hard for me to fail because they threw me into so many different resources, like emotionally. My mom has advocated for me. She is definitely a superhero in that sense. My mom was really involved, because she works in education. She understands it because she works with kids with disabilities. She's the reason I had an Individualized Education Plan (IEP). If she needs to be at a meeting, she's there. No doubt about it. She really puts in the effort. At the doctor, she's like, "She needs this. She needs that." To the point where sometimes I get frustrated because she won't really let me do things for myself. My mom has been on the phone with the university many times. We went to the disability services several times together. I'm really thankful for that. If it wasn't for her, I definitely wouldn't be here, in college, right now.

My dad gets that it is overwhelming. As a child growing up outside the United States, he was constantly told: "You're stupid, you're not amounting to anything. You can't even read a book." He encourages me to not let anyone make me feel like that. So, I guess that's sort of an inspiration. I have definitely gotten a lot closer to my dad because he's understanding. He's definitely been a really great asset in my life.

I'm super close to my sister. She's like my best friend. We talk everyday about anything and everything. I can go to her for anything. I've always been the emotional one. She's always been the rock. We are opposites. We sort of complement each other. Even though she's in [a different state] right now, I still call her all the time. She works with kids with disabilities. She went into teaching kids with disabilities because she saw how high school wronged me. All her teachers loved her. She was a straight-A student. Then I come in, fumbling around. The same teachers that supported her so much told me I wasn't capable of doing things. She was like, "Do they not see that you've done all this stuff? Not see how capable you are? That doesn't make any sense. You weren't given the right support. That's not your fault. You don't learn this way." She's very big into teaching in different ways and understanding that homework isn't for everyone. It doesn't mean that you're not going to learn. It doesn't mean you're not intelligent. She's the best. She's a teacher I wish I had. She's really good about working with each individual kid with disabilities, figuring out how they learn. I sometimes visit her classes and talk to her kids. I try to give them hope that school isn't everything. I'm so grateful to have her as a support system.

My aunt has always been like a second mom to me. She very much understands the world and how things should be. She's one of the most confident human beings I've ever met. She has given me coping mechanisms that she uses, which have been super helpful to me. She says things like, give yourself a date. If things don't change by this date, you're out. It's going to help you so much. When I struggled in the workplace, she's like, "Go to human resources if things are going wrong. Say all these really good arguments. Take care of yourself first.

Stand up for yourself, remembering you're not going to die if you leave this job. Right now, you can survive. You have a place to live and money saved." She's like a really good life coach.

Tippi shared how her disability created social and academic challenges throughout her schooling experiences. She also described the coping strategies she learned and implemented.

It was in 5th grade when I was diagnosed with ADHD. I guess I wasn't doing well for a fifth grader. My desk was just a mess of papers. If I don't take my ADHD medicine, I just can't do anything. I'm not lazy, I just cannot bring myself to do work. A lot of my ADHD is procrastination. I've just been trying as long as I know I stay on top of it. Once I get behind, I get discouraged and procrastinate more. But as long as I know I am on top of my work, and getting everything in on time, I'll stay with it.

I was definitely struggling in high school. Homework and things were really hard for me, especially with ADHD. A six hour day of just sitting there—which isn't easy for anyone—was almost impossible for me. Then, having to go home and sit more and do homework did not work for me. Also, in high school, they like to treat you weirdly. It was pretty difficult in high school. However, looking back, I'm grateful for my K-12 experience because it taught me coping mechanisms and how to deal with school load.

I actually like college a lot. It's easier than high school. Even though college work is more overwhelming, it's not like a bunch of busy work. Having my own schedule, time in between college classes, and having my classes scheduled throughout the day was also a huge change. Walking around campus and doing things at my own pace made me feel like I was always in control of my own life. It's so good for my mental health and academic health. ADHD can make it hard to sit in class for a long time. The hour and fifteen-minute lectures are not happening. Trying to write things down during note-taking, and trying to focus on one thing, is really hard for me—especially with teachers who just lecture and are not really there to help. It's hard when they are teaching at a fast pace. You just fend for yourself.

I think that the biggest difference for me in college was that no one knew me. They just kind of let me do my thing. I was more willing to go and advocate for myself in college. I'm more comfortable asking for something better here than when I was in high school. I feel like in high school, a lot of people want to be like everyone else. So, I was more embarrassed in high school to have to go and be like, "I need help." Versus in college, when I'm struggling, I feel more accepted. Here, you have to advocate for yourself. If you want help, you have to go get it. They don't force it upon you. I have the resources if I need them, but I still make my own decisions.

I've been able to do my own thing and figure out how I work best without people telling me. It's definitely brought my perspective that "I can handle this!"

In college, Tippi lived with roommates and felt comfortable disclosing her disability to them. But, as time went on, one roommate shared frustrations with Tippi's disability.

It's not something that I hide. One of my roommates has anxiety too. I think the other one has depression. We all sort of have our things. One day, one of my roommates said, "Oh my God, I can't study with you at all." She'd ask me to study. When I couldn't focus on something or I'd get distracted, she's like, "Oh my God. You get distracted so easily. You're the worst person to study with." She said it in front of everyone. I was like, "I actually can't help that. It's literally not my fault." She had her insensitive moments. I didn't call her out for it because she didn't mean anything by it. She was just making a joke. It was just a mean joke. Like, God forbid I did something like that to her, the priest would be called! I used to really beat myself up over it. It's not something that I control. People get frustrated with me. I would get frustrated with myself. I'm like, "Come on. Just focus. Just focus." I realized I can't. It actually helped me when she did that kind of stuff because it made me realize like "I'm not doing it on purpose. I'm not doing it just to make you mad. I've told you this. That's your problem. You don't have to study with me." That's when I really realized I work best alone.

Despite the roommate problems, living on campus, living by myself, has definitely been a really positive experience. Being able to figure out stuff on my own. Knowing that I'm going to be okay without my parents' help. I realize how much I'm capable of when I'm by myself because I realize how much I know, and how much my life experiences helped me out. I took it for granted when I was younger because I was like, "When am I ever going to need to know how to fold my laundry?"

Despite roommate challenges, Tippi found it easier to make friends in college. She appreciated the opportunity to forge connections with peers who were also learning to effectively navigate college.

Making friends in high school was a little bit harder for me in general. In college, I got to reset and make friends in different ways. That gave me a different type of confidence. Being in the dorms, and making friends that way, was a nice change from what I was used to. People that I grew up with saw me struggle and wrote me off. In college, talking to people who are also in the same thing (classes, disability status) makes me feel like I'm not alone. Just to have this very clear support group of people that are like me. I know I am not alone. We're going through it together. That helps a lot.

Tippi described her fear of failure and how it motivates her to persevere through difficult situations. She explained how her fears often kept her from applying for jobs and internships. But, once she applied, she was very successful.

I'm definitely someone who is afraid of failure. I've had tons of experiences where I was scared to do something, did it, and learned it was okay. For some reason, it's just constant fear. When I was 16, I wrote in an essay contest that my teacher told me about. The grand prize was a trip to Italy and free airfare. I'm like, "I don't know if I can. But, I want to do this!" Of course, I was nervous. It took me a while to finally get it in. In the end, I did it and ended up winning!

There might be times I won't study for a test because I'm scared I'm going to fail anyways. I feel like it might set me back in the sense that I'm not actually applying for internships or jobs because I'm nervous that I'm going to not get it. I've come to like myself the more I prove to myself that I'm able to do things. It's definitely been an improvement from last year. I kind of got in my own way. My confidence kind of got in my own way. I didn't try doing internships before I started volunteering. I thought I couldn't get them. I didn't think I should try. I've always been kind of holding myself back.

I worked two jobs this summer, like 80-hour weeks! I managed it. Obviously, once I get it, I'm fine. Bringing myself to get it is the iffy part. It's actually a really proud feeling coming out of work after a 16-hour day. Like, "I just earned so much money, but I need a nap." It's weirdly satisfying.

Tippi appreciated the support from disability services on campus. However, she found mixed support from college professors.

I have my disability services counselor who explains everything and waits for me to have questions. They had this orientation that explained all of our options. It was so well developed that I just knew that no matter what my obstacle, no matter what was going to come at me, that I could recover. Because of disability services, I am super covered, especially since my classes were stressing me out. I was overwhelmed by the fact that I might not get into the classes I needed. What am I going to do if I can't get into those classes? Disability services gave me priority in classes. That was a weight lifted off my shoulders, not having to worry about it.

Disability services in college were great. It really helped me out, but no one ever told me, "Okay you're going to have troubles with this, you're gonna have problems with this," because I proved that I was willing to overcome whatever the obstacles were. I'm covered no matter what, but it's on me to be covered. I'm still taking care of me. I went to my professors to get my disability accommodations letter signed saying that I have a disability. Most of them were like "Let me know if you need anything. Here's my office hours. I'm always here. Come talk to me. I hope you have a great year." They were all so friendly. Even though I spent five minutes with them, they established a relationship. It's like a very supportive community.

I have one professor who is really nice. But, he goes so fast in class. He doesn't want laptops. I emailed disability services, but they are not emailing me back about recording his classes. That's my most negative experience because I get really antsy if I can't keep up. He'll put something on the board and he'll go to the next slide in two seconds. I'm like "Are you serious? … like please just let me do this!"

I had one professor that I was just struggling with. To be fair, she was trying that new swapped classroom where you watch the lectures online and you go to class and you discuss it. I actually ended up loving that. When it first happened, I had no idea how to handle it. It was a mixture of me not being great at studying anyways, plus her attempting this new thing. I had a meeting with her. She's like "What are you doing now? What's your job right now?" I'm a receptionist at an animal clinic. She's like "maybe just stick to your strengths and stay a receptionist." No, I refuse. I didn't come to college to be a receptionist. I can do that without college. She was not my mentor. I was like, "I need to prove you wrong!"

In a positive light, another professor was just a completely different type of professor. He was very chill. He was excited to teach. He wanted to see students succeed. He's a passionate teacher. He's also had to figure out how to teach in different ways. I think that's a big asset for him. He can see this person struggling and thinks," Let's try this approach." That really nice professor, I still see him because he's affiliated with the aquarium. I'm able to be like, "Look how well I'm doing!" And he's like, "I'm just so proud of you." That's the positive feedback I've always wanted. I've never had a good relationship with a teacher, so his kindness is just mind-boggling to me.

In college, Tippi started as a wildlife and conservation biology major.

I know I want to work up close and personal with animals. I always wanted to work with animals. I've always loved animals. I have a soft spot. If I ever see an animal hurt in a movie, I'm like balling. I've always wanted to be able to help animals and do something to give back to them—make an impact. I like the idea of working at Yellowstone around wildlife and animals. I think that would be really cool. I want to go more into animal rehabilitation. I did a thesis last semester in my writing class about animals in the entertainment industry.

Eventually, Tippi switched her major to animal management and was getting meaningful hands-on experiences that inspired her sense of purpose.

It turns out wildlife doesn't mean animals so much as it means like plants and dirt. Right now, I'm in soil science because I'm still technically in that major. Animal management is working on farms and zoos—working with actual living animals and not plants. I want to go into rescuing—like at a refuge.

Not all people are bad. It's just that people tend to be really ignorant. They're like, "It was just an animal." They don't want to think about it. I just know I want to do something to counteract that at least. I really want to know that I died doing something good and helping animals. There are at least a few animals out there that are doing good because of my work. I love knowing that I at least helped some animal's life. They are pretty intelligent in the sense that they realize that they're being helped. They're thankful. You see them being really affectionate. I definitely want to know that I left making some sort of impact for any creature.

I went on a conservation trip, like a little excursion to a local island. We built nesting boxes for birds. I liked being out in the field and using my hands. This is how I do things. This is a viable way to learn, versus being in the classroom learning from a book. That was a big turning point. That also helped me realize I want to work with animals and work in conservation. It changed how I thought about everything. It makes me want to go out and work with wild populations of animals and help do research out there. That definitely changed my perspective on what I want to do. Having a goal to work toward is a really nice feeling because even when I was younger, I never really felt I had a goal to work toward because I never knew what I really wanted to be. I knew I wanted to work with animals, but I didn't really know how. Now I know. I'm really excited about this. If I really want to do something, I'll do it. I need to do this.

By the third interview, Tippi earned her college degree. She reflected on her trajectory through high school, college, and into the world of work—and the ways her disability impacted her experiences.

College was really important in building my confidence both academically and socially. High school isn't easy for anyone, but especially those with disabilities. Teachers who don't really understand disabilities brush you off. I had a lot of teachers telling me I couldn't do things and that I wasn't able to do things. I said I wanted to work with animals. I was told I won't be able to handle a four-year college. I was told I'd never work with animals. That's where high school really got me down. In high school, they wouldn't even let me try because they thought I couldn't do it. That definitely shaped me, not being able to try things and attempt things that I never would have pre-college.

My confidence was very low going into college. Once I got there, I was like, "Oh, I am able." I felt a lot more confident doing it because nobody was telling me I couldn't. I was blessed that in the years I was there, a new professor had started who used to be a whale trainer from the aquarium. He's teaching animal behavior and how to train animals. Being able to take his class and learning from him, I got a lot of confidence in being able to work with animals.

I worked at a park zoo in their seasonal education department. We did little skits for kids, educating them about conservation. I actually really enjoyed doing little plays and being able to educate kids about animals and wildlife. That was a parallel step to my major when I changed my major freshman year. After I graduated, I went and volunteered at the aquarium. I interned unpaid. Then I got a job after two years of volunteering and interning as a temp. From there, I got a permanent position. If I told my little high school self what happened, she wouldn't believe me! I'm very grateful for the experience I had in college.

Tippi also reflected on how she changed between college and entering the workforce, noting key shifts in confidence and relationships.

I do really well in the workforce, which has also helped me with my confidence. Knowing that I have been able to be successful—and not that the academics weren't important, but they weren't everything. I felt really disabled when I was in school. I'm a person with ADHD—not I *am* ADHD. I have coping mechanisms that I don't even think about anymore. I honestly can't even tell you what they were. But, somehow it has gotten easier. It's very evident to me now that I am slow at processing. It's okay, but I got to work on it. If I'm working on a wild animal that's about to bite me, I have to be able to think quickly on my feet.

I used to have a really hard time with feedback because I was so insecure. I had such a lack of confidence that with any criticism, I would just shrink into my shell and be like, "I'm the worst!" Now I'm like, "Thank you for the feedback." My mentor during my internship said, "Your greatest strength is that you can take feedback better than anyone I've ever met." I think that was a big coping mechanism for me. Just take what people are telling you and use it. If they're taking their time to tell me, I might as well use it!

Tippi experienced disability-related hurdles in the workplace. She also noted how the work environment and specific job duty of supporting sick animals sometimes increased her anxiety.

I definitely have a hard time with certain things. My job requires a lot of time organization. That's like, a big part of my disability. I get rambling daily. Communicating is really hard for me. I'll kind of get off-topic. I'll get distracted halfway through a sentence. Sometimes you'll see me literally walking back and forth trying to think of what I need to get done. Standing still and having to think about tasks is not super useful.

My job is genuinely anxiety-inducing because it is working with sick animals. It is working with animals that you built relationships with. There's a reason they can't be released. We fall in love with an animal. There's a possibility they could die. There's a chance that you could see them suffer. That is just the nature of the field.

Everyone has that natural anxiety. It depends on what department you're in. I started out working with the outdoor animals. Then I got hired in the show department, which I fell in love with. They are the sweetest group of people. They just have your back. They're so supportive. They'll do anything for each other, even in the worst of times. Then, the department I started out in started struggling so I had to go back down there. It is the most toxic work environment. It gave me so much anxiety and so much depression. We're very short-staffed. I don't know if it is just my ADHD or just being a human, but I feel very out of control of my life at this point. I have no say in what my job is. They didn't ask me if I wanted to go back down. I left this department that I absolutely loved, and these animals that I absolutely love, to go back down to a department where I was miserable. In the last few months, I've definitely not been in a great place, but neither is anybody else. I think now they realize they're overworking us. We're working 14-hour days—so it's definitely exacerbating my anxiety and depression.

Tippi recognized that the environment also took a toll on her co-workers. Sometimes, she would disclose her disability and coping strategies to support struggling co-workers and to develop more authentic relationships with colleagues.

Other people have ADHD at my job too. They have a different type of ADHD. They are better at coping with it. It's hidden better. They're also on medications. They can mask their symptoms better than I do. I can bring it up, "Oh, I get anxiety too." If I see someone having anxiety, I'll be the one to go over and help them get through the panic attack because I've been there. You aren't alone—there are a lot of us with anxiety. I would not bring it up to someone who doesn't have it, because it's not super understood if you don't have it. People think, "Oh, well you're just sad. Oh, you're just tired." They don't understand it's brain chemistry. I used to be really ashamed of my ADHD. Now, it helps me explain things. If I'm talking to someone I'm like, "Sorry I'm rambling. It's pretty common with ADHD. I have trouble organizing my thoughts. Hopefully, that helps you understand me better." I'll say it to people who have known me for a while too. You see how hard I work. You see that I am capable. These are the things that I'm struggling with. So, hopefully that gives them a more well-rounded opinion of me and my desire to succeed too.

Despite her comfort disclosing to coworkers, Tippi wrestled with if, and how, to disclose her disabilities to management—especially after witnessing ableism in the workplace.

I usually don't disclose that I have depression or anxiety. I know that sounds awful. A lot of people in my field do disclose those things. I've noticed they get brushed off very quickly. There are people who are not getting a job. Everyone's kind of in a bad place right now with our career. A lot of people have depression. A lot of people have anxiety. It's one of those things that almost goes without saying. Everyone's struggling. I've seen people when they have panic attacks. Someone is like, "Get over it." It's one of those fields where you know you're lucky to be here. So, therefore, just shut up and put your head down. It's not the best field to be in.

Lately, I felt more empowered to bring my disability up. "Look, I have this disability. I genuinely struggle with this. Other people do too." They expect me to be like the people who are really good at masking it. I'm still figuring out how to do that and how to make it so that it doesn't end up going against me in my workplace. The anxiety and depression is definitely hard at this job because they are not super understanding. They're very old fashioned. Very old fashioned perspectives like "Don't complain about your feelings." I've literally heard them tell people just to shut up and put their head down.

We definitely have had very old school people in charge for a while, who don't understand disabilities. I've heard them call the person with autism that they just hired a pity hire. I've heard them not talk very kindly about people with disabilities. It definitely doesn't send a good message to people with disabilities about, "Hey it's okay we're willing to work with you." I think, if anything, if I were to go to a higher-up and be like "Hey, this is a disability I have." I would almost be set as an example. They'd be like "Look! We hire people with disabilities," rather than you're a person first, more than you're a diverse hire.

After a number of inequitible work experiences, Tippi became a vocal advocate for equity. Tippi was especially passionate about challenging pay inequities in her field.

Men make more money than we do. We've complained about it before. But somehow human resources keeps turning it around where it's our fault because basically they know women are passionate about these animals and will work for terrible wages. We love these animals. I think that's almost what makes this a very toxic field. I have no idea if it is just our aquarium where this happens. They only hire women, but we're paid such a low salary. I think most men wouldn't be interested in it because they can't support their families. That is why you have to be married to be in this field.

I also think it's a very classist field. Very classist. I did an unpaid internship which a lot of people can't do. After COVID, they put a fee to do an internship. It was $750 a semester to work for free 40 hours a week. I'm very open that this is a classist situation which ends up being a racist situation. I'm very passionate about that—so they're going to regret hiring me. I went to an intern and said: "Hey, have you paid your fee yet? Go talk to someone. Say that you can't afford it. Ask what that money is going towards. Question it. Do not let them get away with that."

Yet, when Tippi advocated, sometimes co-workers responded:

"We can't do that. We can't fight what's going on." My response is: "we have to, or how are we going to survive in this field? It's classist, It's sexist, It's racist. It's very clear these people (management) have never dealt with that kind of oppression." I am very frustrated by it. I can definitely see in their eyes, they think I'm radical for wanting human rights.

Tippi also described her cultural background and her experiences with racism throughout her life.

My dad's from India and my mom is white. Indian culture's just such a different culture. I feel like it really gave me the chance to be curious about the rest of the world. I'm finding more diversity in college than I was used to in high school. It's nice to no longer stand out. I used to be pretty ashamed that I was Indian, because my friend when I was little would tell me nobody liked me because I was Indian. That resonated with me for a while. I'm like, "Wait a minute. That doesn't make sense. Why would someone not like me just because I was Indian?"

I definitely feel like I'm a radical thinker because I come from a different background. I actually love being a person that comes from a different background. I'm very open that I'm Indian. Growing up, I was very much *not* open that I was Indian because I wanted to be the same as everyone else. I was almost ashamed of it because the people I was around were definitely racist. I was very quick to hide it. Now I'm very open about it.

I enjoy being a person that people are comfortable talking to about the questions they have about race that they're too afraid to ask. If you don't ask those questions, how are you ever going to learn? I'm really excited to be that person for people.

Most people usually end up accidentally being insensitive because they were too afraid to ask. I have definitely dealt with some people at the aquarium that are very insensitive. They clearly don't realize—I mean I *hope* that they don't realize how insensitive they are being. They will bow to me. Anyone with two brain cells can realize that was not the right thing to do. Once, I was just sitting at a table and someone asked, "What are you?" I look ambiguous. So I tried to make it a joke by responding, "What do you think?" I want people to be able to ask those questions. I think that's still important. But also put yourself in this seat, huh? Maybe next time, you'll think of not asking it like *that*.

My field is white. Every now and again, you see some people of color, but it's rare. Especially in my department, I believe there's maybe three people of color. I've definitely joked that I'm the diversity hire. One time I made that joke and my boss pulled me over. "You know that's not why you were hired right? You were hired because of your skills, you are a skilled person. That's not why you're here."

By the third interview, Tippi was in a romantic relationship and learning from her partner how to live independently.

We live together. I think by sharing a space, I have to clean up after myself and make sure it looks nice. I definitely get positive feedback. One, he's happy. And, also it looks so much better to have a clean space.

My boyfriend has been really important in the fact that he's like "You just need to stop being scared of everything." He's not insensitive, but sometimes he definitely doesn't understand it. But it's almost been good, in a way, where I'm like, "Okay, I just have to get over things." I have to just try things that I'm scared of because then I do and I'm like, "Oh that wasn't scary." He's amazing at talking. He's taught me a lot about communicating with people. I will have him read my text messages. I'm very grateful to have him as a partner. We help each other. I think he's taught me to be a lot more independent because he's a very independent person. He's inspired me to want to do better for myself.

When asked about her dreams for the future, Tippi shared goals of becoming a mom, living simply, and continuing to pursue simple and sustainable living.

I want to be out in the field working with animals and wild populations. I'm kind of all over the place right now, but I know at the end of the day, I want to be helping wildlife and helping the earth as a whole. I'd love to do big-picture stuff, but I would also love to do wildlife rehab. Even if that's a volunteer thing or a part-time job, that's definitely something I want to get into too. I don't have a clear trajectory, but I have a lot of things I want to try and kind of see what feels like the right fit. In talking about the future, I really want to be in education—even if it's still working with the aquarium in the education department—teaching kids about conservation. Education, at the end of the day, is going to be the most important aspect.

I guess I want simplicity—like having a job, being able to make a living, doing what I love, and being able to have a family. I always knew I wanted to be a mom. I want to have kids and raise them in the idea that the earth isn't here to serve us. We're here to serve it and make it better. We could raise a society that understands and isn't as ignorant as the society we have today. I want my kids to also feel like they want to make the world a better place.

Reflection Questions

1 *K-12 vs. college services.* Tippi talks about the disability services she received across her educational trajectory. Discuss how she felt about the "disability person" (aide, special educator) helping her in her elementary classroom. What can we learn from her experience of feeling singled out in front of her peers? Now, consider how Tippi felt about collegiate services. She explained, "I have the resources if I need them, but I still make my own decisions." How did this difference in the delivery of services (based on different disability laws mentioned in Chapter 2), impact Tippi's sense of self and feeling of empowerment?

2 *Workplace rights.* Discuss the numerous forms of prejudice and discrimination, Tippi witnessed in the workplace. What strategies did she use to challenge ableism, racism, sexism, and classism? How were her tactics different? Similar? Reflect on why her approach might have differed when combating these different forms of discrimination. Have you ever experienced discrimination in the workplace? How did you handle it? How might your strategies be different from, or similar to, those used by Tippi?

3 *Educating others about race and culture.* Tippi said, "I enjoy being a person that people are comfortable talking to about questions they have about race." Yet, she also alluded to how frustrating it was when people were "ignorant." Educating others about one's identities and experiences with oppression can be *both* empowering and exhausting. Discuss this complicated reality. Consider the role that allies can play in helping educate so people who experience discrimination, like Tippi, don't always have to use their time and emotional energy to be the educator.

4   *Authentic friendships and disclosure.* Tippi felt like it was easier to make friends in college than it was in elementary and high school. Once she got to college no one knew her as "the disabled student." As such, she felt empowered to develop new relationships by disclosing her disability only when she wanted to. What can we learn from Tippi about the ways environments can foster or inhibit the development of authentic friendships for disabled youth? What strategies can educators and family members use to create opportunities where all youth can develop authentic friendships?

14 Meet Titus

Pronouns: He/him
Age: 35
Self-identified disability: I have learning disabilities that affect how I
  process information.
College major: Nutrition and Dietetics
Current living situation: Living with spouse with a child on the way
Current job/position: I am a health coach and workflow specialist
Passion: I love working on projects where nothing is set in stone—yet I
  need to build it. So, my gift helps a lot!

Despite disability stigma, Titus redefines his disability as a gift and creates a life of purpose. He hated school. Even as a college student, he found most teachers to be discouraging or unhelpful. Yet, he continues to learn and enjoys teaching others. He has social support from some family members, a supervisor, occasional teachers, and, most importantly, his wife. Although he struggled with finding the right job, he now loves his work and finds himself emerging as a leader in his company. He is committed to supporting others and expressing his creativity. Titus is growing increasingly pleased about being recognized by others for his unique talents and skills—or as he calls them, his gifts.

Titus reflected on his early childhood, initial diagnosis, and the asset lens he uses to describe his disability today.

My mom said she knew I had a disability when I started to talk. When I was really, really little, she said I was like a tornado of energy. I did not stop asking questions. I wanted to know everything. I was six when I actually legit got diagnosed. I think I had to go see the therapist or something. I had vivid memories of that. Basically my whole life I've been told that I was dumb, that something was wrong, and that I was different from everyone else, and I had to change.

DOI: 10.4324/9781003495703-14

So, at a very young age, I was like, "No, I'm not dumb. There's nothing wrong with me. There's something wrong with everyone else because they can't see what I can see."

Titus had a number of negative school experiences which led him to hate school. He laments how schools are not designed to effectively support disabled students.

I hate school. I've had a lot of bad experiences in school, especially with other kids and teachers. Every grade, every school was absolutely awful. I've hated every second of it, and I cannot wait to graduate college next spring.

I had teachers specifically go to my mom and tell them that they wanted to put me into a special education class or that I was slow and that I wasn't paying attention. I constantly had detention, constantly got in trouble. School is designed for a specific kind of person, and I am not that kind of person. So, it makes it really, really hard because I want to do good. I want to try. But, it's very discouraging when I go to a teacher, and I'm like, "I'm having a lot of problems with this," and they look at you like you're an idiot or they don't have time for you. They think, "All you do is sit in class, you don't pay attention, you stare off into the stars." It's like, "Well, it's really hard when there's all this going on around me."

I just don't like people who don't get me or my disability. I'm a really good person. I'm a really nice person. It's just that I can't sit still. I can't be quiet. I don't know how to do that. I don't know how to walk into a room without looking at everything and memorizing everything or looking at someone. It's just a lack of people understanding me.

They asked me if I wanted to keep having accommodations when I was a freshman in high school. I said no because high school was freaking scary. I was overweight. I was not very confident. And now here I am about to be thrust into this giant labyrinth of kids who are going to make fun of me and pick on me. Why the hell would I add another thing to the bullying? So, I specifically said no, and my mom told me that I should have, but I didn't want to make myself a bigger target for bullies.

Titus reflected on the potential impact of not utilizing disability accommodations that he was legally due. He struggled academically until meeting a teacher who recognized his talents.

I totally would have done much better. Totally. Totally. Totally. I mean I didn't do really well until my senior year when I had a teacher who was actually like, "Oh, there's something more to this kid than someone who can't stop talking and can't stop moving." It was an English class. The teacher was like, "We're going to write poetry, and we're going to write haikus." Then she's like, "Just write one." I wrote one within a minute, and everyone else was still working. I'm like looking around, and I'm like, "Oh my God, did I do something wrong? I must have done it wrong because I went too fast."

She came over and she read it. She's like, "Titus, this is really beautiful." I'm like, "Really? No, it's not. I just doodled." She's like, "No, this is really good. Have you ever written before?" I'm like, "No." She's like, "Do you want to try?" I'm like, "Sure." Then I developed this whole relationship with her. She believed in me and told me, "You're actually a really good writer." Even today, I write poetry. I don't do it on a regular basis. It's just a good outlet if I have nothing to do, or if I can't exercise, or I can't run around, or can't be outside.

I hated school so much that I was like, "I don't want to go to college." My dad is a really good guy, but I had a strained relationship with him. He was like, "Go to college." And I was like, "No." So, I just worked for a little bit and I kind of farted around with my friends. We made a bunch of movies about characters we'd make up. I did handyman jobs. Then, I worked as a stonemason with my father. I just love rocks, so I wanted to be a geologist. I went to a local community college, and I graduated there with the intent to come to the state four-year university and be a geology major. Then my girlfriend at the time broke up with me through a text. It was my first breakup. I got to the point where I was like, "Alright, I either want to keep going down in this depressing, horrible state, or I've just got to turn myself around." So, I turned everything around, lost like 100 pounds, got wicked in shape, and just started doing things for me. And then got into the nutrition program at the university.

When asked if he planned to go on to graduate school, Titus replied:

Oh God, no. Not unless someone pays for it. I would love to, but I need to get out of school. Just the structure of school, I just don't like it. It's so insanely hard to just sit there and just be quiet and just listen to something that someone is just reading off the board. I sit in class and wonder "How is no one else bored? How are you paying attention?"

Titus reflected back on his experiences with schooling and how they influenced the way he tries to function as a professional coach today.

You know, I think back and I did have one nutrition teacher who everyone did not like, but I thought hers was the best class. I got an A in that class. It was because of how unorthodox it was. She didn't follow a book. She didn't require me to take notes. She fostered class discussion that included everyone. In that class, I thrived versus the other ones. I felt included. She'd be like, Titus, "I know you have something valuable to share." And that's the one class I felt was awesome. In other classes, I was like, "Oh wow. Like I am not thriving here. Like why? Is something wrong with me?" Looking back on it, I realize the structure and teacher interactions in those courses made me feel like I was dumb. That kind of feeling has always stuck with me and informed future decisions. In my current job, I like to help support my teammates so no one ever feels that way. Looking back on it now, I wonder, "Why would you do that to a student? Why would you not support them?" So, all of those negative educational experiences helped inform how I support my colleagues today, because I never want anyone else to feel that way. Never, ever, ever. So, I feel like a teacher in my company now. I teach the new people who come in. I train them and things like that. And, I always have those negative school experiences in mind. So, I always make sure the training is fun and relaxed.

Titus had many things he enjoyed, especially working with his hands. But, he did not have a clear career path or goal for many years. After two years at the local community college, he found a way to turn his love for food into a career by majoring in nutrition.

I have such a heightened sense of touch and feel and smell, so I'm really good at cooking. I love to cook, and I love to cook healthy stuff. It just seemed so easy to me to decide on a nutrition major. I just came into the nutrition program, and I was like, "This seems really cool," and I absolutely love it. I love what I can do afterwards with it.

While working on his bachelor's degree, Titus worked at a community center where his passion for teaching people to live healthy lives led serendipitously into a job where his ADHD allowed him to thrive.

I actually got hired as a kids' counselor in the building, and I went downstairs to work out in the gym. When I was working out, I saw someone doing something wrong. I just went up to them and in a really nice way, I was like, "Hey, I just noticed you were doing that. Maybe you should try doing it this way. This is the right way." And I showed him. He was like, "Thank you." I walked away not thinking about it. The boss at the time came up to me and asked, "Are you a trainer somewhere?" I'm like, "No." She's like "What do you do?" I'm like, "I work with the kids upstairs." She's like, "Have you ever been a trainer?" I'm like, "No." She's like, "Do you want to be a trainer?"

So, I was a personal trainer for like four and a half years. And, I love helping people. I love working with people. Not a lot of trainers have done the same exact thing I have where they've been overweight their entire life and then became healthier. So, I just love working with people who are like, "This is impossible." I'm like, "No, it's really not that impossible. It's only impossible if you say it's impossible. You can definitely do it." So, I also use my degree and do a lot of nutrition with my clients. It's just really, really easy. When I was really young, my best friend and I said we wanted to do things that seemed so insanely easy, but get paid money for it. So, that's how I felt about that job.

As a trainer, I could work with anyone. I could be in a class, and my boss could be like, "One of the staff is out and she can't teach class. Can you teach it?" I'm like, "Sure." I can teach any kind of class, boot camp, chisel, pilates, or yoga. And it's just kind of like brain ecstasy to walk into a room, not know who is going to show up, and then just make up something on the spot. The boss hates it. She hates that I just make up things on the spot because she wants a structured class. I cannot—physically will not—mentally sit down and write something up because I don't know how to do that. But, I do know how to go to a class and just make it up. I also can connect with anyone in my classes. I can have a client who is 13 years old. I know how to talk with him and get him out of his shell. And then I have an 85-year-old client and talk with him too. It really is fun because it's just something different every time. And that's what I really, really liked in that job—it was just different stuff every day.

So out of college, I started as a personal trainer. And then after that, I moved to another state where I was a fitness manager of a gym that turned out to be an extremely negative environment. That negatively impacted my career and my work. I had a lot of moments, a lot of triggers. When I first started work, it was very difficult because I would have moments where I couldn't talk. I would have to stop what I was doing. Or, I had to walk away. As I've gone through my different jobs, I've also learned the types of environments that are triggering and those where I can thrive. I decided to leave that negative environment without having another job lined up. Later, I became a health coach where I realized, "Oh wow, this is great. I can use my gifts."

Titus reflected on how his family pressured him about staying in jobs he didn't like and how he resisted.

It was stressful having so many jobs and not staying at a place for a very long time. I also got so much negative support from my family about that. Family kept asking," Why can't you stay there? Like, what's wrong? A job is a job and you need to stick through it. You're not supposed to love it." And it was a very internal thing for me to be like, "No, I'm not staying somewhere where it's not positive. I did it once and it was a horrible experience. And from that point on, I was just like, never, never again will I stay in a negative work environment. If I feel it deep down in my belly, if this isn't right, if I'm not being supported, or if I'm not able to be me, or be creative and use my strengths, then I have to leave no matter what.

One outcome of COVID was that Titus left his face-to-face work and took a job that involved working remotely, which turned out to be a very positive experience.

In my current job, I always ask, "how can we make this a positive experience for staff and clients? There are no failures. There are no mistakes. It's just learning things." And, honestly I've had such a great time. I could not be in a better place as far as leaving my in-person job to work remotely. COVID was horrible, but I love being a hermit. I love that I get to be home. I don't have to go anywhere. I can just work from my house.

Now, I work remotely for a digital health company where I also help with productivity and workflow and experiments because my brain is all over the place. And, it doesn't matter because it really helps being in a situation where you need to build something really quickly and you need to be creative. I love working on projects where nothing is set in stone yet, and I need to build it. So, my gift helps a lot! Most people come into an undefined work situation and are very frustrated or flustered because they don't have any written directions and it's just a bunch of stuff they have to figure out. But, my brain's just like, "Yes! Let's put it all together. Let's figure it out."

When I initially got to work as a health coach, I immediately became bored after two months. I created work for myself because I was just constantly thinking, "How can I make this better?" I was just constantly trying to figure things out. So, I immediately got tapped for this new position. It was a new department and new role within the company to help with inefficiencies and productivity. And it was daunting to start a new role with so much unknown. But, my brain was just like, "Yes! Like yeah, throw me in the room. Chaos? I love it."

The ten of us coworkers all got along with each other, even though we never worked with each other before. But, we all just came together and worked collectively. And, I know this is not humble for me to say, but I'm like the team captain. I know I am because I've been told by many people. In the beginning I was just a chameleon in the group, learning about other people. And I think that's where my gift of being finely tuned to other people really came into play—being able to understand what is needed. After a while, I thought, "Okay, I know I can lead at this point."

We all kind of grow and learn what is best for us and how our environments help support us. And, I think managers are very important for that. Having a good one helps. I have not had a really good manager up until the one I have now. She doesn't think, "Oh, Titus has learning disabilities or he has issues." Instead, she just thinks, "Oh, wow, Titus is really good at being thrown into a room. And I don't have to give him a lot of instruction. I just tell him, go do whatever. And he just goes and does it!" That's the kind of freedom and the kind of understanding and support that helps me thrive. When something in our organization is not working, she listens when I say "here's why we need to change this"—especially if it's negatively impacting others. That's something that's very important for me. I get very emotional about it and I get overly excited about the ability to solve these issues at work. I am so happy to have a manager who sticks up for me and is like, "Oh no, you're right. We're not gonna do that anymore. Even if we both get in trouble!" That kind of encouragement and support from a supervisor is very, very important. She makes me feel very welcomed and trusted.

Titus reflected on what makes him good at his job and how his particular gifts enabled him to be successful as a remote coach.

One of my strengths is being able to minutely pick up on small changes in people's body language and behavior when they're talking. I was never formally taught these skills in classes, but it's just the way my brain processes information. All my life, I've been teaching myself how to interact in a world where it was very difficult for me. I had to learn very, very quickly about how to read people's body language, how to scan the tone of their voice, and pick up little things when they're maybe a little bit upset or they want to say something, but they're not saying something. Being a coach and being remote, I had to use these skills. I honestly got excited because I was like, "Yes! Another challenge!" I'm gonna have to do this on the phone. I won't be able to see people's faces. And so, I always close my eyes when I talk with people on the phone and I take a breath and then slowly imagine them. I listen to their breath, listen to the sound their lips make, listen to different things like that so I can understand and help them.

Today, Titus recognizes his disabilities as unique and valued features of who he is as a person. He also sees his disability as an asset in his career.

My wife helped me get to this realization that hey, I am different, and maybe I am a little special. And, I can do all these things without thinking about it. My entire life, everyone has told me—and my entire life I've told myself—there's nothing special about that. You're not special. I think now, I'm just becoming more and more aware of how freaking amazing it is. And, I would never change it for the world. I absolutely love who I am. I'm just hyper as hell. I'm just bubbly and bouncy. When I'm at work, I freaking skip! I think I'm a good person because I like to think how everyone else would like to be treated. I can use my gifts of being able to read people, being able to read situations. And, I can use that to help people and to help them support others who maybe are having a rough time.

This level of self-acceptance and self-celebration had not been achieved without facing ongoing and persistent challenges. Titus had to devise coping strategies and take steps to manage periods of feeling overwhelmed.

So, when I first started as a trainer, I was kind of learning about my disabilities and realizing I have a lot more deeper things going on. It was very upsetting and very kind of like triggering. In those triggering moments, I would react by just shutting down. I would internalize things and I wouldn't be able to talk. I would be breathing very deeply or I couldn't breathe. My wife wouldn't know how to react. She would be very upset and she'd want to help. Then, I'd lash out at her. Slowly, it evolved into me being like, "Okay, I can understand that these moments are happening and it's negatively impacting her. People are getting worried about me. I need to do something." And so I learned that in those moments to just focus on breathing and to ask myself: "Why am I upset? How can I convey my thoughts and feelings instead of just internalizing everything?" Then, slowly as I got some strategies down, I realized I needed maybe extra support and so I got a service dog. He would do deep pressure therapy on me when I had those moments when I couldn't breathe. Eventually, they were getting more infrequent because I developed coping strategies like distinguishing the smaller stressors versus the bigger ones, or realizing I needed to go sit down or walk away. We retired my service dog a little while ago. And so it's been really interesting to think about where I came from—not having any coping mechanisms to now, where I have coping mechanisms and I don't take medication or need my service dog. But it's me.

Titus and his wife have a strong relationship and are expecting their first child. He and his father are working together to fix up their house in preparation for that next stage of life.

Right now, we have a house. But, I'm completely remodeling it and fixing it. I want the house to be just a little bit more comfortable for having a new baby. And the only thing I think I can solidly say is I am glad to just be together, be supportive of each other, and just have a good relationship with my wife and my soon to be daughter.

Reflection Questions

1   *Disabled assets and gifts.* Throughout the interviews with Titus, he rejects the deficit-laden messages he has heard from others and has, at times, told himself regarding his disability. Rather than view his ADHD through a deficit lens, he embraces how his disability provides him with a specialized skill set in life and in his career. How does Titus' story influence your thinking about disabilities as deficits or gifts? How has Titus learned to highlight his assets in his life and career? What are your assets and strengths?

2   *Unaccommodating school experiences.* Titus shared that he often felt that he was not supported, welcomed, or accepted in school. He remembered many educators who did not believe he could succeed in school. What do you think Titus meant when he said, "School is designed for a specific kind of person?" Can you recall a memory of a teacher or professor excluding a student? What was the impact of this exclusion on the individual and others in the class? What can educational systems, family advocates, and students themselves do to ensure that schools are designed to help all students thrive? Negative school experiences prompted Titus' desire to help others. How common is it for personal experiences of discouragement and rejection to become a source of determination to help others?

3   *Encouraging colleagues and workplaces.* Throughout Titus' employment history, he shares dissatisfaction with employers who did not see his strengths and assets. Titus finally had experience with a supervisor who trusted his judgment, acknowledged his strengths, and invested in his ability. What are specific ways he felt seen and heard by this supervisor? What were the characteristics of work environments in which Titus thrived? What can we learn from Titus about finding a work environment and supervisors who foster satisfaction and success? How can you recognize assets to support all your coworkers, including disabled colleagues?

15 Meet Willa

Pronouns: She/her
Age: 30
Self-identified disability: Visually impaired/legally blind due to albinism
College major: Therapeutic Recreation
Current living situation: Living with a roommate
Current job/position: Buyer for a hospital
Passions: Advocating for people with disabilities; Proving people with low expectations wrong

Willa identifies as visually impaired/legally blind due to albinism. As early as age 10, she began to advocate for her educational rights, demanding the services, support, and resources she needed to excel. Her talents and passion for disability justice led her to be actively involved in advocacy groups in the community and at college. Those experiences served her well when she experienced discrimination in post-collegiate jobs. Although she strove to be a strong, independent activist, it was challenging to find living accommodations and public transportation that fostered self-sufficient living. Her story concludes with a quote that sums up Willa's perspective and experiences: "I'm just appreciative of what I have, how I got here, those experiences, and to be able to share them with others. Hopefully, I can continue to do that because that's what motivates me. My whole life is health care, healing, and helping others."

Willa begins her story by telling us about her disability.

I am visually impaired/legally blind due to albinism, which is a lack of pigment in my hair, skin, and eyes. No pigment in the eyes causes a visual impairment. I was diagnosed at birth. Growing up with a disability and having a disability since birth is a lot different than being diagnosed with a disability later in life. The further away things are, and if I haven't trained myself to know what

DOI: 10.4324/9781003495703-15

I'm looking at, the less defined they get. A lot of it is training myself to attend to other people's body language to know who people are, listening to people's voices, and honing in on my hearing, which is obviously better than my vision. I try to just adapt and be flexible and make all of that work when albinism creates limitations.

My parents would get really offended when people would call me an albino. My parents say, "She's a person with albinism." Well, I don't care. That's what I am. They want to call me albino, that's fine. However, they can educate themselves because I'm going to tell you about albinism. My parents really never went around saying that they had a child with a disability. It really didn't matter to them. We just went about our daily lives. That was normal for me. That really helped form my opinions and perceptions of life. People are like, "How do you do it every day with a disability?" Well, it's my life.

Over the course of the decade and three different interviews, Willa shared evolving thoughts about her disability. In her first interview, she shared:

My disability gives me purpose. It makes me who I am. Not looking like I have a disability allows me to see from a sighted world, but also understand where people who are blind (or who have different disabilities) are coming from. I understand the disability community as a whole. I'm part of it. But somebody who might not be able to explain having depression or who is bipolar may not know how to represent themselves or their disability in a positive light to other people. That's where my self-advocacy skills come in—although I'm much better at advocating for other people than I am for myself.

College made it easy for me to identify as someone with a disability. We were all looking for something that made us unique and made us stand out, and that told our story. It's part of the growing pains of figuring out who you are as a person. I think that stems from how well someone's disability was managed in high school or how well you were able to connect with others through your upbringing in your schooling. College is that first place that finally allows you to be yourself, talk about those things, and connect with other people on that level. Even if college peers don't have the same disability, you can relate to them on a human level. It's easier to find people to connect with if you identify as disabled and are open to sharing that information right off the bat when you meet someone. It also takes away the awkward situations in case accommodations are required so that other people are aware. College taught me a lot about people. I came in contact with different people with different types of disabilities who were at different points of acceptance in their disability journey. There were people who were just coming into that disability identity journey and who really admired me and my strength and kind of gravitated towards that. Because I was able to be open about my disability and to share my experiences, I helped them a lot through their process.

In the second interview, Willa says her view of her disability hadn't changed drastically, but by then, she had experienced college and workplace situations that shaped how she thinks about disability identity and life choices for herself and disabled people more broadly.

It definitely defines who I am every day in that it decides the choices that I make. Other people make decisions based on their lifestyle and their family situation. Somebody with a disability has to think about their disability, too. First and foremost, I ask myself, "Will this work for you?" Having to make all of those choices can be overwhelming. Part of the decision-making process is the amount of support one has, and where the support comes from. If somebody is able to explain their disability and needs, or walk someone through one step at a time, they have an easier time. It also depends upon how they view their disability. If they embrace it or if they don't identify with it. You have to make people understand and see your attitude toward it. If it's not something that scares you, it's not going to scare them. They'll be more willing to embrace it with you, and figure out what works for you.

In the third interview, Willa defines disability as a clinical diagnosis but also notes that she wants to be seen as a person first and to discuss her accommodation needs once she gets to know another person or employer. Willa continues to feel like an expert of her own disability.

Disability is a limitation that prevents people from completing tasks at a level the general population can. Disabled people need assistance in completing those tasks that other people wouldn't. I used to let it define me. I used to identify very strongly. I'm an albino. It's just like saying blonde. Other people can instinctively recognize hair color, but not my disability. I struggle, because I do consider myself as someone with an invisible disability unless someone knows me. I think it's something that I've managed to navigate for 30 years. That has taught me more about myself and how I react to the world and to people. I now see my disability as how I relate to others more than something I identify as. You acclimate to the world around you as an adult. You can kind of pass without having a disability, so to speak. You find your voice. I now say, "Let's talk about me as an individual, what my talents and skills are first, and *then* we'll talk about what potential accommodations I'll need." I try to make those connections and find common ground with other people. So, that way, they have some way of understanding the difficulties that I go through. We are the experts of our disability.

Willa learned to be an expert about her disability from her parents who advocated for her needs in elementary school. She also started advocating for herself (and others) from a very early age. When she experienced bullying or ignorance, she chose the path of educating people to combat ableism.

When I first started school, they wanted to put me in a special needs school. My parents said, "No. She has a little trouble seeing. She's not intellectually challenged in any way." That is a common misconception for people who are blind or visually impaired because of the delay. Things with sighted people are instinct—somebody's expression, the tone in their voice, and walk. People like me are slower to react to those things because it's not instantaneous like for everybody else who is sighted.

Half the problem with disability is finding somebody to give you a chance to do what you really want to do. Then, when you succeed, you might have more believers in you and your capabilities. I did have a guidance counselor in fourth grade who asked me if I wanted to do a seminar for all of my peers in my grade—100 students! I held a seminar on albinism in each homeroom. I showed them the pictures from the conferences. I let them use the technology that I had. It broke those barriers and the peer bullying that I experienced stopped. People need to become knowledgeable of people's differences. If that means getting to use my cool magnifiers, then I'm all about it. I also did a diversity day at that elementary school after I graduated for the students in regular education classrooms. They got to come around and do different experiences with different disabilities to learn the differences and to see what people use to overcome obstacles. The younger that happens, the easier it is for us to be accepted.

I'm just so appreciative that the adults in my life at the time allowed me to advocate for myself. I knew that I liked advocating and I started young. Most people with disabilities that have a 504 or Individualized Education Plan (IEP) in elementary school don't attend meetings as early as I did. I was 10 when I attended my first meeting with all the specialists from the school and from the Board of Education for the Blind. I started attempting my patient care technician's (PCT) work when I was in third grade. I think it's the job of not only the teacher, but the parent and the service providers, to teach the student how the system works and the processes that are put in place for support.

When I was in middle school, there was another girl who was in a wheelchair and notes were being taken for her because she had cerebral palsy. They told me I couldn't use her note taker anymore. I remember, they cornered me in a classroom. It was just me, the PR professional, and a teacher. But, I said, "You're going to have to get me a copy of the notes." They looked at me funny like—why would she ever speak against us? I was like, "You're going to have to find a way to do it." It felt so weird to speak against someone when your back is literally up against the wall. You can get angry about it in the moment. But, I tell others in similar situations to follow through with the job (of self-advocating) first and then experience the emotions later. I don't think I could have done anything better.

Willa encountered low expectations from many teachers. She defied those ableist assumptions to succeed.

I used to go around the day before school started, meet all my teachers, and explain to them what accommodations I needed. I had an honors English teacher my sophomore year in high school. She didn't have any faith in me whatsoever. She goes, "We read 12 novels. Your vision is not going to be able to keep up with the amount of reading that we have to do." She did not think I could manage the work load. At the end of the year, I must have surprised her. I couldn't believe that someone who didn't believe in me was telling me that I was successful and that I had done well. I came out with a B+. She was one of my biggest supporters after my sophomore year. She supported me and nominated me for the National Honors Society. She wrote letters of recommendation. She turned out to be one of my biggest fans. Unfortunately, I had to prove myself to her before she thought that I was capable of doing it. It was probably my drive and my willingness to work with her, and to show her how to work with me, that allowed me to get through that class. Self-advocacy is so important. If you can't explain how you work best and how you learn best, they're not going to be willing to find out how to teach you. You have to make their jobs easier for them. A lot of us end up playing into the statistics of not being a successful person with a disability. It would have proven her right. It disappoints me that we have to prove ourselves before we can get the support of people, organizations, or even family. I want to be part of that change. I am capable of doing the same things in different ways with different accommodations. For students like me, success is directly related to how well people are willing to work with us.

They tried to take away my accommodations in my senior year. I remember crying in the hallway with my teachers because they couldn't give me the enlarged textbooks or the enlarged paperwork. I couldn't get the work done. I was in all honors classes. I said "You can't take away what got me to my honors classes and expect me to succeed." I went to the headmaster of the high school. I said, "Here's my problem. "They said "You need to go get your IEP from the special ed department because that's the law. They have to give you your accommodations." I got it, made copies, and gave them to everybody who needed one or who had never seen it before. That was my turning point thinking that there were *other* people that went to school who weren't getting what they needed because they didn't know how to ask. If you don't have parents who are forward and willing to be your advocate (or know *how* to be an advocate), then you're not going to get what you need to be successful. That really was the first time that I realized that I wanted to do something in the field of working with people with disabilities.

Despite strong self-advocacy skills and supportive parents, Willa wondered if there may have been other resources that could have helped her be more successful in elementary and high school.

I feel frustrated with the limited services that were given to me in K-12 school. I could have had more had they told me what technology was out there. Whether it was funded by grants or by my own personal family, then at least I would've been able to keep up with some of the work or maybe achieved better grades than I did. Luckily, when I got to my college, they had a beautiful center for adaptive technology that had all of these wonderful devices for the classroom. It had computers on wheels that had cameras to make the board closer to you. They make different flash drives that can read to you. They could take a screenshot of things if the professor's going to wipe off the board and you can still copy down your notes.

Despite the technological resources available at college, Willa still experienced challenges.

College was very challenging. The disability resource center was one of my main reasons for choosing my college. It is one of very few colleges in the state that provides students with weekly appointments as part of their accommodations. A counselor/specialist helps you with time management and self-advocacy. They also help you learn how to represent your disability to your professor, how to work with other people, and to explain how your disability works in a classroom and learning environment. The services were fantastic. They were better than most other universities I had looked at. The disability services were well known throughout the university by the professors and other students. You could walk in, hand your professor the envelope for your exam the week before and they would go drop it off at the resource center. Then, they would go pick it up after you completed it. It was a very well-oiled machine. But, as all systems do, they have flaws. It was mostly communication between housing and facilities and the disability resource center. Things like snow removal was an issue for students with wheelchairs on campus. I had taken a lot of those issues to the president and the vice president. I was invited back to have a conversation with the university vice president about disability services and how accessible they were to students on campus. We started that conversation and the university then put diversity panels and committees in place for students.

Communicating directly with the college president about disability accessibility was one of the many ways Willa strove to make a difference for disabled students on campus. As noted earlier, Willa began advocating for her educational needs by the age of 10. She elaborates on her trajectory.

I always knew I liked people and defending populations that can't necessarily say what they need or have their voices heard right away. I attended these albinism conventions when I was younger. I'm a huge disabilities advocate. I am very active in the state and on different boards. I've sat on all these disability organizations that have been such an advocate for access. I'm also the board member for a summer camp that offers a week of leadership seminars. I was a delegate. Then, I became a staff member and now a facilitator. We teach high school students about their disability and self-advocacy. The seminars give them a place to go where they might not have either ever met somebody else with a disability or with the same disability that they have themselves. I've also provided scholarship opportunities through that organization. I'm really all about trying to get people with disabilities what they need and to teach them how to get it themselves. I always find a connection with other people. I am able to, at a human level, find a baseline of empathy or compassion to relate to others. That's always been most important to me. I want to be able to make other people feel validated. That's just a huge part of who I am. Even if I don't understand you, I can empathize. I can at least find some sort of common ground. I like to think of myself as a peacekeeper.

I find that most people with disabilities try to form some structure to keep some consistency in their lives—whether it's in routine or a support group of friends. In college, my outlet was to give back to the campus community. That's where I feel like my purpose comes in. I was extremely active on campus during all four years that I lived on campus. I was also very active in student government. I was the board chair of clubs and organizational management on campus. I also held a position as a programmer in the program council, which is the major programming body on campus for campus activities. Being the president of the disability advocacy club, I helped students get through their academics. They listened to what I had to say. At the end of the day, they could take what they wanted from my insights, but they also learned something.

During our initial interview, Willa was considering an array of career options that combined her passions for disability advocacy and healthcare.

As early as I could remember, I wanted to be a special education teacher. I also wanted to be a special education attorney so I could teach people about their rights. I would have done a lot of pro bono work because people with disabilities just don't have the money. I also knew I wanted a family and knew a legal career would be time consuming.

I might be one of those people that have a lot of jobs and positions—have my hand in a little bit of everything. Ultimately, I would love to help people with newly found disabilities or newly acquired disabilities, like a traumatic brain injury or the loss of a limb, and help them transition. I'd show them the options and the services that are available to them once the doctors are out of the picture. That's when people really feel it. It's when no one else is around that people might wonder, "Alright, well these services have gotten me this far or this support group has gotten me this far." But, when you're on your own, disabled people wonder, "Where is everybody?"

My calling might change. I might end up working with parents of students with disabilities. I could teach them how their children learn best so they can teach the schools and even teach their children. I've always been the person that always has a plan. It's okay for me right now to not have a plan. I can let whatever's meant to happen, happen.

Willa ultimately selected a major that aligned with her passions for disability advocacy.

In my therapeutic recreation major, the academics were centered around working with people with disabilities. That's what we were going to do when we graduated. Students in that major were more accepting of the accommodations that were needed and more willing to help. The professors already knew how to teach disabled students because of the nature of the major. I would say a good 25% of the people who chose that major had disabilities. You want some place where you'll be accepted in academics, friendships, and whatever else you go through. So, picking that major was just the easiest route for me. The Board of Ed Services for the Blind were definitely supportive of my major choice. They were happy to see somebody who they could use as a positive example of success and who had done all of these advocacy things.

After college graduation, Willa sought a job in a field related to her college major in therapeutic recreation. But, she experienced barriers and had to accept a position outside her desired field.

I tried looking for positions in the field of recreational therapy. They said, "You don't have a driver's license. You can't drive our clients. There's really not a position here for you." That was why I started looking outside of my field. So, I started working for a cable company. But, they let me go. They couldn't provide reasonable accommodations. There was a woman who I didn't know. I was in training. She goes, "Are you albino?" I said, "Yes." She goes, "People with visual impairments don't last long here. I just want to be open with you. I've seen that happen." I did appreciate that honesty and boldness. Most organizations don't share what they're capable of providing unless you ask for it, which has always frustrated me. Budgets restrict people from getting what they need in the workplace.

Willa experienced lack of access, accommodations, and support in many of her post-college jobs. For instance, in one of her early positions, the company could not provide the accommodations she needed, so they transferred her to another role in the company. When she experienced workplace discrimination, Willa considered taking legal action against the organization.

That was my first experience at a full-time job. It was not what I went to school for. And, I had to experience those types of things that normally one wouldn't think that they would have to encounter in their first full time job. They couldn't get the magnifier to work on their computer. So, I took a $6 an hour pay cut and an extra ten-minute commute to a different department in the same company. When they transferred me, they didn't give me a choice. I explained to them that the ADA law states that you have to seamlessly transition me into a position. The new job definitely discriminated against me and gave me the opportunity to enter into a lawsuit. There should have been a lawsuit, but I didn't have any life savings or money for a lawyer. I couldn't find a lawyer to do pro bono work. The lawyers that I did consult said that I definitely had a case. That said, I don't want that (a lawsuit) to be on my record for my future careers. One, two, three years at a company is not worth as much as your reputation, the experience, or the money that you could have saved by staying with the company versus fighting them with a lawsuit. At the end of the day, I had to accept the fact that I was more than capable of completing the task that the job required me to do, but because of my disability, I did not make as much money and had to take an internal transfer just because they couldn't make something work. They weren't trained in any disability etiquette. They weren't trained to support somebody with a visual impairment. That was really hard for me to go through.

When I left that job, people were calling and texting me to offer support and express their frustration. I said, "You can't be mad at what the company did to me because I'm not mad about it." I had the opportunity to teach a lot of people at that organization about having a disability, a visual impairment, and albinism. You're going to have those days when you're like, why did this company do this to me? Why is it always about suing somebody? Why can't they just fix the problem? If you find somebody that's willing to go the extra mile, the issue would become resolved. If you can't find the right people to do that—that's kind of where it hit me the most. They forced me to sign the papers that basically said, "You either have a job or you don't have a job. It all comes down to you and your disability." I was like, hopefully I never have to help somebody else get through that experience, but at least I understand all the legal rights, and all of their process as well as my emotional process. It's been a lot.

The second time we talked to Willa, she had been laid off and was searching for a job related to her interest and background in healthcare. By the third interview, she had found a job in a hospital setting.

The company I worked for decided to lay off everyone. I was out of work for about six months. That was a little difficult. I really wanted to be back at the hospital. I started applying there. I applied for 12 jobs and had four interviews. They hired me for a telecom operator position at the hospital which meshed well with my experience. My bachelor's was in the healthcare industry. Since then, I got a new position with a 10% increase. They gave me a position as an administrative assistant to one of the Vice Presidents of the hospital. I had done all my college internships there. I knew everyone there. They already knew that I had a visual impairment.

Despite support from many hospital colleagues who were familiar with Willa's disability, she still endured ableist concerns about her capabilities and illegal questions during interviews.

A bunch of higher ups were asking dumb questions during interviews. The director of rehabilitation services said, "How is she going to tell the difference between a fat person and somebody carrying a child out of the childbirth center?" The vice president, whom I ended up working for, asked if I could do stairs. Just very ignorant. They should know better being in healthcare! They asked me, "How come you don't use a cane? Do you think you'll be able to do curbs? How are you going to be able to navigate around the building outside?" I said, "You shouldn't be asking me any of those questions because your hospital should be ADA regulated! If you have an issue with me, then you have an issue with your entire population of people coming into your hospital." They tried to weed me out with those questions.

Once I started the job, I brought a lot of safety issues to their attention that they weren't able to see unless they were seeing it through the eyes of a blind person. They really began to realize the security issues that they had and began to make some of those changes.

Eventually, I moved over to purchasing in the same hospital. I've been there for two and a half years. It's fun. I was being promoted for all my expertise, skills, and talents. In the last six months, we've had complete turnover. So, I've trained the new purchasing manager and my new colleagues. I was supposed to receive a supervisor position this week. After four interviews, they said, we've decided we need somebody with more supervisory experience. We're putting the position on hold because everyone's so heartbroken that you won't be filling the position. We're taking the position off the table for now. I struggle with the politics and culture. Knowing that behind the scenes, it might be an accommodation thing. I can prove myself. I prove that I'm worth keeping. It's very difficult to grow in such a small hospital. I'm halfway through my masters at an online program. I never thought I'd go back to school, but I am getting my MBA and healthcare management at my own pace. At the hospital, they just asked me to do a results reporting project this year. Even though I won't have a title of a supervisor, I'm reporting to all these executives on their statistics. And, I'm answering any questions that they have and resolving any issues.

I always knew that I wanted to be in a position to be able to implement policy to make the changes that impact patient care. I always anticipated that I would end up back at this hospital working in administrative roles that were close to executives. But, I did not always have the hope of being one! Never in a million years would I have thought I'd be a buyer in a purchasing department in a hospital during a world pandemic.

Regardless of the position I've been in, the feedback that I've gotten is, "You always take the extra time to figure out how what you do impacts another department or another person. You change that to make it better for people." I think some of that has to do with disability. I feel like I'm the perfect person for the job because I can provide that compassion and empathy. I provide them with as much information as I have access to in order for them to get through difficult times with themselves and their families. Trying to humble myself a little, but I know I'm valued because of the tasks that I am required to complete on a daily basis. My name crosses the CEOs and the vice president's lips positively daily.

In her final interview, Willa ruminated about what her career trajectory and future might look like. Despite the challenges of finding jobs in her field, and receiving accommodations, Willa was inspired and empowered. She reflected on her own growth between the first and last interview.

Wherever life takes me, I'll welcome it and work it out. I wish I could say I didn't expect it with each new opportunity, but I do expect to be discriminated against. I think disability will be a roadblock in my personal life. But I also think it'll be an asset to everyone else around me. Half of the problem is that not enough companies employ people with disabilities. I have to explain to the company what services are out there. I'm a huge asset. Given the right company and the right position, I can help them better their services and accommodations that they're able to provide to employees.

Given the importance of independence for disabled people, we end this story with Willa's experiences. The inability to drive impacted her college living choices, job opportunities, housing options, and independence throughout her life.

I cannot drive. I grew up knowing that I wouldn't be able to drive. Unfortunately, this caused more emotional family issues and definitely some communication issues as far as my parents wanting to see me getting my license at 16 instead of my state ID. When I first got my state ID, my father was upset about it. He was crying all the way to the DMV because he couldn't provide his eldest daughter with an opportunity for a car. That pulls on your heartstrings to know that your parents will always be worried about how successful you are. My sister is the first and only child in the family to get her license and a car. My sister, as close as our bond is, she'll never be able to understand my desire for freedom and my desire to just get up and go. Unfortunately, that's what's holding me back.

During college, there was a silver lining to Willa's inability to drive. Living on campus provided an opportunity to get involved in leadership positions and activist roles that she may not have taken advantage of if she was commuting to campus.

That was my real reason for living on campus. I could've commuted if I was able to drive like everybody else. But, I don't think I would've been as involved on campus because a lot of commuters come, go to class, and then go home.

After college, Willa's inability to drive impacted her career opportunities and independence.

Unfortunately, I live on a main road. I can't get anywhere unless somebody drives me. It's extremely dangerous to walk. I live across the street from a shopping center. But, I can't even get there on my own. Unfortunately, I can't go wherever I want whether it's the state, the job, or the place that I want to live. It has to be determined by the public transportation system and whether it's adaptable and flexible enough for my life, or for the career that I've chosen. I don't have those freedoms.

I've had job interviewers say, "If we hired you as a manager for multiple locations, how would you get there, because we know you can't drive with a visual impairment?" And I just kind of look at them and allow them to ask the question. I don't tell them that it's super illegal and you don't have the right to ask me that. I said, I never had an issue getting to work before. I won't have an issue now. Luckily, I've always had significant others and family that were willing to drive. Uber, Lyft, and ride shares have become more common; it definitely makes things a lot easier. A lot of those services are being utilized by our patients too.

By the second interview, I purchased a condo in the same town, so now I can walk to work. I can walk everywhere. I have a doctor's office, a pharmacy, a grocery store, a strip mall, a Kohl's, Subway, and Dunkin Donuts. Anything that I would want to do on a day off. It's been quite an amazing experience and a turnaround since our last interview. I was living by myself. To help pay the mortgage, I rented it out to a tenant. Everyone in my life does [know about my disability, including the tenant]. That's not really something that I hold back on. The more people I tell, the more people are willing to help. The bigger network I obtain from having them know. They are all really support-ive. My roommate has offered to take me to the grocery store if the weather is bad or we both have the day off. It works out well. Most people don't mind. That's pretty cool. I don't have to depend on my family. I don't know if they expected it to happen that soon. I think they thought that there may have been a transition period for them to get used to the idea of all of the sudden being off duty after 24 years. I have that autonomy and I've come a long way with the help from a lot of people encouraging my independence. Just being able to set some of those boundaries with family members. Letting them know that I still want to spend time with them, even though I don't need them. I also maintain my integrity and my dignity because I feel as though I've built a life for myself.

Willa's joy in gaining independence from her family of origin also shaped her thinking about the kind of romantic and familial relationships she wanted to cultivate for herself.

Honestly, above all else, I hope I have a family within the next 5 to 10 years. I'm even thinking about adopting a child, potentially, with a disability. I do want a big family—two kids. But, I don't know if I'll be able to afford a big family. My hope is to marry someone who has a big family already, that way I can either take it or leave it. Having my own children and raising them in a culture where they're accepting of everything—not just disability—is my hope. [It is important for anyone, especially children] to understand that they can learn from other peoples' experiences. That, ultimately, makes me happy. I love being able to tell people, "Live whatever life you want to live" and to then help them pursue it. I'm definitely a giver, so whatever I can give to everyone else, then help them accomplish, is what I want to do with my life and family.

What I find is that most men are attracted to me because I'm capable of being independent. They know that I don't need them to do anything for me. I can be a strong, independent woman and manage life with a disability. But, they know that I'll be okay, even after them. I make sure that I set that foun-dation for myself with boundaries. People say, "I don't want you to ever have to worry about a ride or I don't want you to ever have to worry about needing your basic needs being met." There's comfort in knowing someone wants to do these things for you. But, I think it is important to try to maintain as much independence as possible—because people will come and go.

Willa reflected on the role her family of origin played in her development and in inspiring her passion for paying support forward.

I appreciate my relationship with my family and what they were able to do for me. I'm in the situation that I am because they were so forward thinking. They let me go out and do my own thing. They stood up for me when I was going to be put in a school for people who are blind or visually impaired. They took that leap of faith and still trusted themselves to be able to support me. I'm just appreciative for what I have, and how I got here. Those experiences shaped me and I am glad to be able to share them with others. Hopefully, I can continue to do that because that's what motivates me. My whole life is health care, healing, and helping others.

Reflection Questions

1 *Educational self-advocacy.* Discuss the instances of self-advocacy in Willa's story. When reflecting on her self-advocacy, Willa shares great insights about navigating the education systems. What are some key takeaways that you learned from reading about her experiences? What are structural protections that K-12 education can employ so that students like Willa don't have to advocate for themselves in the first place? What can higher educators do to adapt systems and cultures to better meet the needs of disabled students?

2 *Workplace discrimination and ADA.* Willa names multiple points in which she experienced discrimination and prejudice at her workplaces. Exclusion was so common that Willa began to expect it. Can you identify points in her story where the Americans with Disabilities Act (ADA) was violated? What are some structural changes that the workplaces could do to prevent such acts of discrimination? How can the ADA be upheld in workplaces to create inclusive environments for workers with disabilities?

3 *Independence.* Independence is often thought of as a sign of adulthood. What insights did you garner from Willa's experiences striving for independence? What were some of the hurdles and successes she experienced in her quest for independence? What can we learn from Willa's experiences seeking, but facing hurdles in achieving, independence? Consider the strategies you adopted to move toward independence? Which tactics were successful? Unsuccessful? Why? What can families, peers, teachers and employers do to foster accessible environments where disabled people can gain independence?

16 Meet Willow

> **Pronouns:** She/her
> **Age:** 27
> **Self-identified disability:** Attention Deficit Disorder (ADD), Dyslexia, Reading Comprehension
> **College major:** Biomedical Engineering
> **Current living situation:** Living on her own in an apartment
> **Current job/position:** Prosthetist
> **Passions:** Dance, Helping children and people with disabilities

Willow is committed to paying forward the social support that she received throughout her education and during her transition from childhood to adulthood. Her parents demonstrated love, care, and dedication. Willow is inspired to foster that kind of support through her career goals and with her own family one day. Despite self-doubts and transferring from one college to another, she is committed to pursuing happiness in her professional and personal life. Playing to her strengths, she was able to creatively combine her interests of working with children and in medicine to be a prosthetist. She plans to make a difference in the lives of disabled children through her career.

Willow described her disability and reflected on what it means to her. She also talked about how it has influenced her sense of self over time.

I have dyslexia and reading comprehension troubles. It makes me less confident in a way that I have a disability. It's a lot harder for me to go through life and work on projects. Everyone is already done with them; I haven't figured out how to start it. But, I'm glad I have the disability because if I didn't, I would probably coast through life. It taught me that you have to work hard.

Disability is something that affects a person in a very specific way, but it doesn't stop them from achieving what they want to achieve. It's a certain hurdle

DOI: 10.4324/9781003495703-16

that you figure out how to work with or work through. When I was in school, my disability was always in my mind. It affected absolutely everything about my life because I was a full-time student—reading, calculations, and all of the assignments. With ADD, dyslexia, and reading comprehension, I had to listen to all my textbooks on tape. If I read a paragraph to you, I cannot tell you what I just read unless I read it a few times slowly, stop after every sentence, and think about it. It's easier for me to think and hear it. Hate to say it, but when I don't understand something, I give up. Then, I take a few days and I go back to it. I work it out. Usually at that moment, I'm just so frustrated. I think, "I'm not able to do this." I've always been that way. I don't really know why. My mom used to tell me all the time; "You're shutting down." It probably goes back to reading. I had to read summer books all the time when I was in high school and middle school. We had to give book reports. I had no idea what I had read. But, I had already put all the time into reading it. When I was writing the paper, it just didn't make sense at all. My mom would read the book, too, and be like, "This is not what the book is about." I was like, "Fine, I give up. I quit school." I was seven. I'm a science major because reading is so not fun for me. Not that I've gotten over it, but I've learned to cope with it in an easier way. I have easy access to websites that can read text to me if it's something too long. I don't read-read textbooks.

In K-12, there were always so many other kids who were in my situation that I had class with. I never felt alone, which was great. In high school, I actually took special education classes and training classes on how to learn. I heard that college was going to be extremely difficult for me. I had to take these tricks and learn how to adapt my learning to what the professors were trying to teach. I really don't remember a huge time in college, where anyone was like "yeah life with dyslexia after college looks like XYZ." But, I was told that it was going to be very difficult to go from high-school-level work to college-level work. I take my work seriously, so it really wasn't much of a difference for me. I take the same amount of time on homework and studying. It's difficult in that the work and workload is harder, but it's still doable. Last year, I took extra time on exams and took all that time. This semester, I wanted to see if I could not use all that time. I didn't get the papers that said I needed extra time until later in the game so that I could see if I needed it. I didn't really need it for any of my classes, which was good for me. Can it be possible that I evolve out of my disability? I don't think it is, but that's what it feels like.

My disability doesn't super define me. Back then (at the time of my first interview), I was really defined by it. I remember getting really emotional in my first interview for some reason, really feeling like I hadn't talked about my disability in a while. It helped me to realize that I do need to kind of refocus on the tactics that I learned in high school and special education classes. I had put a lot of pressure on myself that I needed to be perfect. Talking in the first [interview] and then reflecting before the second interview helped me reevaluate how I can best help myself, rather than "I can't do it. I have a disability." That was cool. My family and I joke about things like that all the time. If you read me this number, I will say okay I'm dyslexic, just in case I get it wrong. I always keep it upbeat and humorous. I'm not ashamed of it. It's fun that I have dyslexia. I pronounce things wrong. My texts will make no sense sometimes. It's just my quirk, I think. Positivity is something that I always try to go toward, even if I'm struggling or if something is not going my way or I can't do something. Just being positive has kept me going. Like, "Fine, I can't do it. That's okay, I can do something else." When I was little, I went to therapy. They used to tell me to make journals and boards. Now, I keep it in my head. No one else really needs to know what I'm thinking.

Since I've finished with college, my vocabulary seems to be better. Within my specific field, I can read things easier and kind of understand them more. Commitment to not avoiding reading or having to focus on a specific task for a long period of time, has brought me to an easier way of life now. I've always been told disability is going to be part of my life forever. It's not really present anymore, which is weird. When I struggle with something, I'm not embarrassed. I'm not mad at myself. I'm like "oh okay, let's try that again." Back in school, I would be like "why can't I do this? I have to get this done. I'm on a deadline." I have a much more positive outlook now. Education and learning are where the disability thrives. It's a very different life now than when I was in college.

Willow had a variety of important sources of support, including family and friends as well as educators on campus (e.g., disability office, student life) who helped her not only survive, but also thrive along her educational journey.

I was lucky enough to grow up where I grew up and who I grew up with. My disability was looked after. I was given every tool that I needed. I know that a lot of other people with my same disability were not given those opportunities because of where they were geographically or class wise or things like that. It's definitely made me more aware. I definitely don't take it for granted. My mom has all the patience in the world. She would literally learn what I was learning in school and then teach it to me after school in her own way. My mom will always help me no matter what I need help in. I'm like, "Mom, I'm getting a little anxious. I don't know how to handle this," She'll be like, "All right, I'll do it for you." Then, she tells me what she did. She's taught me that I can do what I need to do. I just have to ask the right questions and do the right things. It'll work out.

Looking back from K-16, I am extremely grateful for everyone who helped me. I'm a lot better of a reader. I used to read in an influx pattern. It was like duh duh duh. So I'm really glad I don't talk like that now. Learning little tricks—like if I'm reading a book, getting two rulers out or a special Window tool where I could just hit one sentence at a time—was really helpful. I still do that now when I have to read something really long. I know these tactics are beneficial now. But, at the time, I was like this is the dumbest thing ever.

Definitely the college student disability office and student life office provided me support. I have Rachel as a disability advisor and she's awesome. She's really cool. They give me pens and paper that talk back to me and read the lectures. I wanted note takers and extra time on tests. I got that in high school too. It was nice to know that I could still get it in college. Both colleges obviously want to help me succeed and do the best that I can. At my first college, there is only one disability counsel woman on my campus for a thousand kids. It was stressful to try to get a meeting with her. After I did, I felt that she was very helpful. We figured out what I needed to do.

When I told my roommates I was dyslexic, they were surprised. They were like, "But you're an engineer. You have to do math." I was like, "Numbers are easier for me than letters. I don't know why." I'm really good at math and figuring out problems. When I got tested for my disability, I could say 16 numbers backward and forwards to you. But, I couldn't do it with letters. It was weird.

My sophomore year was my last year at my first college. I was having a really hard time with this specific math class. Basically, I had jumped three levels and was kind of expected to know what was going on. I wasn't doing well, which for me is really hard. I always tried, even with my disabilities to get, you know A's. B's would bother me. No matter how much work I put into it, I felt like I wasn't doing something that made me happy. It wasn't going to help me get to my goal of what I wanted to do with working with people and healthcare.

I had been thinking about switching colleges for a long time. Yesterday, my parents were like, "You know what? If this is what you want to do, we'll make it happen." They've always been number one. Before I went to my current college, I was second-guessing myself. Should I just stay where I have friends? I know kind of what's going on in the classes. Be miserable, but finish and sound like I got a smart degree? Or, do I go excel and be what I want to be at a different college? I just didn't know if I could handle coming here to this new campus on my own. But, it turned out really well. My family and friends have been so supportive of me. I get text messages every day asking, "How's school down there?" Like, "So proud of you." It's just so encouraging. At my first college, I always had other kids in my class who needed note-takers or extra time on exams, which was great. When I got here, I said I needed extra time. One kid in my class said, "Well, I could get extra time too, but I feel like that's such a crutch." I was like, "That's kind of rude to say." Luckily, other kids heard that and knocked him down a peg. That was okay. Some people don't really understand what they're saying, even if they do have a disability. They certainly don't really understand what that means. They don't want to sound dumb, so they try to build themselves up. It's like, "You're not dumb. You need a little help to get to where everyone else is at. It's not a crutch."

When we have time off from school, we all like to hang out. We also study together. Someone asked me to read the chapter out loud for everyone so that they could all listen. I was like, "I really would learn better if someone else read it to me." They were all so cool with that and accepting, which was really awesome.

I have two parents and a little sister. I love my sister. I miss her a lot. We were really close back at home. Now, I barely ever get to talk to her or see her because I'm always busy and she never has time. I've never been taught that my disability was a disadvantage. My mom always said "it's not bad. You don't learn wrong, you just learn different." My parents are really good at not focusing on my disability too much. If I wanted to do something, there was no chance I couldn't do it. That was their attitude. I never had the attitude of, "I can't do this because of my disability," until I got older and realized maybe I really shouldn't be an English major. Yeah, I have a very good relationship with my family. It took a downturn because of my past relationship for a few years. But, over the past seven months, it's been building back up, which has been really great. My dad flew and drove with me to unpack all my stuff every time I've moved. They've always been very supportive of what I'm doing.

As you get older you start to care less or, in my experience, about how you're perceived by people. You want to focus more on spending time with, or connecting with, your family because they will be there for you, no matter what. At least in my little family world, that's how it is. I used to really care about what my friends, or my boyfriend, would think. And, I wouldn't talk to my family for a while. That was a bad idea. I lost four family members that were all very close to me through old age, accidents, and suicide. It surprises me that I pushed my mom, dad, and my sister away with my next relationship. I was trying to hold on to someone without being afraid. Now, I realized how important that family dynamic and that relationship is. I'm not going to jeopardize it in any way.

I've worked my butt off. It's hard sometimes to feel like I can't do something. That's probably my biggest depressor in life. That sucks, but I stay positive. I have friends and family to support me and have the opportunity to make the decisions that I want to help me in life. That is really what keeps me going basically.

Willow discussed her academic journey, including transferring colleges, transitioning into the workforce, and living independently. Willow settled into her new major and college.

My passions pretty much made me come into this program. This is where I was meant to be. There's not much that I can't do here because it's all with my hands or it's all thinking about problems. I'm really happy here. I came to realize that I'm not really alone. I honestly don't think my disability will be an asset or a roadblock [in my career]. That's who I am. I've learned to adapt to what I need to do. I've picked a program where I can utilize my good skills and not be taken down by the bad.

Happiness, for me, is doing what you want to do. For example, I finally made the decision to go somewhere else for school and mood completely changed. I've loved it so much. I'm doing a different program. I'm more into prosthetics, more orthotics. That's what my program is called instead of biomed engineering. Surprisingly, I'm doing better. It's more hands-on. I'm building things and learning more about the body instead of doing a lot of things with numbers and reading. Because I was never really good at that with my learning disability, this is a better fit for me. After my master's program, they set us up with a residency. For two years, I can go somewhere in the country and work for someone else, which is cool. Then after that, I want to own my own practice back up where I'm from, which would be nice. When I'm old I want to make a school for prosthetics because the only ones on the East Coast are in Connecticut and Florida. I feel like that's not enough. I want to do my residency in California. I went there over the summer. It's so awesome. I want to go somewhere different because— why not?

So, after leaving the first college, I finished my bachelor's in two years. I had my two years at the first college and then two years at the second college. Then, I did my master's program for engineering management. It had a high focus in orthotics and prosthetics. Last week, I just completed my residency program. I had two years of residency to do. In between that, I traveled. I lived in a van for a couple of months, traveled the country trying to make the best of my time before starting residency. I just moved and will be working at the children's hospital here, so that's very exciting! I did live by myself for a year for my first residency. I was the healthiest I had ever been. Living on my own now and looking at this little apartment that I created. I feel very confident in myself and very ready to bring other people into my life if I feel they deserve it. I absolutely love living alone and being independent. It's different for me. I've always had roommates between home, school, and camp. Now that I have my own space, I really like it.

Willow reflected on integrating learning techniques, exercise, and part time jobs while in college. In these settings, she tried out and honed a variety of strategies that informed the ways she thought about and planned for her future.

My life is school, work, and dance. I'm at a dance company. I'm the hip-hop teacher, so that's really fun. I work at a restaurant right now. I don't really have much time for fun, to be quite honest. It's making me a very good multi-tasker. It's helping me to not become a procrastinator because I'm very much a procrastinator. It's getting me ready for the professional world, which is exciting and terrifying. I don't think I'll need accommodations in my future work. Right now, I have time and a half for lab practical exams. Other than that, I don't utilize any accommodations. I don't really think I would need any in the professional world because I chose a career path where I wouldn't. I think that is what I did subconsciously.

In my part time job waiting on tables, I have to input orders into a computer system. I write down orders. Then, I go to this little box computer where there's options like steak, salad, chicken. Sometimes we have letters in front of it, like WW or WH, like two-letter codes and then the meal. When I go to a restaurant,

I'm never going to modify anything ever again. It is so annoying for servers! Sometimes I mess up on the orders because I typed in the wrong number or modification. They get really mad; it's awkward. But it's okay. My bosses don't really care because everyone gets stuff wrong. I just take it. That's whatever. I would never tell a customer, "Sorry, I'm dyslexic. I got your order wrong." They wouldn't care at all.

My new university doesn't have a dance club or anything. I found a studio where I can take adult classes, which is really awesome. I'm getting a job teaching soccer to two-to-five-year-olds, which is …terrifying. But it's only twice a week, so I'll do it.

Willow felt that her disability had not changed the nature of her work experiences, partially because she would not let it.

No, I don't let it. I felt very stern about saying that, but I've never had an issue with my dyslexia in a workplace. Reading comprehension-wise and dyslexia-wise, I would take my time. But I never felt like I was rushed. If anyone ever gave me a problem for it, I would fight back. That's not allowed. I would say that disability doesn't mean that you're not able. It's a different ability type thing. I could quote my mom for years.

Willow worked in different environments and shared the role of her disability in those environments.

At my last job, my residency, my director actually asked if I had any learning challenges that she would have to adapt to. She was amazing. The hospital that I worked at was also a center for dyslexia research, so I made a comment once that I have dyslexia. They all knew. They were all aware, which was really helpful. Any writing assignments, they would make sure that I felt comfortable with. I was just very blessed to have that. But, I do not think that anyone at my new job knows about any sort of disability, which is interesting, because I've always told people.

Willow talked about the influences on her major choice and career aspirations, and the strategies she used to achieve her dream job of creating prosthetics for children.

It's a combination of everything. My mom and dad are both in healthcare. I always wanted to work with patients because that's what I had seen. I really liked engineering and art. I was always really good at math and science. I wasn't allowed to take either art or music because of my disability. They had to take one of those away, so I could do my special education classes. In high school, I was looking at engineering courses. I knew I wanted to work with kids. How am I going to do health care and engineering and art? It doesn't make sense. Then, the Boston marathon bombing happened. I was set to shadow a prosthetist randomly. It happened to be one of the marathon bombing victims. We saw him walk for the first time. I was like, I want to do this. How do I get to do this? Maybe there's a specialty for kids. Now, that's literally my job title! That was exciting.

So, I ended up leaving my first college and going to a more specified program in another state for Orthotics and Prosthetics. Orthotics is basically bracing a body part. Prosthetics is replacing a body part. My slogan is literally brace it or replace it©. For prosthetics, the kid will come in. I'll cast their residual, whatever's left, fill that with plaster, and then it's basically like an art project with anatomy trying to carve out certain areas of the plaster. And then I'll pull hot plastics over it, they'll come back and try it on, make sure everything fits right, and then I'll finish it out, whatever color they need and attach you know knees, feet elbows, arms, hands, whatever they're missing, and then they come back in to pick it up. It's so cute.

I've always wanted to be a prosthetist and do prosthetic patient care. I didn't know that was an option to do, not just as a Masters, but as a bachelor's program. I was going to take my bio-med engineering degree and go to prosthetic mastering school. But, I figured out recently that I could just transfer and keep all the credits that I've done still and do exactly what I want.

I've always wanted to help people in some way or another; also because I've been helped when I needed it. I wanted to grow up and be someone who I would have wanted as a kid to help me. I feel like I'm giving kids back their childhood. It's my life's purpose, definitely. Every time I give a kid their first leg, it's life-changing for me and for them.

I'm lucky that I had such a specific goal in mind. I went for the jobs that would help me get there. I've moved every single year since leaving my first college. To be in one place for a long time, I haven't done that since I left for college. I have big goals for my company as far as getting more kids to come to our clinics. We're a private company in the children's hospital. They don't really have a prosthetic lab fully made yet. They outsource. I make all my stuff on my own based on my last year residency, which I really can't talk highly enough about. They said that they would buy me the equipment and any tools that I needed. I have big goals to make it a known program in the area that doctors feel confident sending their kids to me specifically. I couldn't be happier with my current life.

Willow's personal goals evolved over time. Yet, Willow consistently hoped for marriage and a family.

I want to be married. That would take so much stress off. I don't have to go searching for a partner and family; it's just there when I get home. That would be fabulous. I talked about this with my roommate. We're like, "Let's be married now; then, we don't have to worry about that. We can focus on school and not love life."

I love kids! Three psychics told me I'm going to have twin boys, which is devastating and exciting. I also really, really would like to adopt a limb-disabled child of any age. I have two aunts that have been adopted. Two of my cousins on my dad's side, and one cousin on my mom's side, or vice versa, are adopted. I've had friends who have been adopted. Growing up and working in my field, I get to work with a lot of disabled kids who are in the foster care systems. I've always wanted to help kids. I feel like that's a great way to do it, especially if I'm already trained in what they need. Making this kid's life better and easier would be really great. I would love to have a learning disabled kid. I can see disability from a different perspective.

Reflection Questions

1 *Combining art and science.* Willow noted how she could not take art or music in K-12 school "so I could do my special education classes." Yet, in her dream career, Willow now combines engineering and art to create prosthetics for children. Given her passions and life goals of being a prosthetist, how might this restriction from art classes have affected her life? What can educators and families do to ensure that all youth have equitable access to arts and other enriching activities in elementary, middle, and high school?

2 *Relationships and family bonds.* What does Willow's case illustrate about the role of strong and supportive relationships for disabled youth? Willow alludes to a time when a romantic relationship caused some tension within her family. After that relationship ended, she vowed to not let anything get in the way of her strong family bonds. Have you experienced something similar? What strategies can individuals use to foster strong and positive relationships with loved ones—even when the people we care about might not get along with each other?

3 *Purpose.* How would you describe Willow's sense of purpose? How is her sense of purpose related to experiences with her own disability? Consider your sense of purpose—and if/how it might be related to your lived experiences. How have your life experiences reinforced, or led you to modify, your sense of purpose?

4 *Positivity.* Throughout Willow's story, she explains how keeping a positive outlook helped her persevere. As you think about Willow's experiences, where are times that she chose positivity over negativity or defeat? Imagine how Willow might be paying her sense of positivity forward in her career as a prosthetist. Can you recall instances in your own life where you channeled positivity—even during a tough time?

17 Meet Yolanda

Pronouns: They/them
Age: 29
Self-identified disability: Autistic; Hypermobile
College major: Undergraduate: Math, Mechanical Engineering, and
   Chinese; Graduate Degrees: Mathematics, Neuroscience
Current living situation: Living with roommates
Current job/position: Teacher, Researcher, Consultant

Yolanda shares their story as an autistic and hypermobile individual who was not diagnosed until college. Despite bullying from peers, and even teachers, Yolanda thrived academically, earning a bachelor's, master's, and doctoral degree during a ten year time frame. Yolanda enacts a passion for disability education and activism through teaching and writing. Specifically, they critique neurotypical societal norms, deficit-laden language, and incomplete research about autistic people. Their story highlights how disability activism often stems from one's disability experiences and identity development. Moreover, we see that support, friendship, and a sense of belonging can be fostered by finding a disability community—whether in person or online. Yolanda's story also points to the complexity of intersecting identities and how one's sense of self evolves over time.

Yolanda shared insights about disability generally, and what it means to have a sense of self rooted deeply in autism.

Disability means for me that there's a mismatch between what I'm actually able to do and what other people expect people to be able to do. Like yes, my vision is not that great. I wear glasses. But, when people think of needing glasses, they assume that with them, being able to see across the room is within what's expected. So, that's not a disability. But people do expect that I'm always going to be able to express myself pretty well using oral speech. That's not true. That

DOI: 10.4324/9781003495703-17

is part of a disability. The word *special* tends to piss me off in a disability context because it's like, "This is a need that actually a decent bunch of people have. But, as soon as you have it because you're disabled, it's *special*."

People wondered if autism might be a thing with me, even as early as kindergarten. My teachers were fairly sure that something was up. I don't think the word autism was even mentioned by a teacher until I was 13 or 14. It actually took until I got to college for anybody to finally put it on a piece of paper—both autism and hypermobility. On the autism thing, I could talk and I'm a girl. People kind of assume that if you're a girl and you can talk, you're not autistic. This doesn't work. But people assume it. Hypermobility tends to not get diagnosed until you get one of those anatomically impossible injuries.

I'm autistic. I'm also hypermobile. Neurodivergent is another word that I would use related to being autistic. It's kind of a broader umbrella. My body and brain are weird. I'm not going to say that my body and brain are wrong because I don't think they are. But it's pretty clear that they're not typical. It's the entire way my brain is wired. People seem to think I'm smart. That's one thing. I definitely tend to have offbeat ideas for solutions, just because the way my brain works is not typical. Therefore, some of the solutions that I will come to, and that make immediate sense to me, are not typical. This apparently winds up looking like creativity, which I might even agree that it is. I don't know, but it comes in handy. Offbeat perspectives are definitely useful when you're trying to make new things. Also, pattern recognition. I have really, really good pattern recognition.

A lot of the problems that I run into as an autistic person are based around people thinking that they can separate the autism from the person. If you can be a person with autism, you can be a person without autism and then attempt to enforce said separation. This doesn't actually work. It goes fairly badly, especially because a lot of people conflate acting autistic with autistic expressions of distress. When people are trying to separate the autism from the person, then I'm getting stressed out. From the perspective of anybody who makes that kind of conflation, I'm suddenly acting a lot more autistic, which is the opposite of what they wanted.

While navigating a world designed for neurotypical people, Yolanda found camaraderie, understanding, and support from friends and in online communities.

Being autistic means navigating a world that's designed for not quite how I actually work. My executive functioning is kind of overall not great. That varies from my homework is a problem to initiating a new activity on my own is a problem. I need to be reminded to go eat food, go shower. I have friends who will do that for me. They'll send me a message that says, "Go food" or "Go hydrate." Okay, thank you.

Autism is, in a big way, kind of a community thing. In-person ones are great, where they exist. I have found lots of other people who are like me. Autistic online communities are great. It lets me find other people who are like me. Friends who make sense. This is huge. It's a community. It's identity. I mean yes, it's a disability, but it's not just a disability. The Internet has been huge for autistic stuff because, while we actually do tend to like community type stuff, actually going into a space full of people can be overwhelming. So the internet is good. Online, I am involved in an autistic community and it's great.

Yolanda talked about the ways prejudice against autistic people was rooted in misinformation. Yolanda experienced bullying from other students and teachers.

Autism means fairly often being described, or being referred to, as "the scary thing." They think, "We need to find an answer because autism is scary. The rates are increasing. This is a crisis for our children." And of course, every month or two, you'll get a headline about a parent who killed their autistic kid because autism is so difficult to deal with. The media will be sympathetic to the parent who just killed their kid. A lot of public perception stuff is pretty terrible, like attempting to blame mass shootings on autism. Autism comes with sensory processing issues. Most of us can't really be in the same area as a gun that's going off. But, supposedly *we're* going to shoot everybody? I don't know how this works. It really doesn't.

When I was in elementary school, I got bullied fairly badly. Mostly, it was other students but there were a lot of teachers seeing it and deciding they didn't actually care because maybe it would teach me to act a little bit more normal. It didn't, by the way. Getting hit with a book was the one incident I can actually remember—and that was actually a teacher.

Yolanda explained how prejudice and discrimination towards autistic people was heightened for autistic people of color who are often misdiagnosed, denied accommodations, or harmed when unable to communicate with authority figures.

A lot of black children who, properly speaking, are autistic get diagnosed with oppositional defiant disorder instead. Or, they are just thought of as being misbehaving or bad and may not have access to disability services. Whether or not they get diagnosed or recognized as being autistic, that doesn't necessarily mean that they're going to be accommodated or have actual access to things the same way that I generally have. Whether the diagnosis is used in useful ways, or whether it's used against you, definitely differs by race. Like, they talk about autism identification cards—you give the police a card to say that you're autistic. Ah yes, because a Black autistic person is definitely going to be able to reach in their pocket for this card and not get shot. No. That is an extremely white solution.

During college, Yolanda had an opportunity to study abroad but experienced discrimination from the international school which negatively impacted their wellbeing and academic success.

My program apparently did let the Chinese university know, "Heads up, one of our students is autistic." They heard the A word and the administrative people flipped out. They did not want me to come at all. And, they made attempts a few times in the first semester to have me sent home. "People like that shouldn't be in college." They said that. I am not a fan of people who say that for reasons that I'm in college. I'm good at this. Stop that.

I was very, very stressed that year. It kind of sucked. It definitely did have a little bit of a vicious cycle effect. I'm stressed because they want to get rid of me. So, I don't do as well. So they use that as an excuse to want to get rid of me. So, I'm stressed because they want to get rid of me. So, I don't do as well.

By the second interview, with the encouragement of professors, Yolanda was completing a Master's degree and applying to Ph.D. programs. Lived experiences as an autistic student who studied abroad informed their research interests in disability related communication.

I am a disability studies scholar. As an American in China, it's a cultural difference that we can work with. What happens if we start treating these kinds of disability related communication issues as cultural differences that we can work with as problems of translation? Machine translation and computer assisted translation both exist. I had a general idea that research related to autism communication and improving communication for autistic people had issues and needed to do better. I had an idea of how it might be improved technologically. But, I don't think we're near implementing the idea. But, there are other ways that I'm still addressing that general goal.

By the third interview, Yolanda finished their doctoral program in neuroscience.

My dissertation research was on a specific kind of brain computer interface called the P300 brain computer interface for people with amyotrophic lateral sclerosis. This is used for augmented and alternative communication, which is the fancy pants technical term in the field for communication tools and strategies used by people who cannot fully rely on speech.

Yolanda expressed a passion for education though writing, specifically within disability-related genres. They also wrote a blog designed to help readers support autistic children.

My writing has been in some books. I've done a couple of book reviews. I won a poetry competition with a submission about, "What is a monster?" Is it about the characteristics of the monster, or is it about the people who are defining it, and erasure and what's not reflected? I've written about topics of disability and queerness and both. More disability, but definitely both. I've done a decent bit with representation of neurodiversity in fiction. Let's see...I've also done a decent bit about augmented and alternative communication (AAC), as I use it personally. I won an award because I helped moderate a group on Facebook. That group isn't specific to any particular disability in practice, but it is very autism heavy. At least half the admins are autistic. All of the admins use AAC and may also lose speech as I do.

My blog ranges from explaining about autism to answering questions from parents about, "So there's this idea of neurodiversity that you're talking about. Does it mean that XYZ?" Usually the answer is no, because they're like, "Does that mean that you want us to just not do anything to teach our kids?" Oh my God, how do you even conclude that? What the hell? Just because I think that torturing children until they obey you is bad does *not* mean that I think you should not teach. Those are different things. If offering gummy bears, or offering a quarter of an M&M to your child when he looks you in the eye is the only way of teaching him that you can think of, you are a bad teacher. Like no, I want you to teach your children the skills that they need as they grow up into autistic adults instead of you trying to teach them to stop being autistic. That second one isn't going to work.

A passion for educating others led to various positions as a consultant and teacher. Yolanda received unhelpful suggestions from neurotypical colleagues about navigating teaching situations when they lost the ability to speak. Leaning into the autonomy given to college teachers, Yolanda developed more authentic ways to be effective in the classroom.

I am working as an independent contractor for a company who primarily works on augmentative and alternative communication. My research with them involves working with anonymous language use data collected from AAC users who use their applications. In addition, I teach math online. I am also going to be teaching developmental neurobiology at the undergraduate level.

For teaching, it is good to let the supervisor know about my disability. The accommodation suggestions that the math department was able to offer me were not helpful. Their first suggestion; if I lost speech, I should call the math department. I appreciate the thought of contacting the department and they might be able to send somebody. But, the problems are actually several fold. First, if I cannot speak, I cannot make a phone call. There actually are technological ways around that with AAC, but I don't have any of them set up in my classroom. So, for me, it is currently true that if I cannot speak, I cannot make a phone call. Two, I was not teaching in the main math department building at the time. There was construction. If somebody started walking the instant the phone started ringing, I could have somebody in my classroom in 10–15 minutes. If I can hold out for 10–15 minutes I can make it the remainder of the 50-minute class. If I can't, they're too late to help. Sending somebody else to make me not do my job is not actually an acceptable solution.

But, mostly they trust me to handle it myself if I think that I can. For example, I have taught in rooms where I had a projector, in which case typing into the projector is an option. I have taught in labs where, after the initial explanation for the class, I'm largely dealing with individual students one on one helping answer issues with their individual lab experiments or projects. In this case, I have often written my answers on an index card and left the index cards with students.

I have written on the whiteboard (without accompanying mouth words) instead of writing on the whiteboard with the words that most teachers are using. It works. That is kind of one of the things that are, by and large, covered under "teachers have some autonomy in how they run their own classroom."

Over the course of three interviews, Yolanda shared their family's journey of acceptance. In their first and second interviews, they explained:

My dad still denies that I'm autistic. Fail. He's pretty good about the needs that I actually have. He's just very much against the idea that autism is a descriptor for those needs. As long as I don't say the A word, we're okay. My dad was pretty actively discouraging about identifying me as being autistic. What actually happens is that I just don't talk about it with him anymore. I still hang out in autistic communities and I actually do disability study stuff. I have my disability blog, but he doesn't know about any of it.

There's this thing about autism, it runs in families. I'd actually brought up the word autism to my mom when I was about eight, but her reaction meant that kind of fell off the radar for a while. My mother said, "No, you're not. They (autistic people) can't talk. They can't do things. They're not smart." I was like, "Oh. Okay. I don't understand. What?" I mean all of those things are false, but it's a fairly common way that people think of autism as being. She had a realization upon finding out that I really do meet criteria for the initial screening for autism. Her response has basically been along the line of, "Oh, the whole family does that." So, that came with a nice big realization of, "Oh my God! The entire family is autistic." So, I had very different reactions on different sides of the family.

By the third interview, subtle changes occurred in how Yolanda's family acknowledged their autism.

My mom's understanding of what autism is has updated a bit. With it, she kind of realized, "Oh my God. It is so much of the family"—which makes sense because with the screening questions my mom answered a lot of them with "no more than the rest of the family." This was completely true. It was also wildly misinterpreted. If you, your parents, and your siblings are all autistic, are you really going to notice that anything is different when your kid is autistic? I'd mentioned something being related to autism and she would be like, "Oh, doesn't everybody do that?" I'm like, No, no…most people do not. There's this thing about autism; it runs in families Mama. She was under the impression that she made eye contact. Then she realized that she didn't know what color eyes anybody had. My dad still doesn't particularly like to talk about it, but he has recognized that describing me as autistic is not inaccurate. He's not a fan of labels, but he recognizes that I am autistic.

In addition to centering autism in their identity, Yolanda consistently reflected on the intersectionality of their gender, race, and religion.

So, in terms of the gender thing, none of the neurotypical gender definitions make particularly much sense to me. It's like, "Here is a definition of what it is to be a man. I don't think that matches. Here is a definition of what it is to be a woman. No." At one point, I've also wondered, "Is autism just taking up the spot that my gender is supposed to go in?" It might be. People talk about knowing that they are women or knowing that they are men. I'm like, "No. I don't have anything that looks like that." I definitely have this whole knowing I'm autistic identity thing. A lot of the stuff I do that looks gendered is actually for sensory reasons. Like loose long skirts are more comfortable; I can't wear tight pants. I'm fairly sure the way my brain works is related to my not quite getting any of the neurotypical ways of defining gender.

By the second interview Yolanda shared evolving thoughts and feelings about gender, asexuality, and autism.

I'm a little bit louder about being nonbinary. People say, "You're a woman in math?" I respond, "Actually, no. I am a nonbinary in math." I think that, to some extent, gender just looks like a system that people made up that doesn't actually quite work with biology, or with how people's brains work. I look at this system and I go, "What the fuck?" Are you this one? No. You are that one. No. "You have to choose." Says who? I don't believe you. This entire system makes no sense and I'm going to ignore it, thank you very much.

I think my asexuality actually does relate to my autism, because I have sensory processing issues. Sensory overload is a fairly common issue for me in everyday situations. Sex stuff, which is like, "Yes, let's really heavily stimulate some of the most sensitive parts of my body." Sensory overload is an issue in typical situations. This sounds like a terrible idea. I actually am asexual in part because I am autistic. This does not invalidate the fact that I am asexual.

In the third interview, Yolanda was asked about the following identities they listed on the demographic form: "asexual, pan romantic asexual and then gender queer, non binary, gender vague, transgender."

I mean—pick a gender? No. What kind of person do you want to have sex with? No. Who are you romantically attracted to? Yes? I mean it's not quite that simple. Like, as far as romantic attraction, I actually have a definite preference for neurodivergent people.

My gender is a part of me and I'm autistic. So my gender is also autistic. Autistic ways of doing gender are not necessarily the same as neurotypical ways of doing gender—even if somebody is cisgender—which I am not cis. I am nonbinary. I am trans. But, I'm not convinced that autistic women and neurotypical women have the same gender experience either. Is my hair long for sensory reasons or is my hair long for gender reasons? Yes. Did I get my boobs chopped off for sensory reasons or for gender reasons? Yes. Do I need to separate them (autism and gender)? But internally, it's like, "Do I even necessarily always need to separate it out?" I'm not little pieces—like this piece is autistic and this piece is nonbinary and never the twain shall meet. That's not how humans work. My pronouns are not a grammatical error, my pronouns are they/them/theirs. Use them!

Reflection Questions

1 *Family dynamics.* Yolanda's story reveals how family dynamics can be complex and evolve over time. Discuss the ways family members dealt with autism diagnoses and treated Yolanda. How did Yolanda react to these attitudes and treatment? Discuss this family situation in light of Yolanda's choice to blog and select a career path where they advocated for autism awareness and support? What can allies do to support autistic people who are not fully accepted by their families? What can professionals do to support disabled youth struggling with unhelpful and/or challenging family dynamics?

2 *Intersectionality and identity.* Yolanda shares many thoughts about how their intersectional identities shaped their evolving sense of self and worldview. How does intersectionality appear in Yolanda's story? How does intersectionality impact your identity and experience in the world? What strategies can you use to support the complex, intersecting, and evolving identities of people in your spheres of influence?

3 *Harm reduction.* Yolanda experienced prejudice and bullying. They also referenced the abuse and harm directed toward autistic people due to misinformation and hate. Disabled people are more likely to be abused than any minoritized group. How can you create welcoming, supportive, and safe spaces for autistic people? What specific strategies might you use if you witness bullying or violence toward autistic people? What specific strategies do/can you use if you experience bullying or violence?

18 Unfiltered Advice from Participants

In the preceding chapters, we learned how participants navigated life, school, work, healthcare, and family. In this chapter, we categorize advice from numerous participants to emphasize the common recommendations they offered to readers. This approach allowed us to streamline the advice and organize the chapter into three recommendation sections for: educators, disabled youth, and families.

By asking our participants for their advice, we are recognizing the value of their experiences, validating their insights, and providing a means for them to impact others. In Chapter 1, we noted how stories told by disabled people can be viewed as radical acts and a form of cultural activism (Kafai, 2021). We can challenge ableist assumptions, stereotypes, and norms by asserting that stories by, and about, disabled people are valid and have worth (Kafai, 2021). In this chapter, we continue these radical acts by centering advice from disabled people. This approach is different from many educational texts where experts (often non-disabled people) offer advice and recommendations to readers. We believe that those most impacted by prejudice and discrimination should be the ones to speak their truths and offer advice to others. Disabled people have invaluable expertise and sage advice for combating oppression (Berne et al., 2018). We hope that through the advice offered by disabled participants, readers glean insights for promoting positive change in their homes, schools, workplaces, and communities.

Advice for Educators

As the preceding chapters showed, disabled youth navigated a variety of challenges in educational settings. In listening to participants, we heard about the behaviors and attitudes that they experienced as obstacles or undermined their confidence as students. Conversely, participants shared ways in which educators validated, supported, and sustained their well-being. Based upon these experiences, participants offered five types of advice for educators: (1) See us; (2) Believe us; (3) Teach us; (4) Believe *in* us; and (5) Advocate for and with us.

DOI: 10.4324/9781003495703-18

See Us—Make an Effort to Build Relationships

Participants felt that to be effective, educators had to focus on building relationships, getting to know individual students, and understanding that disability impacts every person differently. They were adamant that educators who took the time to know them, and *see* their talents, were more effective. Participants noted that the time and effort educators took to build relationships with them was invaluable. Alice shared, "People with disabilities kind of get pushed aside a lot [by educators]. It's not fair. Take the time. Make the time. Disability or not, everybody deserves to succeed." Similarly, Peter appreciated when educators acted like "less of an authority figure. When they're there to help you. When they show interest and get to know the kid." Titus agreed that educators should take the time and provide care support for students. In jest, Titus suggested that to deal with teachers who disregard students with disabilities he would, "fire them all!" He elaborated, "New teachers have to be more educated in what's going on, in what's happening, and how to deal with disabled students." More than just "dealing" with disabled students, Titus urges teachers to the time to sit down and ask students: "Hey, you say you have ADHD, but what can you do [well]?" Titus felt that by getting to know a student and showing interest in their strengths, teachers could be not only more compassionate, but also more effective. Indeed, decades of educational research on equitable teaching practices shows that the most successful educators care about their students and foster their unique talents (Argus et al., 2022; hooks, 1994; Noddings, 1992).

Yolanda stressed that educators should not solely focus on a student's disability. All people are complex; including people with disabilities. They warned teachers to not assume that student behavior was always related to autism. Yolanda's advice to teachers:

> Dear teachers, it is totally developmentally appropriate for an autistic teenager to not do what you want them to do. This is not autism. This is teenager. It's autistic teenager, but teenager. React to it with the fact that they are teenagers, not with the assumption that they don't know any better. They do.

Yolanda's message reminds us that seeing disabled people means seeing their whole selves.

Peter discussed the importance of educators being aware of their biases and how their assumptions shape the ways they treat students. He shared,

> We're humans. You are going to label different kids. You know which ones are the well-behaved ones and which ones are pretending. That label isn't helpful. Be conscious of how you're categorizing your kids. And, be

very cautious in how you project that. It's something that teachers should be aware of.

Peter, and many of our participants, call upon educators to see students as unique and complex individuals. Only then can educators build authentic and supportive relationships with their students.

Believe Us—Trust That We Know What We Need

Participants in our study wished that educators would believe them when they disclosed their disability and described their educational needs. Unfortunately, many of our participants had educators question the legitimacy of their disability and accommodation requests. Often, this skepticism felt like judgements about their ability and worth. As noted in Chapter 2, higher education systems require individuals to provide documentation of their disability and related learning needs. To our participants, these processes felt disrespectful and served as barriers to success. Correspondingly, participants wanted individual teachers and university systems to simply *believe* them.

Yolanda and Justice spoke of the process that students with disabilities have to follow to receive accommodations in college. Yolanda shared, "the idea that in order to have your needs met, you need to get paperwork from *able* people demonstrating that you actually do have this need, seems pretty screwed up to me." Similarly, Justice lamented about the collegiate process that requires written proof from an "expert" that a student has a disability and deserves accommodations. Justice wanted educators to:

Take [students] seriously even if they don't have that magical piece of paper saying exactly what's going on. Trust people's judgment on what's going on with their brain. Do not assume that this specific doctor is the only person who can tell you what's up with this student.

As we noted in Chapter 2, the accommodation process in educational institutions change when students move from high school to college, shifting the responsibility to students to provide documentation and request accommodations. The advice from our participants is to trust that students are the experts about their disabilities and learning needs.

Titus urged educators to not only believe a student when they disclose their disability, but to also recognize that every person's disability uniquely impacts how they learn. Titus recalled,

I had a teacher once, and I brought her my learning disability [paperwork]. And a week later, I said I had a problem [understanding the material]. And she said, "Well no one else had a problem." I said, "But I have ADHD. This is going on." She's like, "Well I have other students that have disabilities, and they don't seem to have a problem with this." Obviously, they do not have the same thing going on!

To his dismay, this teacher was unwilling to believe Titus when he reached out for help and explained his specific learning needs. All of our participants advise educators to believe students when they express their unique learning needs and ask for accommodations.

Teach Us—Use Strategies that Support

Many of the participants wished educators would find ways to meaningfully engage disabled students in the teaching and learning process. Educational practices that are used in classrooms today are often inherited from previous decades. Sometimes these classic forms of pedagogy do not tap into hands-on, real-world experiences. Nor are they very inclusive of all learner's needs. Teaching with one mode of delivery—like a lecture—shows little regard for students who struggle with accessing the information in that way. Titus suggested,

> Maybe instead of just reading everything off a damn screen, just have more tangible classroom activities. Maybe get us to be more interactive, something that we can do as a group. Or even a field trip. Or something else instead of just sitting there and expecting us to absorb this information for 50 minutes.

Indeed, many students wished that teachers would use multiple instructional methods to engage them within the classroom.

Participants also wished teachers would use a variety of methods to allow them to demonstrate their knowledge and understanding of a topic. Traditional assessment procedures may not be conducive to everyone, particularly students with disabilities. In his classes, Titus was graded mostly on traditional pencil and paper tests. As he shared, teachers are quick to say, "Off you go. Here is an exam." Titus implores educators to,

> Change up the exams to something else! I'm a horrible tester because I sit down and have 50 million questions going through my head. I know this! I don't know it this way, though. You're just testing me in one way. Schools should offer different ways of testing; maybe verbal or something like that.

Tippi agreed. She lamented how narrowly designed assessment practices negatively impacted her ability to demonstrate her knowledge. Tippi explained how frustrating this was.

Not everybody tests well. Maybe don't only focus on tests. Focus on other assignments. There are tests where I'd studied hours, but I still failed. My anxiety makes it hard for me to take tests. It's not that I don't care about your class. I just can't do it. I'm frustrated.

Just because a student does poorly on a test does not mean that they haven't mastered the material. Teachers have an array of tools at their disposal to measure if, and how well, a student is learning. By using varied forms of assessment, educators can more effectively and equitably assess student learning.

Yolanda also urged educators to understand the nuances of how a disability impacts a person's ability to perform a task. They remarked,

When [people with disabilities] run into something that we actually just don't have the ability to do, increasing the consequences for not doing it isn't going to magically make us able to do it. It doesn't work. Find a different goal.

Instead of fixating on a student's compliance to a perceived educational norm, Yolanda wishes educators would rethink the goals and help students achieve success. It should be noted that some participants did have positive interactions with outstanding educators. For instance, Alice described how two professors in particular "were so open and interested in helping me."

The advice offered by our participants aligns with best practices for inclusive and equity-minded teaching. For instance, as mentioned in Chapter 2, Universal Design for Learning (UDL) focuses on how educators can use multiple ways to represent, engage, and assess students (Rose & Meyer, 2002). As participants pointed out, more inclusive and engaging teaching would better honor unique learner needs and talents—and most importantly help disabled learners thrive.

Believe in Us—Presume Competence and Set High Expectations

Educators can support and inspire, as well as deflate and harm. An educator's attitude toward a disabled student can impact the student's self-concept and ultimately success in school. Our participants urged educators to presume competence and set high expectations. Their specific advice encompasses many ways that teachers can show support by believing in disabled students' ability to succeed. Kalani shared,

Never tell somebody that they can't do something because some people won't be able to take that and challenge it. I hear that over and over again. I hear those people doubting me. "You're not going to make it. You're not going to be successful." Don't tell somebody [that]! Tell them what they *can* do to achieve it. Help them! Point out the positives. Don't point out the negatives. Those positive people play such a role. Disabled students will remember them more and thank them more than all those negative people who said: "You're not going to make it." Those positive people make it ten times better.

As Kalani notes, truly supporting disabled students means believing in their capabilities, recognizing their strengths, and offering positive feedback and encouragement.

Peter points out that while sometimes there are challenges that disabled students face, it does not mean they are not capable of success. He said that educators:

definitely have to have the attitude that this kid can have the same amount of success as any other student. You are a huge influencer on whether they drop behind. I would say [teachers should understand] that every student has potential. How you treat and interact with that student vastly changes their outlook on life.

Decades of research measuring the impact of expectations on student achievement confirms that educators play a pivotal role in whether a student rises to a challenge (Wang et al., 2018). Individual educators (and educational systems) cause immense harm when they perpetuate disability biases, set low expectations, or assume students are unable to succeed. Our participants, thus, advise educators to see strengths, set high expectations, and believe in the capabilities of disabled students.

Advocate for and with Us—Disrupt Ableism and Bullying

The last theme of advice for educators centers around advocating for, and with, students. In some cases, especially when participants were recalling early childhood bullying, young people absolutely wanted educators to advocate on their behalf. For instance, Alice explained, "it's always been my experience that professionals don't always stand up and advocate for the students. Help [your students] get through school. Be somebody who can advocate in an honest way and help pay it forward." Like Alice, many participants reflected on their early school experiences and lamented the lack of advocacy by educators.

However, collective advice from our participants also calls attention to the importance of honoring the perspectives and agency of disabled people. For decades, a central tenet of disability activism has been the concept of *nothing about us, without us* (Charlton, 1998). This approach calls for decisions that impact the lives of disabled people to be made by people with disabilities. Certainly, decision making can include non-disabled allies. But, action should only be taken in conjunction *with* disabled people whose lived realities, perspectives, and wishes should guide decision making. Yolanda noted how students with disabilities, specifically students on the Autism Spectrum, can be targets of bullying in school. Yolanda suggests interventions by professionals and family members can be misguided if the advocacy does not include or respect disabled student input. Even worse, educators can put the onus to stop bullying on the victims instead of holding perpetrators accountable. Yolonda shared,

> A lot of parents tend to go in, and most of the professionals even are going in with an idea of, "We're going to teach this social skill of how the neuro-typical people do social things, and this is going to solve some problem." And then it turns out to not solve the problem. Problem: autistic students tend to get bullied. Attempted solution: teach autistic children social skills. That doesn't actually work. It really, really doesn't even a little bit. Other attempted solution: teach the typical kids not to suck actually does work. Teach the bullies to stop sucking.

Yolanda urges educators to take a stance to disrupt bullying by focusing on perpetrators, not by trying to fix or blame disabled youth. Advice, like this, reinforces how important it is for non-disabled people to listen to the perspectives and solutions offered by disabled people and to advocate *with* them.

Advice for Students with Disabilities

During the interviews, we asked participants what advice they would offer their younger selves. Their responses included not only specific advice they'd give themselves, but also more general advice for disabled youth. Participants hope that disabled youth will stand up for their needs, self-advocate, ask for support, embrace their disability, and actively reject discouragement. Participants also ruminated on the wisdom gained by overcoming hurdles. We've organized their advice into five sections that capture their collective advice to disabled youth: (1) Self-advocate; (2) Connect; (3) Push back; (4) Believe in yourself; and (5) Persist.

Self-Advocate—It's Okay to Ask for Help

Our participants urged students with disabilities to advocate for themselves. Crucial elements of self-advocacy include knowing oneself and being able to articulate one's specific needs. These aspects of self-advocacy are especially important for college students (Daly-Cano et al., 2015), and they appeared throughout participant advice. For example, Alice suggested, "you've really got to know yourself." Poppy also explained how being "open about [one's] disability and needs" is crucial in the transition from high school to college. She continued,

> Tell them about your disability. Be open and honest about what it means, how that affects you, and what you need from them. Be as explicit as

possible because if people don't get it, they won't think about it any harder than they have to. Many times people might resist you at first. Say it anyway. Then, after a while, you can tell that they benefited from you saying something.

Tippi also emphasized how being persistent when self-advocating is critical. She advises people to:

Do it. Because when I was younger I never did for some reason. For some reason, I was so afraid of it. Now that I'm older, I'm up in people's faces. I'm like, "Hi, you're going to help me because I need help." You realize how important it is the more you do it and how easy it is to get things to go your way if you just do it. People can't read your mind. If you need help, they don't know until you tell them. Definitely self-advocate.

Most of our participants wished they had told their younger selves (and other youth with disabilities) how important it is to ask for help. Kalani shared, "Don't hesitate to ask for help. Don't wait until it's too late. Know that there is help; that there are resources and people out there to help you. Don't wait until you're almost failing a class to find out." Alice also advised, "It's okay to ask for help. People shouldn't settle. Just because you advocate, it doesn't mean that you're not grateful."

Willow echoed the advice and resisted the stigma sometimes attached to help seeking. She urged students to adopt the attitude that "there's no shame in asking for help or saying that you can't quite do something, because you can. You just need help to do it." Kalani further stressed that, "It's okay to show weakness. It doesn't make *you* weak to show weakness."

Self-advocacy is critical to student success. In many of the stories, you read about participants being denied accommodations they were entitled to. For instance, educators and employers disregarded accommodations that Willa was legally due. In response, she had to self-advocate to get her needs met. Willa's advice for other disabled youth:

Know your rights. It is the teacher's responsibility to get you what you need. Just keep talking and someone will listen. If you don't get an answer, go to the top. Even if people don't respond well to you at the top, they still have to do it because it's the law. Whether it's school, or whether it's your employer, you will always have some sort of assistance. Don't take no for an answer. Make sure you document everything. It will serve you well.

Collectively, our participants encouraged disabled people to self advocate by asking for (and sometimes even demanding) the resources and support they needed to thrive.

Connect—Find Your Community

When considering advice to other disabled people, several participants focused on the importance of connection and community. They advised disabled people to surround themselves with friends, allies, and support systems. In reflecting back on his time in college, Titus wished he would have advocated for an affinity group that brought together disabled students. He remarked that he should have, "mentioned it to disability services ... about some kind of meeting" for disabled students. He thought a student club could foster a sense of connection by providing a space where students might collectively realize, "Hey, we've all got the same kind of thing going on!" Although Titus never suggested his university create a student organization for disabled students, many campuses do offer clubs or affinity spaces where disabled students can meet, connect, and organize. And, in some of the stories, you read about students who made important connections in disability activist communities.

Disability affirming spaces are one type of space where people can find connection. Our participants also found a sense of community in various other places. As such, they advise readers to find the people and places where they are accepted and affirmed for their authentic selves. For example, Willow recommended finding an instant community by living in a college residence hall designed for specific majors.

> It helps *so* much with studying. The first year in college is hard for everyone. If you have other people who are going through the exact same thing as you, no matter if they have the same disability or not, they're going to be able to help you, which I think was great.

Many of our participants hoped to find a connection with their college roommate. As you read in the stories, collegiate roommate relationships varied widely among participants. Tippi offered the following advice for living with roommates during college:

> Compromise is part of living with someone else. If they're making you feel like you can't do anything right, just be honest with yourself. Just do you. Remember they're your roommate, they don't need to be your best friend. Just be kind to yourself.

Along the same vein, many participants recommended finding a community with people who know and appreciate the authentic you. Kalani explained that when you find "people who understand what you're going through, you're going to go a lot farther." She also stressed the importance of reciprocity in relationships, and specifically being a supportive friend. Kalani shared,

When they're having a bad day, help them because they're going to help you when you have a bad day. Those are going to be the people that help make or break you … You're going to be a lot more successful in everything you do if you have a support system.

The advice about developing authentic relationships also extended into finding a partner. As adults, our participants understood that finding and fostering meaningful and mutually reciprocal relationships was directly related to one's sense of self. For instance, Tippi shared the following insight and advice.

Now, I'm finding myself and realizing that I want to be with someone who wants to be with me. I'm not going to change myself for someone … You're not going to be happy in a relationship if you're not happy by yourself. Relationships don't mean happiness. Relationships means having someone to share your experiences with.

Above all, the advice from participants was to find authentic connections, mutually supportive relationships, and a sense of community. And, to those who are struggling to find those kinds of connections, Kennedy also hopes that disabled people will, "Try not to worry about where you fit in. You'll find it … don't give up."

Push Back—Don't Listen to 'Em

Too often, our participants received discouraging and ableist messages. Their stories illustrated numerous ways educators, family members, medical providers, and significant others discouraged decisions and/or pathways *because* of their disability. In this section, participants offer the advice to "push back" against deniers and naysayers.

Titus shared how educators often "tell you that you are wrong and that you have to learn to do it a different way." His advice to disabled students: "Don't listen to 'em. Do it your way. Figure out your way." He further explained that "if you have that feeling deep down inside you, listen to it, and use those things as gifts. Cuz that's what they are [gifts]. Just nurture it, use it, and push yourself through it (the discouragement)." This advice highlights the power of pushing back against negative messaging while also harnessing positive self-talk to persist. Titus' advice builds upon his story where he reframes his disability as a gift. Here, he suggests that all disabled people should be proud of, and nurture, their gifts.

Kalani had specific educators who came to mind when she reflected on advice to disabled students.

I've had teachers and professors say, "You know, maybe you should look into a different career path, you're not going to be a nurse." I was able to take that and work even harder to prove to them how badly I wanted it. I do belong here!

Like Kalani, many participants experienced educators who discouraged them from particular majors or career paths. This discouragement often stemmed from assumptions and deficit notions about disabled people. But, as you also read in the stories, many of these educators were proved wrong by participants, like Kalani, who followed their dreams and succeeded.

Yolanda learned to more covertly push back against well intentioned professionals who offered poor advice. Yolanda's advice to autistic students who get bad advice from neurotypical people was as follows:

Master the art of smiling, nodding and doing whatever the heck you want … because people are going to have some truly terrible advice. Most of the things that are evidence-based for autism are evidence-based for reaching goals that you might not share. It's the goals they think you *should* have, which is not necessarily the same as the goals you *do* have. Decide accordingly.

Yolanda's advice was to push back by setting one's own goals, following them, and ignoring bad advice.

Willa's advice to push back related to her challenges receiving disability accommodations. She needed specific technologies to make class materials accessible to her through braille and text to speech software. Yet, she encountered instances where educators denied her access requests. Her advice,

Don't stop when you hear the word NO. Keep going until you find somebody that'll tell you YES. You have to know how to find the grants and services that'll provide you with the technology that you need. There is a way. There are people out there that are willing to help you find that way.

Willa also recalled a time in elementary school where she had to push back at an educator who was not providing accommodations. Even at age 10, she was confident conveying her lived experiences and educational needs. Her advice to disabled youth stems from that experience.

You are the expert of what you need to be successful and to get the job done. It feels so taboo to stick up for yourself when you're so young. You have all these people in the room that are supposed to be sticking up for you. Make sure you tell people what you need. People don't know unless you tell them. It's okay to speak against people. At the end of the day, you're taught that you could rely on so many other people, but you really need to set yourself up to rely on yourself. You can trust yourself. Keep doing what you're doing because … it's the right thing to do.

Tippi also remembered a time when college advisors discouraged her career choice. Instead of deterring her, it sparked a commitment to making her dreams come true. Tippi recalled the story and offers this advice to others:

> I'm kind of grateful that they told me, "I'll never work with animals" because it made me prove myself. That kind of lit that fire to be like, "No this is what I'm going to do no matter what. I will not let myself fail at this." Don't let it get you down. Don't knock your confidence. Don't be afraid to fail. It's okay to fail.

Tippi's advice reminds us that part of growing includes learning from failure. As you recall from Tippi's story, today she has a successful career working with animals. Had she not pushed back, and experienced some failures along her journey, she may not be where she is today.

Believe in Yourself—Embrace Your Disability

Our participants want disabled readers to believe in themselves and to embrace their disability. They collectively want disabled people to believe that you can succeed. Willa's advice is to, "accept and embrace your disability. Work with it. Make it part of you." Willow advises young people to identify their passions, work toward things that bring them joy, and not be deterred.

> Find something that you love and something that you know you can do. Definitely find something that you can put your best skills towards, instead of always worrying about your disability. I liked what I was doing at my first college. But I always had the question in my mind, "Can I do it?" Obviously, anyone can do anything ... and you're going to make mistakes! But, if you're constantly questioning yourself, it's not going to be any fun.

Like advice provided by others, Willow explains how everyone makes mistakes. Yet, believing in yourself fosters success. Moreover, self-confidence can also help an individual have fun along the way!

Many of our participants talked about the long road to believing in themselves. Some specifically recalled how harmful self-doubt was to their younger selves. Mercedes explained,

> There's moments when I was younger that I never thought I'd be successful. I never thought that I would grow up and have a good job and things like that. So it's definitely difficult, but I think that not beating yourself up when you're a kid is really important. Enjoy the fun parts of being a kid, rather than focusing on the stressful things.

Mercedes wishes that she would have been easier on herself as a child. In offering this advice, she also hopes that disabled readers will stop beating themselves up with self-doubt. Collectively, our participants hope readers will embrace their disability and believe in themselves—despite what others might think, say, or do.

Persist—It Gets Better and Your Future Self Will Thank You

The last piece of advice for disabled people is to persist, even when things are challenging. As we've noted throughout the book, ableism is pervasive and impacts every aspect of a disabled person's life. And, as you'll see in this section, participants offered advice about not merely surviving prejudice and discrimination, but thriving and finding joy.

Participants shared how persistence ultimately helped them get where they are today. Kalani explained, "You gotta keep fighting after those lowest days." Willa similarly advised, "It gets better. The struggles you feel and face now will build you to be the person that you need to be for the experiences that you're going to have."

Tippi reflected on past challenges and how she persevered. Based on her experience, she advises disabled youth to focus on their strengths instead of discouraging messages from others.

> Don't let people tell you that you can't do stuff because you can. It's almost an advantage [to have ADHD] because it makes you think differently. You work more hands-on. Just don't listen to people because they don't always know what they're talking about. It does get better. I promise.

Tippi's advice reminds us that everyone hits rough patches in life. But, with perseverance, it can get better. Alice agreed. She offered this advice to college students with disabilities.

> Hold on because it's such a crazy ride. Know that it gets better. It's harder to hear that when you're in really dark places, but it really does. Part of what makes college difficult is when you're in a mainstream setting. You just live life a little differently. That makes it a little difficult. Just remember that you deserve to be here in school, like everybody else. It's wild. Able bodied kids are figuring out who they are, where they fit in, and so are you! But it's harder for you. Work hard. There's always something better [out there for you, even] when it feels like there's no opportunity.

Alice offered this advice in hopes of inspiring college students to persist, even during tough times and even when it means doing things differently. Her advice, like others in this section, ends on a hopeful note that there is always something better out there. Indeed, a number of participants explained how perseverance through struggle ultimately leads to long term growth and success.

Kalani explained, "We're all going to struggle. You're going to keep struggling no matter what. But, you just gotta keep fighting. As annoying as it can be at times, it's the best thing in the world." Kalani believed that struggle promotes growth, and thus, can end up being the best thing in the world! Willow also advises young people to see the big picture and to have hope for the future. She explained,

> Learning new ways to learn is going to help you flourish in the future. Don't feel packed down from what's happening to you now. Have fun. Don't worry so much. Be patient with yourself.

We conclude this section with Willow's advice because it is a good reminder that despite very real disability-related barriers, individuals can grow, flourish, and maybe even have some fun on their journey. Importantly, our participants hope that disabled people—especially those in rough patches—also hear their message that it does get better.

Advice to Families/Caregivers

Participants had some advice for families and caregivers about supporting disabled people in their lives. In addition to the explicit advice, we also drew some quotations directly from interview transcripts when the story was recounted in hopes of offering a lesson to families. Although not worded specifically as advice, we included some of those story excerpts here because they contain important guidance to families. The advice to families is categorized into three topics: (1) Love us unconditionally; (2) Empathetically listen to us; and (3) Advocate for, and stand with us.

Love Us Unconditionally

Overwhelmingly, our participants appreciated (or in some cases wished for) unconditional love from family members. In their opinion, unconditional love includes valuing *every* aspect of a person's body, mind, and soul—including their disability. Several participants shared painful memories of feeling like their parents wanted to change them to fit into societal ideals of normalcy. In those cases, the message that they received was that we love you—but we don't like, or fully accept, this disabled part of you. Such messages were painful and had long-lasting effects. Titus remembers feeling like his parents were embarrassed by his quirkiness as a child. One memory when he was six years old particularly stood out to him. Titus shared,

> I've always been into woodworking and making things with my hands. I made a tomahawk from a pair of garden shears and a stick after I watched the movie *Dances with Wolves*. When I showed my parents, they lost their

minds–started treating me like something was wrong with me and put me in therapy. I immediately shut down and started to not trust any adult in my life. I was the quirky kid who hid my true self, because the adults in my life didn't know how to support me. I often think about what my life would be like if, instead of shunning my quirks, they embraced them.

As Titus was recalling this incident, it was clear how proud he was of his youthful creativity and how hurtful his parent's response was. Embedded in this memory is Titus' desire to have his parents embrace, appreciate, and love every aspect of himself—including what he referred to as his disability-related quirks. Justice shared a similar story of feeling rejected and alone with trying to get their mother to listen to their needs. Justice recalled,

My mom was in deep denial about my disabilities when I was growing up. Any time a healthcare professional suggested there may be anything wrong with me, my mom would refuse to take me back to them. If I expressed concerns about my own health, especially my mental health, she would usually respond with an angry lecture about how I was imagining things. As a result, many health problems that began in middle school went undiagnosed and untreated until well into my 20s.

Angry lectures from parents related to an undiagnosed disability certainly do not evoke feelings of unconditional love and support. In Yolanda's story, we also heard about parents who refused to consider that their child might be autistic. In response, they, and many others, pushed Yolanda to think, act, and be neurotypical. As such, Yolanda urges families to understand that "Normalcy isn't the goal; ability to do things (possibly with help) is a goal." Unfortunately, instead of unconditional love and support in working toward achievable goals, Yolanda received familial encouragement to be someone they were not. By contrast, many of the stories illustrated the deep and unconditional love and support that families provided to our participants. For instance, Peter's parents were a beacon of support. As we were finalizing this book, he said to us, "if it's possible I think it's important to mention the parental support I received. Especially since parents of disabled kids will read this book." Resoundingly, participants wish for families to provide unconditional love and support to the disabled people in their lives.

Empathetically Listen to Us

Our participants shared how important it is for family members to listen to a person with a disability. Some felt listened to, while others felt ignored by family. Justice shared their frustration with not being listened to by relatives. They stated, "ignoring my disabilities won't make them go away; it will just make them worse." Based upon these experiences, Justice advises families to:

Trust that they are the ultimate authority on what they're experiencing and what they need. Don't withhold help when they ask for it, and (unless it's an urgent matter of safety) don't force help on them when they say they don't want it.

Titus also reflected on how important it is for families to not only listen, but to also *hear* and respond with empathy. Titus shared, "Above all else, listen to your kid's true voice about how they feel. And, be empathetic. Be the person that they go to even if you don't have answers." All of these pieces of advice reinforce how important it is for family members to deeply listen to, and empathize with, youth so they can grow.

Advocate for and Stand with Us

In all of the stories, you witnessed journeys of young people coming of age and becoming autonomous adults. In those stories, self-advocacy was a recurring theme as young people moved through college and into the workforce. As noted in many places in this book, participants appreciated learning how to stand up for themselves. Yet, when offering advice to families of young children who often cannot advocate for themselves (or are ignored when they try to do so), our participants advise adults to offer support and advocacy. Some participants in our study even shared that they wished their family would have advocated more for their needs in home, school, healthcare, and other settings. Justice spoke directly to their family when stating, "My advice to my family would be: get me the physical and mental health support I need." Kennedy reflected on the challenges he faced trying to self-advocate. While he preferred to figure out challenges for himself, he feels that he "would have been better off to have been given more suggestions or guidance along the way."

Yolanda and Titus urged families to adopt an attitude of inclusion with navigating spaces for their disabled child. To parents, Yolanda implores, "Don't ask *if* your kid can be included in an activity. Act like you know that *OF COURSE* they will be. And, if necessary, ask about *how*." Similarly, Titus suggested that families "learn about the support programs schools offer and find resources that can support your child. If none exist, then be innovative in helping your child be successful in an area where it may be difficult to adapt."

Alice urged families to advocate not only for their own child, but for all children with disabilities in their community. Her advice stems from seeing families struggle with systemic educational barriers. Alice explained that:

Advocacy is always worth it, no matter how overwhelming it can be. The person with a disability is human and should be treated as such. People often forget that. Do what you can to ensure this person is thriving and not just surviving. If you are in a terrible school system, make it better than you found it for the next person and their family.

Alice's advice points to the importance of fighting for disabled rights today and in the future.

Finally, a decade after our first conversation, Poppy shared a story about a recent trip with her sister. The story illustrates how being deaf in one ear impacts her as an adult. It also offers families insight into the ways support efforts can, and should, evolve over time.

> I got auditory sensory overload. When the noise became too much, I just left to sit in the bathroom at the back of the farthest room with the door shut, my hat over my eyes, and a finger in my good ear. Everything to minimize the sensory input. At some point, my sister came in and just sat with me on the bathroom floor. My disability hadn't changed, but my sister and I were better equipped to tackle the challenge. We sat in silence until I was ready to talk. And when I did, she knew what I needed to hear. When I reflected on this moment, I was grateful for the lifetime of moments of frustration. While [family support] initially seemed chaotic and unhelpful, they gradually created more and more space for something better. They led to that moment. And, in that moment, I felt so supported.

We end with this quote from Poppy to reinforce how important it is for families to make the effort to understand their disabled relatives. As she noted, familial efforts sometimes felt unhelpful. But, over her lifetime, and as her family continued to listen and understand her needs, Poppy's relatives began to intuitively know how to be helpful. We encourage families to continue to listen to disabled loved ones so that they, too, can act in ways that foster deep feelings of support.

Final Thoughts

In this chapter, disabled people offered their advice directly to readers. Scholars might call these pieces of advice radical acts (Kafai, 2021). And, in many ways the advice is radical, in that it invites us to center the wishes, hopes, and needs of disabled people in a world where their bodies, minds, and identities are viewed as outside the norm. And, in other ways, the advice is not very radical at all. Our participants wish to be seen, heard, believed, supported, and loved. Aren't these things all humans deserve and need to thrive? We hope you will reflect upon the advice and respond to disabled people in your life with these wisdoms in mind. The advice, shared by our participants, echo what we as scholars, educators, and activists believe. Disabled people are the experts of their own bodies, minds, and hearts. It is important to really listen to, and support, their requests, hopes, and dreams.

As you read this chapter, you may have recognized how participants advised readers to provide disabled people various levels and types of support. As such, we hope you will ruminate on the complexity of support. Not all participants asked for the same type of support. Moreover, the suggestions offered here reveal how the type and delivery of support might (and should) evolve over time. This chapter contained many requests for support and advocacy from teachers and family members. As participants reflected back to their childhood, they wished that adults in their lives would have stood up to bullies and advocated on their behalf. But, there were also requests for self-determination and support as they advocated for themselves. As our participants moved into adolescence and adulthood, they wished for more independence and autonomy in decision making—and support in doing so. As we learned from Poppy's last quote, when non-disabled people really listen, they can begin to intuitively know when, and how, to offer meaningful support.

Much of the advice urged disabled people to find connection and community—but not just any connection or community. Participants advised disabled peers to surround themselves with people who hear them, see them, know them, *and* who love them unconditionally. Relationships are important, but authentic, mutually beneficial, and empathetic relationships are the real key to happiness at home, work, school, and in community.

The advice was filled with positive messaging to disabled people about loving yourself and believing in your ability to accomplish your goals. A repeating suggestion was to find the strength to persevere despite prejudice and discrimination. As educators and scholars we feel obligated to add a note of caution here. Most of the advice does not specifically call upon readers to address the systematic, institutionalized, and societal barriers that disabled people face in schools, workplaces, healthcare settings, and society in general. There is a real danger in suggesting that supporting disabled people in resisting oppression is the ultimate goal. That puts the responsibility and burden on marginalized people to make the best of a broken system that does not work for them. That is not, and should never be, the ultimate goal. Changing the system should be the goal. That said, this book was designed to focus on individual stories—stories of people who navigate systemic barriers and challenges every day. And, it is their experiences, hopes, and advice that we've promised to hold front and center. We hope that readers will be inspired to act in ways that support disabled people individually *and* also in ways that change systems, policies, and environments to be more inclusive.

As noted throughout the stories and this advice chapter, navigating institutionalized and ableist systems can be exhausting. Ableism can feel insurmountable. Yet, as the advice in this chapter suggests, individual people *can* make a difference within their spheres of influence. Indeed, the advice emphasizes how disabled people, and their allies, can make a positive impact in the ways in which disabled people experience the world. Whether you are an educator, family member, supervisor, disabled person (or all of the above!), we hope that the advice in this chapter resonated with you. Creating a world where disabled people experience equity and inclusion requires action from all of us. We invite you to keep this advice in mind as you move into the conclusion where we call upon readers to take action to foster family, school, workplace, healthcare, and community environments where disabled people can thrive.

Reflection Questions

1 *Educator expectations.* Participants shared how they experienced varying degrees of educator support and discouragement as they navigated their PreK-college journeys. How can educators ensure that students with disabilities are supported in ways that foster their unique talents?

2 *Advocating for better.* Much of the advice shared in this chapter asks for family members, educators, and allies to stand alongside disabled people. What can you do *with* disabled people to enact positive changes for individuals, communities, and systems? If you are a disabled person, what kinds of advocacy do you (or don't you) need to thrive?

3 *Relationships.* The experiences of many participants in our study illustrated how positive relationships had a significant impact on their lives. Where do you find authentic connections and a sense of community? Consider your relationships. How do they positively (or not so positively) impact your sense of self, outlook, success, and happiness?

4 *Teaching for all.* Universal Design for Learning (UDL) is a framework whereby educators use multiple and flexible strategies to teach and assess learning. What pieces of advice offered in this chapter align with the use of UDL? Have you ever had an educator who was able to reach all students in their classroom? What strategies did that teacher use to value the needs and strengths of all learners?

5 *Do the work.* Too often disabled people are unfairly burdened with having to educate others about their lived experience and to explain what oppression looks and feels like. Educating others can feel exploitative, traumatizing, and laborious. To non-disabled readers, how can you further understand the roles disability and ableism play in society without burdening disabled people to be your educator? If you are a disabled person, how do you make choices about whether (and how) to educate people about ableism, and disability, and your lived experiences?

19 Conclusion

The disability life stories shared in the prior pages illuminate vast differences in the experiences and perspectives of 14 disabled people. Even though there is no single disability story, there *are* common themes in the stories shared in this book. In the following pages, we synthesize these insights and lessons learned. For readability, we've organized the recurring concepts into four themes—each with their own section. They are: (1) Sense of self; (2) Relationships and interactions with others; (3) Success strategies, self-advocacy, and activism; and (4) Career trajectories and finding purpose.

As with the stories themselves, we hope the patterned themes resonate with you. We invite you to consider how recurring concepts, insights, and themes are applicable to your personal and professional life. How have the stories, shared out of generosity and hope, inspired you to act? We hope you have many ideas in response to this question. And, to evoke even more possibilities, we conclude the chapter with a series of questions in a section entitled "Gratitude and a Final Call to Action." Over the course of a decade, our participants took time to recount their powerful, joyful, and painful experiences—their extraordinary and ordinary stories—with us. Their stories inspired us to take action in our homes, classrooms, workplaces, and, most importantly, their experiences prompted us to compose this book. We hope that you will ruminate on the stories, insights, and takeaways and be inspired to enact positive change in your spheres of influence—whether that be a classroom, workplace, healthcare setting, community space, or home.

Insights and Lessons Learned

What insights can we glean, and what lessons can we learn, from the 14 disability life stories shared in this volume? As a team, we asked ourselves this question regularly. While preparing this book, we had many conversations about what these stories, individually and collectively, taught us. Moreover, we wondered how to best share them with you. Our team compiled a running list of insights and lessons learned. The list quickly became quite lengthy. We learned

DOI: 10.4324/9781003495703-19

so much from these participants! And, we hope you did too! Instead of offering an unwieldy list, we decided to synthesize our insights and takeaways into four themes—each with its own section in this chapter. Please note, however, that the boundaries of these four sections are constructed by us for readability. In real life, all of these topics intertwine and reflect complex lived experiences and lessons learned from our participants.

Before moving into our four categories of insights and lessons learned, it is important to keep some overarching ideas in mind. As we've noted throughout the book, all of these stories are context-dependent and shaped by the realities of the ableist world we inhabit. Moreover, the stories are incredibly powerful in that they illuminate how humans grow and change over time. While ruminating on insights and lessons learned, we invite you to remember Chapter 3 where we brought your attention to the significance of ableism, time, and context. As you continue to read this chapter, we ask you to reflect on the ways that context, time, and ableism appeared in the participant stories. You'll also see how these concepts influence the four recurring themes we describe below: (1) Sense of self; (2) Relationships and interactions with others; (3) Success strategies, self-advocacy and activism; and (4) Career trajectories and finding purpose.

Theme 1: Sense of Self

How our participants felt about their disability varied widely, which aligns with the array of definitions and models of disability. Chapter 2 described the ways that various conceptualizations of disability can influence how disabled people think about themselves, and how they are viewed and treated by others. In Chapter 2, we also provided a cursory overview of the expansive research on human development, highlighting the great changes that happen between childhood and adulthood. We hope that readers saw many of those research-informed concepts come to life in the participants' stories.

Through the stories, you witnessed vast differences in the ways our participants thought about disability and how that thinking informed their sense of self. A key takeaway from the collective stories is that there is much variation from person to person and within the same person over time. Some individuals believed ableist societal views and internalized deficit notions of disability. Others resisted negative views and cherished their disability as a positive aspect of their personhood. For some, disability was a central and overarching aspect of their sense of self, while it was far less important to others. Despite the range of experiences and outlooks, disability identity evolved and proved more or less salient within various contexts for everyone.

From these stories, we learned that one important influence on the trajectory of disability was a formal diagnosis. As noted in Chapter 2, educational accommodations, social services, medical resources, and legal protections for disabled people typically require a formal diagnosis rendered by a diagnostician. Among our participants, the process of being formally identified as a person with a diagnosed disability varied greatly. Moreover, obtaining a formal diagnosis is not necessarily sufficient. As was evidenced in the self-reported disabilities of our participants, many had co-occurring physical impairments or illnesses. These co-occurrences uniquely influenced the experiences and corresponding identity trajectories of our participants. For instance, many of our participants self-identified as having attention deficit hyperactivity disorder (ADHD). Although many described co-occurring issues, none were the same. As you read, the experiences and identity development of Kalani who also had anxiety, depression, and PTSD was quite different from Willow whose co-occurrences with ADHD were dyslexia and reading comprehension difficulties. In short, varied constellations of co-occurrences inform not only daily experience, but also identity development, in ways that were only cursorily illuminated in these stories.

The stories also highlighted significant differences in the age and process by which individuals were formally diagnosed. Some, like Landers, Tippi, and Juno talked about how their parents recognized something different about them early in life and actively sought a diagnosis and demanded legally-due services. Others, like Yolanda and Justice, encountered family denial or dismissal of potential disabilities—which led to much later formal diagnoses. Connected to this spectrum of early to late diagnoses is a corresponding developmental reality of having more or less time to experience life as a disabled person; in turn, participants had more or less time for that diagnosis to shape their sense of self. A person diagnosed as a young child has many formative years to experience life as a disabled person. Those years of experience can shape the ways young people develop their sense of self—likely in very different ways than a person not diagnosed until high school or college. Those who obtained later diagnoses had already begun to form their identity based upon lived experiences and labels (or lack thereof) accrued over their lifetime. Kennedy's story illustrates this poignantly and reminds us that any of us can become disabled at any point in our lifetime.

For some, a disability diagnosis was recalled as stigma-inducing time. It was an unwelcome label that made them feel different as a child. Yet, we also learned from others like Titus and Peter that a diagnosis helped explain thoughts, feelings, and behaviors that were previously misunderstood and mislabeled as bad behavior or lack of intelligence. Prior to his dyslexia diagnosis, Peter thought he was "dumb." It was a great relief to learn that he had a disability that could be named, "treated," and managed.

The stories in this book point to the ways that a disability can foster negative feelings about self. This should come as no surprise, especially given the social stigma attached to disability and the countless ways disabled people are mistreated by others. Such experiences have immense impacts on one's sense of self. Participants made meaning of their diagnoses and disability-related labels in a world not set up for disabled people. Correspondingly, all of our participants described feeling different and being treated differently, at some point in their life because of their disability. This mistreatment varied by context and magnitude. Some withstood bullying from peers during early schooling while others did not experience this kind of mistreatment. For others, the usage of educational accommodations evoked a sense of shame as they encountered peers, teachers, and a society who believed that those accommodations were somehow unfair advantages instead of efforts to provide equitable access to education and learning. Recall the story of Tippi who felt a constant source of shame during early schooling when an aide sat next to her in the classroom. Or, the countless college students who, at some point, attempted to go without disability services to avoid being viewed and treated differently by peers and faculty. This choice of college students forgoing services legally due to them is not unique to our participants. Literature suggests that many disabled youth try to unshackle themselves from disability stigma by trying to succeed in college without using accommodations that might help them succeed (e.g., Lightner et al., 2015; Mamboleo et al., 2020).

As young people traverse various home, school, work, healthcare, and community environments, sometimes their disability becomes more or less salient. And, as was evidenced in the stories, the ways people thought about disability, and integrated it into their sense of self, changed over time. For some, disability became less salient as they transitioned into and through college and then into the workforce. Some, like Juno, even explained how their disability was something that they thought about less often in their adult and professional lives. Or Landers, who feels that his disability does not affect his work now as much as it did when he was in college. Yet, both Juno and Landers recognize the value of self-disclosure and the importance of advocacy. Conversely, disability was at the core of the adult identity for others. For instance, Titus came to see his disability as not only a strength, but a gift or superpower that he applied in his job. For others, disability justice was such a core tenet of their identity that it shaped the ways they engaged in community service and activism.

The title of this book signals our specific focus on sharing disabled life stories. Yet, disability is only one of the many identities people find important over the lifespan. We learned how other social identities such as religion, social class, race, gender, and sexuality (among others) were central to the ways our participants saw themselves and how others treated them. For some, like Landers and Peter, religion served as a constant influence in guiding their worldview, sense of self, and life choices. In other stories, we saw evolving ideas about gender and sexual identity as participants moved from adolescence into adulthood. Race, ethnicity, and culture also shaped the ways participants understood themselves within a world where people of color are discriminated against regularly. As Yolanda noted, a non-verbal autistic person of color reaching in their pocket for a card to communicate with law enforcement officers could risk bodily harm if officers perceived that action as a move for a weapon. Given that over 60%

of incarcerated adults in the United States report having a disability, with Black and Latino inmates being overrepresented in this group, Yolanda's thoughts of harm are warranted (Bixby et al., 2022). These intersecting identities also shaped the ways our participants thought about parenting. The stories tell of parental choices that participants made to foster positive identity development in their children. Consider Juno's intentionality in choosing toys for her children that simultaneously resisted limiting gender norms while also showing positive representations of women of color. Although this book focuses on illuminating disability life stories, it is crucial to remember that life stories are rich and complicated because of the myriad of other identities each person finds important.

Theme 2: Relationships and Interactions with Others

People matter in shaping someone's experience. Earlier in the chapter, we reminded you of the importance of context when considering disability life stories. But, contexts are not merely physical and virtual spaces. Influential environments are shaped by a combination of people, policies, and norms. The disability life stories throughout this text are replete with tales of positive, and not-so-positive, interactions and relationships with peers, teachers, coworkers, supervisors, counselors, medical professionals, family members, and a host of others. You read of interactions and relationships that were affirming, encouraging, supportive, and transformative as well as those that were discouraging, unsupportive, and disempowering. All of the stories in this book illuminate the many ways that interactions and relationships with others shaped participant's sense of self, educational experiences, career trajectories, and decisions about current and future relationships.

At different ages, different people become significant in a person's life. Across the stories, we learned of important relationships with peers, teachers, advisors, disability services providers, coworkers, supervisors, mentors, partners, and children. Because we had the opportunity to follow participants over a decade, we got to hear how interactions and relationships with different people made an impact on their lives at various points in time. Childhood bullies were left behind as individuals transitioned into college where they interacted with new peers—some supportive and some not. And, these relationships, while very important during the college years, often became just a memory as our participants transitioned into new relationships with work colleagues, developed romantic relationships, and planned for their futures.

Throughout the stories, we learned how family members provided a range of support and encouragement. Primary caregivers were instrumental early in life. In addition to parents who played an integral role in obtaining a diagnosis, family members were also critical in setting the tone for children in regard to what having a disability meant. Many of our participants described the ways that parents and other family members offered unconditional support and positive framing of disability. These caregivers anticipated needs, removed obstacles, and offered unwavering support. They sent the message to participants that they could accomplish anything if they set their minds to it. Even if familial support efforts were not always experienced as intended, many participants appreciated the effort. Recall Kennedy giving his father "an A+ for effort." Other family members were less supportive. Some were in denial about their child's disability. Others focused on limitations instead of the talents and gifts of our participants. Unfortunately, some of the young people were discouraged from following certain paths by significant others, including family members and teachers. These young people got the message that they could not accomplish certain things and many ultimately made important life decisions based on these discouraging interactions.

From these stories, we also learned how family relationships can change over time, both as the person and the family members grow and develop. As relationships evolved, the way our participants thought about relationships did too. Take for instance Titus, who at different times in his life, had varying types of relationships with his parents. As a young person, Titus described a "strained relationship" with his father. However, by the end of his story, Titus had developed a strong relationship with his dad and was hoping that his unborn child would too. In other cases, participants reflected on the ways that childhood, and early adulthood interactions and relationships, informed the ways they approached parenting. For example, Kalani's negative interpersonal interactions shaped her desire to raise her son to "be a respectful human ... who respects himself and others."

Almost all our participants described instances of being judged by others. Judgments by peers and teachers about their disability, and assumed capabilities, deeply influenced how our participants thought about themselves. External ableist messaging for young people can be internalized and, as noted in the prior section, can impact one's sense of self. Here, we focus on the ways that negative perceptions and interactions with significant others also shape the expectations that young people have of their current and future relationships. Many of our participants recounted childhood stories of being bullied or looked down upon for having accommodations in elementary and high school. Sometimes those experiences led participants to try to succeed in college and workplaces without legally due accommodations—often to avoid disability stigma and judgments from peers, teachers, coworkers, and supervisors. Of course, some of our participants did make use of college or workplace accommodations, and many felt judged by peers and faculty members for doing so. Recall Mercedes who explained the self-consciousness she felt when peers expressed how unfair it was that she got extra time for assignments or could take a test in another setting. Or, Kalani who felt judged, and was left out of social events by college peers. Despite this exclusion, she did find connection and camaraderie in another disabled classmate who received similar extended test time accommodations. In essence, negative childhood and collegiate interactions and relationships often informed the ways in which disabled people approached new interactions and relationships. The next time you hear someone downplaying the significance of a dismissive comment by a teacher or name-calling by a classmate, we hope you'll remember the ways these interactions can have lasting impacts on a person's sense of self and the ways they approach relationships and important life choices in the future.

As participants grew, they also began to reflect differently on everyday interactions with others, especially the negative ones. When they developed confidence in themselves and their capabilities, participants simultaneously began to resist negative and ableist projections from others. Take for instance, Tippi who shared, "My confidence was very low going into college. Once I got there, I was like, 'Oh, I am able.' I felt a lot more confident doing it because nobody was telling me I couldn't." With time, experience, and success, our participants developed into autonomous adults who, of course, cared about interactions with, and perceptions of, others, but, they no longer let those interactions define them. Willow expressed this sentiment beautifully, when she said, "As you get older you start to care less, in my experience, about how you're perceived by people."

We must point out that not all interactions were negative or bad. Our participants also encountered individuals—family members, friends, teachers, mentors, supervisors, partners—who inspired them. In many of the stories, we learned about someone who took the time to really get to know a young person. Instead of focusing on the "dis" in disability and making assumptions about what they could not do, these significant others believed in, encouraged, and supported the talents of our participants. These supportive individuals rejected ableist norms and typical ways of doing and being. Instead, they focused on possibility. For Titus, support came from a teacher who recognized his talents for writing poetry and a supervisor who valued his interpersonal and leadership skills and promoted him to team leader. For Peter, it came in the form of encouragement to apply for a campus chaplain position that he would have never otherwise considered—and ultimately found to be a perfect match personally and professionally. Unconditional acceptance, understanding, and support also came from the individuals who they chose as life partners. Many of our participants found spouses and significant others who loved them for the ordinary and extraordinary people they were.

As we conclude this section, we hope that readers will not be overwhelmed by the ways significant others can shape a disabled person's experience only in negative ways. Certainly, our participants encountered their share of naysayers, bullies, and unsupportive people. Yet, the stories also included at least one person who made a positive difference. Whether it was a supportive parent, inspirational aunt, creative teacher, open-minded supervisor, or partner, we hope that readers takeaway the message that one supportive person *can* make a big difference. And, we hope that one person can be you.

Theme 3: Success Strategies, Self-Advocacy, and Activism

The pages of this book are replete with stories about obstacles in the pathways to success for disabled people. Participants encountered exclusion from peers, inaccessible learning spaces, discouragement from educators, and various hurdles in obtaining and maintaining jobs. Yet, we *also* heard about numerous strategies that participants used to orient themselves—*and to succeed*—in a world not designed for disabled people. We encourage readers to revisit the stories, paying attention to the explicit, and more subtle ways, that participants developed and enacted a sense of agency in their home, school, and work settings. In this section, we synthesize a few of the recurring strategies participants used to navigate challenges, by developing unique success strategies, advocating for themselves, and engaging in activism.

Strategies for Success

Across the stories, we learned about a variety of strategies that disabled people used to manage their disability and succeed in different settings. Over time, participants developed and honed a plethora of tactics to successfully navigate environmental and interpersonal hurdles in schools, workplaces, and at home. These life hacks were sometimes learned from others, or by trial and error. But, most often, they were strategies our participants developed as they learned their strengths and weaknesses and developed a personalized toolkit of tactics that they could draw upon to succeed in various settings. We even witnessed some of these strategies during our interviews. For example, Titus knew he needed something to focus on in order to sit through an hour-long interview for our study. So, he brought a stress ball to the first interview to get out excess energy by fidgeting while we talked. And, during the third interview, he was walking on an under-desk treadmill—a strategy he uses to successfully focus during Zoom calls for work. Like Titus, our participants all developed personalized strategies to achieve success in life.

One of the recurring phrases we heard from participants was feeling that they had to "prove" themselves. Sometimes this meant that they had to work harder or differently to achieve similar successes as non-disabled peers. In other cases, participants felt they had to prove people's deficit-based assumptions wrong. For instance, Alice shared, "You have to prove that you can do things." Kalani even felt like she had "to doubly prove" herself because of the assumptions others made about her capabilities. Most participants talked about experiences where family, teachers, peers, coworkers, supervisors, and others doubted their capabilities. Doubt, whether overtly communicated, or subtly felt by participants, prompted them to work harder to prove that they were able to accomplish a task, degree, or job. Such efforts were exhausting, and often required extra mental and physical effort—actions that our participants knew their non-disabled peers did not have to expend.

One of the strategies that many participants used was humor—sometimes to make light of difficult situations, or to put others at ease. Some used humor because that was a core aspect of their personality. We certainly found ourselves laughing with participants during many of the interviews as they told jokes, used sarcasm, and described enjoyable situations. As they shared the gift of their stories, we witnessed expressions of joy and laughter in their experience. For some, disabled joy included finding connection and belongingness with others through humor and inside jokes. Author Teresa Milbrodt (2018) wrote about how disabled people use humor and storytelling to express independence, agency, and to position themselves in the world on their own terms. We certainly saw humor as an expression of empowerment in some of the stories. We also saw humor as a coping mechanism to deal with prejudice and discrimination. For some, it might have even been a protective factor to avoid violence in various forms. No matter what prompted the humor, it was a recurring theme worth mentioning here. Yet, we struggled with how to convey this repeating theme in this conclusion. Why? Because humor can be used as a tool of hate and exclusion—for example when someone laughs *at*, not *with*, disabled people. As such, we would be remiss if we did not acknowledge the oppressive history of using disabled people *for* entertainment. As Longmore (2015) and McDonagh (2008) have detailed, there is a long history of treating disabled people as spectacles to be laughed at in carnivals and sideshows. Therefore, we invite readers to consider humor as both a tool of oppression as well as one of empowerment.

Self-Advocacy

As seen throughout the stories, parental and familial advocacy was often essential for participants' success early in life. However, as we've noted in other publications (Daly-Cano et al., 2024), as young people grow, it is vital to foster self-advocacy skills so that disabled people can ask for (and sometimes demand) programs, services, and adapted environments they need to succeed (Daly-Cano et al., 2024). We saw this preparation in many of the stories—sometimes with explicit mentoring from relatives, teachers, or healthcare providers. And, in other cases, young people learned to self-advocate by simply watching others, or learning by trial and error. The self-advocacy strategies used by participants varied by context. Some participants felt very confident advocating for their rights in some spaces and not confident in others. At times, relationships influenced how likely a person was to advocate for themself. Were they interacting with a trusted friend, beloved teacher, or supportive supervisor? Or were they dealing with a bully, dismissive professor, or supervisor who might discipline them for standing up for their rights? Poppy, who was deaf in her right ear, explained how differently she might respond to someone talking on her right side: "If I'm not comfortable, I try to do a weird little half-step and go to the right, like square dancing." But, if she was comfortable, she'd either ask them to move or if she was *really* comfortable, she might "just grab the person's arm and yank them." This single example illustrates how disabled people advocate for their needs in radically different ways depending on the context.

Self-advocacy skills were particularly important in arguing for changes to inequitable or inaccessible educational systems (Kimball et al., 2016) as well as in pushing back against bullying or stigmatizing behavior (Vaccaro et al., 2024). In the stories, it was also apparent that self-advocacy strategies evolved over time and across different contexts. For example, in middle school, Willa advocated for herself when her school suddenly told her she would lose access to a notetaker. Channeling her self-confidence, she told the principal and teachers, "You're going to have to find a way to do it." Then, in college, she took a proactive approach to self-advocacy by meeting all her professors before each semester to introduce herself, disclose her disability, and describe her specific learning needs.

Another prominent theme related to self-advocacy was the decision to utilize collegiate disability services. As we noted in Chapter 2, the legal context shifts once students move from secondary school into college. In post-secondary education, individuals must formally request services and provide documentation to show that they have a disability. Colleges and universities are not legally required to provide services to students who they believe have inadequate documentation or do not request services. Studies show that disabled students without accommodations achieve lower grades and persist at much lower rates than would be predicted based on the strength of their earlier academic records (Mamboleo et al., 2020). Stories in this book reflected a great diversity in usage of, and satisfaction with, college disability services and accommodations. Some students like Poppy, tried to succeed without disability accommodation when they started college. The reluctance to disclose their disability and request services was sometimes rooted in the desire for a fresh start in an educational setting without the shroud of disability stigma following them from high school. Kalani did not use disability services during her initial transition to campus because she did not know the office existed and was available to her. Luckily, she eventually got connected with disability resources. Interestingly, both stories reveal a desire to have reached out to disability services programs sooner and even speculate the possibility that doing so would have led to more successful outcomes during their college years. Still others like Willa and Mercedes, actually selected their college based on the availability and reputation of campus disability services. Throughout the stories, we heard about wide variations in student experiences with campus disability service providers. Those who requested accommodations, and received support from campus disability services, reported mixed experiences—from marginally useful to incredibly helpful.

In the workplace, some participants disclosed their disabilities while others did not. The choice to not disclose a disability was either because they feared the repercussions or felt like they could succeed by using their toolkit of strategies described earlier. Poppy was someone who shared her needs in the workplace, saying, "I try to let my employers and co-workers know as soon as my needs come to my mind." Others had less success when it came to advocating for themselves in work settings. For instance, Justice was good about disclosing their disability and requesting accommodations, but their requests were sometimes met with resistance or outright rejection. In one role, Justice had a supervisor tell them to "pretend to not be disabled because being visibly disabled was bad publicity."

We even experienced participant self-advocacy strategies during the research process. For instance, Yolanda made two requests to make sure the interview space would be accessible and comfortable. To reduce unnecessary stimulation, Yolanda asked that the fluorescent lights be turned off. They also sat on the floor instead of the chair reserved for interviewees because it was more comfortable. Other participants requested Zoom interviews (even before virtual meetings became popular). Although these self-advocacy skills did not appear in the printed stories, they speak to the myriad of ways that participants advocated for themselves every day.

Activism

In the stories, you read about many forms and expressions of activism. As we noted in the introduction, even the act of telling one's story can be a form of activism. Some participants referred to themselves as activists and advocates, while others did not use those terms. Willa specifically described herself as "a huge disabilities advocate." Her activism came in many forms, including serving on the board of directors for numerous state and national disability organizations. Alice engaged in activism through multiple educational, community, and political organizations. We have no doubt that our participants, who were active in local, state, and national organizations as young people, will continue to serve as activists and advocates throughout their lives.

Even those who did not proclaim an activist identity participated in educational strategies to increase disability awareness. Some engaged in school organizations focused on justice. For instance, Willa was the president of the disability club on her campus. Even as early as high school, Peter participated in a group that traveled to local colleges to run dyslexia simulations so that people could experience what it might be like to learn with dyslexia. Yolanda wrote a blog and published academic papers to spread autism awareness. Others promoted disability awareness by sharing their stories more informally. Recall how Landers gladly agreed to share his story with other teachers in his school. By sharing his personal journey, he hoped to raise awareness and ideally equip teachers to more effectively support children in their classrooms. In sum, participant stories were replete with instances where they educated others about disability topics in hopes of raising awareness and fostering inclusion.

We would be remiss if we only focused on the ways that our participants served as disability activists. Most understood that ableism was one of the many ways people were excluded and harmed. As such, they expressed the need to raise awareness about inclusion more broadly. Sometimes, this activism was sparked by personal experiences with other forms of discrimination. For instance, many women—like Poppy and Tippi—experienced gender discrimination in school, community, and/or job settings. These experiences fueled their desire to fight for women's rights. In fact, Poppy's story ends with a quote that captures a broader activist stance. She explained, "Being a woman, I'm ready to tackle discrimination, educate others, and fight." Or, recall the stories of Tippi and Juno, who identified as women of color who fought against ableism, sexism, and racism in their work environments. And, although she may not have struggled as much as others financially, Tippi advocated for the rights of all disenfranchised coworkers when she explained how her field was racist, classist, and sexist. She was both annoyed and amused by managers referring to her as "radical for wanting human rights!" Collectively, the stories show how participants sought inclusion and equity for all by standing up for everyone's rights.

Theme 4: Career Trajectories and Finding Purpose

As we noted in the introduction, one of the main interests of our initial study was to understand the career choices and purpose development of disabled college students. Of course, over the years, the focus became much broader. These stories reflect multifaceted life experiences and goals that extend far beyond a narrow focus on career and purpose. However, given our focus on those two areas, recurring trends regarding career development and purpose certainly came through in participant stories. We summarize some of those here.

As noted in Chapter 2, finding one's purpose in life is a large part of the developmental process as individuals move through adolescence into adulthood. Chickering and Reisser (1993) described college students' development of purpose as "an increasing ability to be intentional, to assess interests and options, to clarify goals, to make plans, and to persist despite obstacles" (p. 209). In their work with college students, they also noted that an important aspect of developing purpose is finding a vocation, which can be as specific as finding a job or career or as general as "discovering what we love to do [and] what energizes and fulfills us" (Chickering & Reisser, 1993, p. 212). In 2018, we drew from the narratives of our entire sample of 59 participants to construct a model explaining the process by which disabled people develop a sense of purpose (Vaccaro et al., 2018). We titled the work, *Narrating the Self* to foreground the agentic nature of this process in spite of the many people, processes, and systems that serve as obstacles to disabled youth as they consider their life goals and plan for their future. More recently, we have delved into the specific career decision-making process for college students and found that a number of factors came into play including passions, interests, and encouragement/discouragement from others (Vaccaro et al., 2024). Lived medical and psychological disability experiences also played a central role in student's major and career choices. All of these decisions, however, were made within a context where students, family members, teachers, and employers possessed and reinforced normative notions of what someone in a particular career *should* be able to know, be, and do. Those perspectives rarely include disabled people's ways of knowing, being, and doing. Such exclusionary assumptions were often internalized by our participants, who then ruled out certain majors and careers without fully understanding the career duties or potential accommodations that could be made. As you read the stories in this book, you likely noticed all of these career and purpose-related phenomena. In the following paragraphs, we synthesize some of the many insights and takeaways gleaned from these 14 stories.

When it came to choosing a college major and career path, numerous factors were at play. For many of our participants, their lived disability (or fears about disability-related needs) impacted their major and career decisions. Some students worried that they would not be able to do certain jobs because of medical or psychological disability-related realities. For instance, Mercedes admitted, "I think my disability did affect my career goals because I was very worried about what jobs I could do that didn't involve a lot of memory." We should note, however, that very few of our participants actually talked to career advisors or professionals to determine if, or how, accommodations could allow them to be successful in those careers. Many simply opted out of career paths that may have brought them joy.

For some of the participants, the detours into other careers and unexpected life directions were the result of roadblocks. Recall that Willa had a hard time finding a job in recreational therapy because she could not drive. Yet, she persisted through numerous discriminatory job settings and ultimately found a job she loved. Currently, she works as a purchasing agent in a hospital setting, a position that brings together her passions for healthcare and disability justice. In her story, she explained how regardless of the position she's in, she works to make life "better for people." Indeed, many of our participants chose careers in helping professions such as healthcare, education, or chaplaincy because of the desire to help others. Remember Willa who felt like the perfect person for her job because she provided "compassion and empathy" many of these "helping" professions require. And, Peter who majored in Public Health, but found his purpose in a campus chaplain role where he supported the development of college students and served as a partner to the college administration working toward creating a campus that was inclusive of everyone.

Even when their ultimate career was not in a helping field, many of our participants wove their commitment to inclusion into their daily lives. For some, the desire for justice and inclusion came in hobbies, community engagement, or volunteerism. Take, for instance, Justice whose passion for equity led them to the AmeriCorps program. Or, Willa who volunteered to coach soccer, offer children's yoga lessons, and to teach adapted aquatics and skiing. In all of the stories, we witnessed a deep desire of our participants to engage in various forms of care work—both paid and unpaid. In effect, we can see how care for others was deeply rooted in their sense of purpose in life.

Across the stories, we witnessed journeys from childhood to adolescence and adulthood. For all people, the quest for independence and autonomy is a natural part of the process of becoming an adult (Chickering & Reisser, 1993). However, the stories show that disabled people may encounter unique challenges in this journey. Data show that people with disabilities are unemployed or underemployed at higher rates than their non-disabled counterparts (U.S. Bureau of Labor Statistics, 2024). Unemployment and underemployment can be a challenge to gaining one's independence. Indeed, many of our participants had to live at home with family—at least temporarily after college—because they did not have a job or sufficient wages to live independently. Lack of accessible transportation, discriminatory employment practices, employer resistance to accommodations, and discouragement from others also restricted independence and autonomy. Recall Alice's struggles to find work. She also had a hard time finding reliable transportation to get to work, doctors' appointments, and the grocery store. Her desire to live independently was hampered by lack of access to transportation. In one of the most dire cases, we learned that Justice could not find stable employment and was relying on Social Security Income to survive. Having a job, even a full-time one, sometimes was not enough to live on one's own. Many disabled people, including some of our participants, incurred high costs for services, medications, equipment, etc. All of these expenses can be additional financial burdens for disabled people, which restrict their ability to live independently.

In some stories, participants described overt or covert discrimination in the workplace. For example, Willa knew the ways her employer treated her were against the law. Yet, she was worried about the cost of a lawsuit and her professional reputation—which she believed would be tarnished if she brought a lawsuit against the company. In other instances, workplace prejudice and discrimination were more subtle. In those instances, participants weighed the pros and cons of speaking up. Given their orientation towards care for others, many spoke up against workplace exclusion not just for themselves, but to support their coworkers. We can see this in Tippi's story where she identified various forms of discrimination (sexism, classism, racism) and demanded better working conditions for all. Others, including Landers, Peter, and Titus also believed it was their mission to create work environments where everyone felt valued and included.

One of the trends we saw in the stories was the notion that some environments can be more disabling than others. Participants talked about feeling more, or less, disabled in one setting versus another (e.g., school, workplace, home, community). Many chose careers and jobs where they could use their talents to achieve success and not feel disabled. For example, Willow chose a career path where she would not need accommodations to succeed. In the last series of interviews, we even heard from many participants that they felt that the workplace was actually less disabling than school. Recall the experiences of Juno who has never disclosed her disability to an employer because she did not believe it was necessary. Juno reported that her learning disability doesn't really impact her daily work tasks. We also heard stories where sub-environments or units within the same organization felt more, or less, exclusionary. One of the stories that illustrates this phenomenon is from Tippi who worked in various departments in the same aquarium—one that was joyful and fulfilling while the other felt toxic. All of the stories draw attention to the notion that when environments are constructed using non-disabled bodies and minds as a standard, that environment becomes disabling to anyone whose mind or body does not fit that norm.

The final point we wish to make is that, despite the very real ableist obstacles, participants were all successful in their own ways. Two of our interviewees had earned doctoral degrees in the ten-year time span. Recall Mercedes who dropped a nursing major because she struggled to remember all the bones in the body. She also worried if she could succeed as a nurse. Yet, a decade later, she was earning her doctoral degree in occupational therapy, owned a small business, and volunteered in many community organizations. Yolanda also earned master's and doctoral degrees, using that knowledge to educate about autism via teaching, research, and activism. Like Mercedes and Yolanda, all of our participants experienced disability-related obstacles in life. And, they found a way to persevere and foster a sense of purpose. Therefore, we find it fitting to end this section with a quote from Mercedes who offers perspective on navigating the hurdles and obstacles when searching for a sense of purpose as a young disabled person. In her story, Mercedes said, "You become an adult and you learn how to find, and figure out, your way." We hope that this quote, and all the stories in this book, offer insight into the many ordinary and extraordinary ways disabled people develop their own unique life of purpose.

Gratitude and a Final Call to Action

Throughout this book, participants told their most intimate and personal life stories. They shared these stories out of grace, vulnerability, and hope of inspiring change. We did our best to take the utmost care with their stories. As we close this book, we invite readers to continue this care work by considering how to be a disability activist or ally.

Many of our participants benefited from recounting their stories. The act of verbalizing their story contributed to their own personal growth and insight. Many even had *ah-ha* moments during, or after, the interviews. But, that was not *why* our participants shared their evolving experiences with us. Participants gave us the gifts of their time and stories so that their experiences would be useful to others. Participants hoped disabled people would see some of their own story reflected in these pages—and hopefully feel a connection. Participants ideally wanted to be able to help a young person with a disability feel that they were not alone. Others hoped that disabled readers would not only be validated, but also inspired to demand justice and to enact change. Still others shared their stories to educate family members, teachers, employers, and community members about the lived realities that disabled people face everyday. No matter their motivation, they understood that there was value, and a great deal of power, in their stories and their capacity to create lasting, powerful change. Participants wished for a more inclusive world. And, they hoped that by sharing their stories, readers would not only be educated, but also inspired to take action to foster more inclusive home, school, work, and community environments. As with the participants, we hope that these stories help all readers to imagine *and* enact a world where disabled people are valued and can thrive.

Throughout the stories told here, we have seen how others (families, educators, employers, healthcare workers, social service providers, etc.) wielded a great deal of power. In some cases, that power was used to make a positive impact in the lives of disabled people. And, in other cases, that use of power resulted in a great deal of harm. As such, we invite all readers to think critically about how to use the knowledge offered in this book to enact positive change. Every one of us can make a difference within our spheres of influence—whether that be our family, workplace, community, or other setting. This chapter is undergirded by the hope that, when you know better, you can do better.

Everyone can play an important role in fostering family, school, workplace, healthcare, and community environments where disabled people can thrive. We conclude this book by asking questions to help you determine what your action steps will be. For consistency, we organize the questions into the four themes presented in this chapter: (1) Sense of self; (2) Relationships and interactions with others; (3) Success strategies, self-advocacy, and activism; and (4) Career trajectories and finding purpose. We added one additional section to capture some final, overarching ideas and actions.

Sense of Self

- What stigmatizing messages have you heard (or perpetuated) about disability? What everyday actions can you take to resist stigmatizing messages about yourself or others?
- What ideas do you have about how to help young people not internalize ableist messages/stigma?
- How has your own sense of self been influenced by the attitudes of others? What did that experience feel like? What did it teach you about your potential influence on the identities of others?

Relationships and Interactions with Others

- What can you learn from these stories about navigating your own relationships?
- Consider the relationships you have with disabled people in your spheres of influence. In those relationships, are your words and actions affirming, encouraging, supportive, and transformative? Or, are they discouraging, unsupportive, and disempowering? What specific things can you do to honor the expertise and autonomy of disabled people in your life through your interactions and relationships?
- How can educators and other helping professionals foster supportive relationships with disabled people?

Success Strategies, Self-Advocacy, and Activism

- As you saw in this book, individuals can develop a toolkit of strategies to succeed. What strategies have you found successful? Or unsuccessful?
- In your interactions with friends, family, and colleagues, how can you honor and support the unique success strategies that they use—even when they might be different from yours?
- Who, or what, galvanizes your commitment to disability culture and advocacy?
- What strategies can you implement to advocate for greater accessibility and inclusion in your spheres of influence—home, work, school, community, etc.?
- What specific resources, organizations, activists, or authors can you connect with to engage in as you take action?
- What can educators, and other helping professionals, do to foster leadership and self-advocacy skills with disabled people?

Career Trajectories and Finding Purpose

- What are your passions and life goals? How, if at all, have they been shaped by your disability, or other people's perceptions about your disability? What strategies might you borrow from the stories in this book about finding and living your purpose?

- Consider the youth you interact with. Have you ever intentionally or unintentionally discouraged them from particular goals? In what ways can you encourage youth to recognize their talents and skills and to imagine a future where they can live their passions, and thrive?
- Consider the ways in which your work environment could be more inclusive to disabled people's ways of knowing, being, and doing? How can you change the environment, policies, or workplace culture to not only include, but also celebrate the contributions of all people?

Final Call to Action

- How has this book informed your understanding of disability? And, what will you *do* with that learning?
- Ruminate on your key takeaways from this book. Consider how the insights and lessons learned can inform action in your spheres of influence.
- Consider the actions you can take today, tomorrow, and in the future. Identify 2–3 specific strategies you can use to implement in the coming weeks, months, and years to foster disability inclusion.
- Taking inspiration from the stories in this book, consider how you can use your lived experience to inform change within your home, school, work, or community environments.

We bring this text to a close by reiterating our hopes for the book. First, we hope that disabled readers find a connection and affirmation of their own extraordinary and ordinary stories. Second, we hope readers without disabilities will apply what they learned to foster more inclusive home, school, work, and community environments. Mostly, we hope that, like us, *all* readers glean invaluable insights for action, advocacy, and change. Our participants imagined and wished for a more inclusive world. And, we hope that after reading these stories, readers can help enact it.

We began this book with a quote from Alice about the importance of sharing stories to raise awareness and incite advocacy. Her words, as well as the stories throughout the book, point to joy and success, as well as challenges disabled people experience in a world not designed for them. We conclude this book with a direct quote from Poppy. This quote highlights the importance of expressing gratitude and taking action. She calls upon *all of us* to use our knowledge, skills, resources, and power to make a difference. She also reminds us that change can take time. Indeed, systems are big and messy and complicated. Yet, a consistent theme in this book is that if we all make intentional choices, and take actions (no matter how small in our spheres of influence), the world we inhabit will hopefully, become better—albeit in small or incremental ways. Everyday actions and choices can add up in powerful and profound ways. Indeed, as educators ourselves, we deeply believe that one person can make a difference. One teacher. One supervisor. One family member. One friend. One stranger. One disabled person. Every one of us can make a difference in making the world a better place. With these hopes for a better future in mind, we close with Poppy's ideas about the role we *all* play in creating a more inclusive future.

"It gets better with time. We–the disabled, family, and friends–learn how to better communicate our needs and effectively utilize the resources available. We learn to appreciate what was given to us and to do the best we can with the tools we have."

—Poppy

References

Abes, E. S., & Wallace, M. M. (2020). Using Crip Theory to Reimagine Student Development Theory as Disability Justice. *Journal of College Student Development, 61*(5), 574–592. https://doi.org/10.1353/csd.2020.0056

Acevedo, S. M., Yoshizaki, H. M., Abustan, P., & Pearson, H. (2022). Disability Justice Praxis: Sick, Disabled, Deaf Women and Non-Binary Educators of Color Holding Each Other in Radical Love and Accessible Kinship. *Research in Arts and Education, 2022*(3), 26–35. https://doi.org/10.54916/rae.125083

Angrist, J. D., & Pischke, J. S. (2009). *Mostly Harmless Econometrics: An Empiricist's Companion.* Princeton University Press.

Archer, S. L., & Waterman, A. S. (1990). Varieties of Identity Diffusions and Foreclosures: An Exploration of Subcategories of the Identity Statuses. *Journal of Adolescent Research, 5*(1), 96–111. https://doi.org/10.1177/074355489051009

Argus, S., Vaccaro, A., Coiro, J. Hos, R. & Deeney, T. (2022). Equitable Teaching Practices in Higher Education: Key Insights from the Literature. In S. Keengwe (Ed.), *Handbook of Research on Social Justice and Equity in Education* (pp. 92–113). IGI Global.

Arnett, J. J. (2007). Emerging Adulthood: What Is It, and What Is It Good for? *Child Development Perspectives, 1*(2), 68–73. https://doi.org/10.1111/j.1750-8606.2007.00016.x

Basile, K. C., Breiding, M. J., & Smith, S. G. (2016). Disability and Risk of Recent Sexual Violence in the United States. *American Journal of Public Health, 106*(5), 928–933. https://doi.org/10.2105/ajph.2015.303004

Baxter Magolda, M. B., & King, P. M. (2007). Interview Strategies for Assessing Self-Authorship: Constructing Conversations to Assess Meaning Making. *Journal of College Student Development, 48*(5), 491–508. https://doi.org/10.1353/csd.2007.0055

Beauchamp-Pryor, K. (2011). Impairment, Cure and Identity: 'Where Do I Fit In?' *Disability & Society, 26*(1), 5–17. https://doi.org/10.1080/09687599.2011.529662

Ben-Moshe, L., & Magaña, S. (2014). An Introduction to Race, Gender, and Disability: Intersectionality, Disability Studies, and Families of Color. *Women, Gender, and Families of Color, 2*(2), 105–114. https://doi.org/10.5406/womgenfamcol.2.2.0105

Berne, P., Morales, A. L., Langstaff, D., & Invalid, S. (2018). Ten Principles of Disability Justice. *WSQ: Women's Studies Quarterly, 46*(1), 227–230. https://doi.org/10.1353/wsq.2018.0003

Bixby, L., Bevan, S., & Boen, C. (2022). The Links Between Disability, Incarceration, and Social Exclusion. *Health Affairs, 41*(10), 1460–1469. https://doi.org/10.1377/hlthaff.2022.00495

Blasey, J., Wang, C., & Blasey, R. (2023). Accommodation Use and Academic Outcomes for College Students with Disabilities. *Psychological Reports*, *126*(4), 1891–1909. https://doi.org/10.1177/00332941221078011

Bronk, K. C., Hill, P. L., Lapsley, D. K., Talib, T. L. & Finch, H. (2009). Purpose, Hope, and Life Satisfaction in Three Groups. *The Journal of Positive Psychology*, *4*, 500–510. https://doi.org/10.1080/17439760903271439

Brown, T. J., & Clark, C. (2017, December). Employed Parents of Children with Disabilities and Work Family Life Balance: A Literature Review. *Child & Youth Care Forum*, *46*, 857–876. Springer US. https://doi.org/10.1007/s10566-017-9407-0

Brueggemann, A. E., Kamphaus, R. W., & Dombrowski, S. C. (2008). An Impairment Model of Learning Disability Diagnosis. *Professional Psychology: Research and Practice*, *39*(4), 424. https://doi.org/10.1037/0735-7028.39.4.424

Burgstahler, S. (2009). *Universal Design of Instruction (UDI): Definition, Principles, Guidelines, and Examples*. Do-It. https://files.eric.ed.gov/fulltext/ED506547.pdf

Burrow, A. L., & Hill, P. L. (2011). Purpose as a Form of Identity Capital for Positive Youth Adjustment. *Developmental Psychology*, *47*(4), 1196. https://doi.org/10.1037/a0023818

Capp, M. J. (2017). The Effectiveness of Universal Design for Learning: A Meta-Analysis of Literature between 2013 and 2016. *International Journal of Inclusive Education*, *21*(8), 791–807. https://doi.org/10.1080/13603116.2017.1325074

Charlton, J. (1998). *Nothing about Us Without Us: Disability, Oppression and Empowerment*. University of California Press. https://doi.org/10.1525/9780520925441

Chiang, E. S. (2020). Disability Cultural Centers: How Colleges Can Move Beyond Access to Inclusion. *Disability & Society*, *35*(7), 1183–1188. https://doi.org/10.1080/09687599.2019.1679536

Chickering, A. W. & Reisser, L. (1993). *Education and Identity* (2nd ed.). Jossey-Bass.

Cobb, R. B., & Alwell, M. (2009). Transition Planning/Coordinating Interventions for Youth with Disabilities: A Systematic Review. *Career Development for Exceptional Individuals*, *32*(2), 70–81. https://doi.org/10.1177/0885728809336655

Cohen, O. (2005). How Do We Recover? An Analysis of Psychiatric Survivor Oral Histories. *Journal of Humanistic Psychology*, *45*(3), 333–354. https://doi.org/10.1177/0022167805277107

Cooper, B. (2016). Intersectionality. In L. Disch & M. Hawkesworth (Eds.), *The Oxford Handbook of Feminist Theory* (pp. 385 –406). Oxford University Press.

Côté, J. E. (2014). The Dangerous Myth of Emerging Adulthood: An Evidence-Based Critique of a Flawed Developmental Theory. *Applied Developmental Science*, *18*(4), 177–188. https://doi.org/10.1080/10888691.2014.954451

Creasman, M. W. (2021). How Pregnancy Unmasked My Internalized Ableism. *JAMA*, *326*(24), 2473–2474. https://doi.org/10.1001/jama.2021.22116

Crenshaw, K. (1989). Demarginalizing the Intersection of Race and Sex: A Black Feminist Critique of Antidiscrimination Doctrine, Feminist Theory, and Antiracist Politics. *University of Chicago Legal Forum*, *1989*, 139–167.

Crenshaw, K. (1991). Mapping the Margins: Intersectionality, Identity Politics, and Violence Against Women of Color. *Stanford Law Review*, *43*(6), 1241–1299. https://doi.org/10.2307/1229039

Daly-Cano, M., Ruise, B. L., Moore, A., Vaccaro, A., Newman, B. M., & Newman, P. R. (2024). Family social support for college students with disabilities. *Family Relations*, *73*, 3567–3585. https://doi.org/10.1111/fare.13077

Daly-Cano, M., Vaccaro, A., & Newman, B. (2015). College Student Narratives about Learning and Using Self-Advocacy Skills. *Journal of Postsecondary Education and Disability*, *28*(2), 213–227.

Damon, W. (2008) *The Path to Purpose: How Young People Find their Calling in Life*. The Free Press.

Davis, L. J. (2015). *Enabling Acts: The Hidden Story of how the Americans with Disabilities Act Gave the Largest US Minority its Rights*. Beacon Press.

Deans, C., & Maggert, K. A. (2015). What Do You Mean, "Epigenetic"? *Genetics, 199*(4), 887–896. https://doi.org/10.1534/genetics.114.173492

DeWitz, S. J., Woolsey, M. L., & Walsh, W. B. (2009). College Student Retention: An Exploration of the Relationship between Self-Efficacy Beliefs and Purpose in Life among College Students. *Journal of College Student Development, 50*(1), 19–34. https://doi.org/10.1353/csd.0.0049

Dolmage, J. T. (2017). *Academic Ableism: Disability and Higher Education*. University of Michigan Press.

Dwyer, P. (2022). The Neurodiversity Approach(es): What Are they and What do they Mean for Researchers? *Human Development, 66*(2), 73–92. https://doi.org/10.1159/000523723

Edwards, M., Poed, S., Al-Nawab, H., & Penna, O. (2022). Academic Accommodations for University Students Living with Disability and the Potential of Universal Design to Address Their Needs. *Higher Education, 84*(4), 779–799. https://doi.org/10.1007/s10734-021-00800-w

Edwards, R. A. R. (2012). *Words Made Flesh: Nineteenth-Century Deaf Education and the Growth of Deaf Culture*. New York University Press.

Egner, J. E. (2019). "The Disability Rights Community Was Never Mine": Neuroqueer Disidentification. *Gender & Society, 33*(1), 123–147. https://doi.org/10.1177/0891243218803284

Evans, N. J., Broido, E. M., Brown, K. R., & Wilke, A. K. (2017). *Disability in Higher Education: A Social Justice Approach*. John Wiley & Sons.

Ferguson, R. A. (2012). *The Reorder of Things: The University and Its Pedagogies of Minority Difference*. University of Minnesota Press. https://doi.org/10.5749/minnesota/9780816672783.001.0001

Fine, M., & Asch, A. (1988). Disability beyond Stigma: Social Interaction, Discrimination, and Activism. *Journal of Social Issues, 44*(1), 3–21. https://doi.org/10.1111/j.1540-4560.1988.tb02045.x

Fleming, A. R., & Fairweather, J. S. (2012). The Role of Postsecondary Education in the Path from High School to Work for Youth with Disabilities. *Rehabilitation Counseling Bulletin, 55*(2), 71–81. https://doi.org/10.1177/0034355211423303

Foley-Nicpon, M., Assouline, S. G., & Colangelo, N. (2013). Twice-Exceptional Learners: Who Needs to Know What? *Gifted Child Quarterly, 57*(3), 169–180. https://doi.org/10.1177/0016986213490021

Frankl, V. (1959). *Man's Search for Meaning: An Introduction to Logotherapy*. Beacon.

Friedensen, R.E. and Kimball, E. (2017). Disability and College Students: A Critical Examination of a Multivalent Identity. *Theory and Method in Higher Education Research, 3*, 227–245. Emerald Publishing. https://doi.org/10.1108/s2056-375220170000003013

Friedensen, R., Lauterbach, A., Mwangi, C. G., & Kimball, E. (2022). Examining the Role of Family in the Development of Pre-college STEM Aspirations among Students with Disabilities. *Journal of Postsecondary Student Success, 1*(3), 13–31. https://doi.org/10.33009/fsop_jpss128231

Galván, A. (2013). Neural Systems Underlying Reward and Approach Behaviors in Childhood and Adolescence. In S. Andersen, & D. Pine (Eds.), *The Neurobiology of Childhood. Current Topics in Behavioral Neurosciences, 16*, 167–188. Springer, Berlin, Heidelberg. https://doi.org/10.1007/7854_2013_240

Galván, A. (2018). *The Neuroscience of Adolescence*. Cambridge University Press.

Garagiola, E. R., Lam, Q., Wachsmuth, L. S., Tan, T. Y., Ghali, S., Asafo, S., & Swarna, M. (2022). Adolescent Resilience during the COVID-19 Pandemic: A Review of the Impact of the Pandemic on Developmental Milestones. *Behavioral Sciences, 12*(7), 220. https://doi.org/10.3390/bs12070220

Gill, M. (2005). The Myth of Transition: Contractualizing Disability in the Sheltered Workshop. *Disability & Society, 20*(6), 613–623. https://doi.org/10.1080/09687590500248399

Grigal, M., Madaus, J. W., Dukes, L. L., & Hart, D. (2018). *Navigating the Transition from High School to College for Students with Disabilities.* Routledge.

Hartblay, C. (2020). Disability Expertise: Claiming Disability Anthropology. *Current Anthropology, 61*(S21), S26–S36. https://doi.org/10.1086/705781

Hayes, J., & Hannold, E. L. M. (2007). The Road to Empowerment: A Historical Perspective on the Medicalization of Disability. *Journal of Health and Human Services Administration, 30*(3), 352–377. https://doi.org/10.1177/107937390703000303

Hogg, L. (2011). Funds of Knowledge: An Investigation of Coherence within the Literature. *Teaching and Teacher Education, 27*, 666–667. https://doi.org/10.1016/j.tate.20110.11.005

hooks, b. (1994) *Teaching to Transgress: Education as the Practice of Freedom.* Routledge

Horowitz, A. W., & Souza, A. P. (2011). The Impact of Parental Income on the Intra-Household Distribution of School Attainment: A Measurement Strategy and Evidence. *The Quarterly Review of Economics and Finance, 51*(1), 1–18. https://doi.org/10.1016/j.qref.2010.09.002

Imrie, R. (1997). Rethinking the Relationships between Disability, Rehabilitation, and Society. *Disability and Rehabilitation, 19*(7), 263–271. https://doi.org/10.3109/09638289709166537

Jenks, A. (2019). Crip Theory and the Disabled Identity: Why Disability Politics Needs Impairment. *Disability & Society, 34*(3), 449–469. https://doi.org/10.1080/09687599.2018.1545116

Kafai, S. (2021). *Crip Kinship: The Disability Justice & Art Activism of Sins Invalid.* Arsenal Pulp Press.

Kennedy, C. H., Meyer, K. A., Knowles, T., & Shukla, S. (2000). Analyzing the Multiple Functions of Stereotypical Behavior for Students with Autism: Implications for Assessment and Treatment. *Journal of Applied Behavior Analysis, 33*(4), 559–571. https://doi.org/10.1901/jaba.2000.33-559

Kett, J. F. (2003). Reflections on the History of Adolescence in America. *The History of the Family, 8*(3), 355–373. https://doi.org/10.1016/s1081-602x(03)00042-3

Kimball, E. W., Moore, A., Vaccaro, A., Troiano, P. F., & Newman, B. M. (2016). College Students with Disabilities Redefine Activism: Self-Advocacy, Storytelling, and Collective Action. *Journal of Diversity in Higher Education, 9*(3), 245–260. https://doi.org/10.1037/dhe0000031

Kimball, E.W., Vaccaro, A., Tissi-Gassoway, N., Bobot, D., Moore, A. M, Troiano, P. F., & Newman, B. M. (2018). Gender, Sexuality, & (Dis)ability: Queer Perspectives on the Experiences of Students with Disabilities. *Disability Studies Quarterly, 38*(2), 1–35. http://dsq-sds.org/article/view/5937/4907

Kimball, E., Wells, R. S., Ostiguy, B., Manly, C., & Lauterbach, A. (2016). Students with Disabilities in Higher Education: A Review of the Literature and an Agenda for Future Research. In M. B. Paulsen (Ed.), *Higher Education: Handbook of Theory and Research, 31*, 91–156. Springer. https://doi.org/10.1007/978-3-319-26829-3_3

Kitta, A. (2024). "You May Now Become Who You Thought Was Disposable": COVID-19 Politics and Ableism. *Journal of American Folklore, 137*(545), 321–330. https://doi.org/10.5406/15351882.137.545.04

Krieger, L. H. (Ed.). (2010). *Backlash against the ADA: Reinterpreting Disability Rights.* University of Michigan Press.

Leonardo, Z., & Broderick, A. A. (2011). Smartness as Property: A Critical Exploration of Intersections Between Whiteness and Disability Studies. *Teachers College Record, 113*(10), 2206–2232. https://doi.org/10.1177/016146811111301008

Lightner, K. L., Kipps-Vaughan, D., Schulte, T., & Trice, A. D. (2012). Reasons University Students with a Learning Disability Wait to Seek Disability Services. *Journal of Postsecondary Education and Disability, 25*(2), 145–159.

Longmore, P. K. (2015). *Telethons: Spectacle, Disability, and the Business of Charity.* Oxford University Press.

Maddocks, D. L. (2018). The Identification of Students Who Are Gifted and Have a Learning Disability: A Comparison of Different Diagnostic Criteria. *Gifted Child Quarterly, 62*(2), 175–192. https://doi.org/10.1177/0016986217752096

Malin, H., Ballard, P. J., & Damon, W. (2015). Civic Purpose: An Integrated Construct for Understanding Civic Development in Adolescence. *Human Development, 58*(2), 103–130. https://doi.org/10.1159/000381655

Malli, M. A., Sams, L., Forrester-Jones, R., Murphy, G., & Henwood, M. (2018). Austerity and the Lives of People with Learning Disabilities. A Thematic Synthesis of Current Literature. *Disability & Society, 33*(9), 1412–1435. https://doi.org/10.1080/09687599.2018.1497950

Mamboleo, G., Dong, S., Anderson, S., & Molder, A. (2020). Accommodation Experience: Challenges and Facilitators of Requesting and Implementing Accommodations among College Students with Disabilities. *Journal of Vocational Rehabilitation, 53*(1), 43–54. https://doi.org/10.3233/jvr-201084

Masten, A. S., & Reed, M. G. J. (2002). Resilience in Development. In C. R. Snyder & S. J. Lopez (Eds.), *Handbook of Positive Psychology* (pp. 74–88). Oxford University Press.

McDonagh, P. (2008). *Idiocy: A Cultural History.* Liverpool University Press.

McNicholas, P. J., Floyd, R. G., Woods Jr, I. L., Singh, L. J., Manguno, M. S., & Maki, K. E. (2018). State Special Education Criteria for Identifying Intellectual Disability: A Review Following Revised Diagnostic Criteria and Rosa's Law. *School Psychology Quarterly, 33*(1), 75. https://doi.org/10.1037/spq0000208

McRuer, R. (2018). *Crip Times: Disability, Globalization, and Resistance.* NYU Press.

Milbrodt, T. (2018). "Today I Had an Eye Appointment, and I'm Still Blind": Crip Humor, Storytelling, and Narrative Positioning of the Disabled Self. *Disability Studies Quarterly, 38*(2), 1–33. https://doi.org/10.18061/dsq.v38i2.6163

Mingus, M. (2011, May 5). *Access Intimacy: The Missing Link.* Leaving Evidence. https://leavingevidence.wordpress.com/2011/05/05/access-intimacy-the-missing-link/

Moore, A. M., Vaccaro, A., Newman, B. M., & Daly-Cano, M. (2024). "I Shouldn't Have To Rely on Them Anymore": College Students With Disabilities on the Journey Toward Self-Advocacy. *Journal of the First-Year Experience & Students in Transition, 36*(1), 93–112.

Moore, A. M., Kern, V., Carlson, A., Vaccaro, A., Kimball, E. W., Abbotte, J. A., Troiano, P. F. & Newman, B. M. (2020). Constructing a Sense of Purpose and a Professional Teaching Identity: Experiences of Teacher Candidates with Disabilities. *The Educational Forum, 84*(3), 272–285. https://doi.org/10.1080/00131725.2020.1738608

Moser, I. (2000). Against Normalisation: Subverting Norms of Ability and Disability. *Science as Culture, 9*(2), 201–240. https://doi.org/10.1080/713695234

Nash, R. J., & Murray, M. C. (2010). *Helping College Students Find Purpose: The Campus Guide to Meaning-Making.* Jossey-Bass.

Nathan, M. J., & Brown, J. M. (2018). An Ecological Approach to Modeling Disability. *Bioethics*, *32*(9), 593–601. https://doi.org/10.1111/bioe.12497

National Center for Education Statistics (2024). Digest of Education Statistics. Institute of Education Sciences. Retrieved from https://nces.ed.gov/programs/digest/2024menu_tables.asp

Newman, B. M., & Newman, P. R. (2018). *Development Through Life: A Psychosocial Approach* (13th ed.). Cengage.

Newman, B. M., Kimball, E. W., Vaccaro, A., Moore, A. M. & Troiano, P. F. (2019). Diverse Pathways to Purpose for College Students with Disabilities. *Career Development and Transition for Exceptional Individuals*, *42*(2), 111–121. https://doi.org/10.1177/2165143418758985

Nielsen, K. E. (2012). *A Disability History of the United States* (2nd ed.). Beacon.

Noddings, N. (1992). *The Challenge to Care in Schools: An Alternative Approach to Education.* Teachers College Press.

Olsen, S. H., Cork, S., Anders, P., Padrón, R., Peterson, A., Strausser, A., & Jaeger, P. T. (2022). The Disability Tax and the Accessibility Tax: The Extra Intellectual, Emotional, and Technological Labor and Financial Expenditures Required of Disabled People in a World Gone Wrong… and Mostly Online. *Including Disability*, 1, 51–86. https://doi.org/10.51357/id.vi1.170

Padden, C. A., & Humphries, T. L. (2006). *Inside Deaf Culture.* Harvard University Press.

Patton, L. D., Renn, K. A., Guido, F. M., & Quaye, S. J. (2016). *Student Development in College: Theory, Research, and Practice.* John Wiley & Sons.

Parekh, G., & Brown, R. S. (2020). Naming and Claiming: The Tension Between Institutional and Self-Identification of Disability. *Canadian Journal of Disability Studies*, *9*(5), 347–379. https://doi.org/10.15353/cjds.v9i5.701

Peters, M. (2022). Caring Classrooms in Crisis: COVID-19, Interest Convergence, and Universal Design for Learning. *Disability Studies Quarterly*, *42*(1). https://doi.org/10.18061/dsq.v42i1.7929

Piepzna-Samarasinha, L. L. (2018). *Care Work: Dreaming Disability Justice* (1st ed.). Arsenal Pulp Press.

Pizzolato, J. E., Brown, E. L., & Kanny, M. A. (2011). Purpose Plus: Supporting Youth Purpose, Control, and Academic Achievement. *New Directions for Student Leadership*, 132, 75–88. https://doi.org/10.1002/yd.429

Radulski, E. M. (2022). Conceptualising Autistic Masking, Camouflaging, and Neurotypical Privilege: Towards a Minority Group Model of Neurodiversity. *Human Development*, *66*(2), 113–127. https://doi.org/10.1159/000524122

Raue, K., & Lewis, L. (2011). *Students with Disabilities at Degree-Granting Postsecondary Institutions (NCES 2011–018).* U.S. Department of Education, National Center for Education Statistics. Washington, DC: U.S. Government Printing Office.

Rehm, R. S., Fisher, L. T., Fuentes-Afflick, E., & Chesla, C. A. (2013). Parental Advocacy Styles for Special Education Students during the Transition to Adulthood. *Qualitative Health Research*, *23*(10), 1377–1387. https://doi.org/10.1177/1049732313505915

Reis, S. M., Baum, S. M., & Burke, E. (2014). An Operational Definition of Twice-Exceptional Learners: Implications and Applications. *Gifted Child Quarterly*, *58*(3), 217–230. https://doi.org/10.1177/0016986214534976

Rivera Drew, J. A. (2009). Disability and the Self-Reliant Family: Revisiting the Literature on Parents with Disabilities. *Marriage & Family Review*, *45*(5), 431–447. https://doi.org/10.1080/01494920903048734

Rockenbach, A. B., Hudson, T. D., & Tuchmayer, J. B. (2014). Fostering Meaning, Purpose, and Enduring Commitments to Community Service in College: A Multidimensional Conceptual Model. *The Journal of Higher Education*, *85*(3), 312–338. https://doi.org/10.1353/jhe.2014.0014

Rose, C. A., Stormont, M., Wang, Z., Simpson, C. G., Preast, J. L., & Green, A. L. (2015). Bullying and Students with Disabilities: Examination of Disability Status and Educational Placement. *School Psychology Review*, *44*(4), 425–444. https://doi.org/10.17105/spr-15-0080.1

Rose, D. (2000). Universal Design for Learning. *Journal of Special Education Technology*, *15*(4), 47–51. https://doi.org/10.1177/016264340001500407

Rose, D.H. and Meyer, A. (2002). *Teaching Every Student in the Digital Age: Universal Design for Learning*. Association for Supervision and Curriculum Development.

Rose, S. F. (2017). *No Right to Be Idle: The Invention of Disability, 1840s–1930s*. UNC Press Books.

Schalk, S. (2013). Coming to Claim Crip: Disidentification With/in Disability Studies. *Disability Studies Quarterly*, *33*(2), 1–23. https://doi.org/10.18061/dsq.v33i2.3705

Schalk, S. (2017). Coming to Claim Crip: Disidentification With/in Disability. In L. Davis (Ed.), *Beginning with Disability* (pp. 123–136). Routledge.

Schalk, S. (2016). Reevaluating the Supercrip. *Journal of Literary & Cultural Disability Studies*, *10*(1), 71–86. https://doi.org/10.3828/jlcds.2016.5

Schuelka, M. J. (2013). A Faith in Humanness: Disability, Religion and Development. *Disability & Society*, *28*(4), 500–513. https://doi.org/10.1080/09687599.2012.717880

Sevak, P., Houtenville, A. J., Brucker, D. L., & O'Neill, J. (2015). Individual Characteristics and the Disability Employment Gap. *Journal of Disability Policy Studies*, *26*(2), 80–88. https://doi.org/10.1177/1044207315585823

Shaheen, N. L., & Lohnes Watulak, S. (2019). Bringing Disability into the Discussion: Examining Technology Accessibility as an Equity Concern in the Field of Instructional Technology. *Journal of Research on Technology in Education*, *51*(2), 187–201. https://doi.org/10.1080/15391523.2019.1566037

Shakespeare, T. (2012). Still a Health Issue. *Disability and Health Journal*, *5*(3), 129–131. https://doi.org/10.1016/j.dhjo.2012.04.002

Shakespeare, T., Iezzoni, L. I., & Groce, N. E. (2009). Disability and the Training of Health Professionals. *The Lancet*, *374*(9704), 1815–1816. https://doi.org/10.1016/s0140-6736(09)62050-x

Silván-Ferrero, P., Recio, P., Molero, F., & Nouvilas-Pallejà, E. (2020). Psychological Quality of Life in People with Physical Disability: The Effect of Internalized Stigma, Collective Action and Resilience. *International Journal of Environmental Research and Public Health*, *17*(5), 1802. https://doi.org/10.3390/ijerph17051802

Son, J., Debono, D., Leitner, R., Lenroot, R., & Johnson, J. (2019). Pass the Parcel: Service Provider Views on Bridging Gaps for Youth with Dual Diagnosis of Intellectual Disability and Mental Health Disorders in Regional Areas. *Journal of Paediatrics and Child Health*, *55*(6), 666–672. https://doi.org/10.1111/jpc.14266

Taylor, A. (2018). Knowledge Citizens? Intellectual Disability and the Production of Social Meanings within Educational Research. *Harvard Educational Review*, *88*(1), 1–25. https://doi.org/10.17763/1943-5045-88.1.1

Thomas, S. B. (2000). College Students and Disability Law. *The Journal of Special Education*, *33*(4), 248–257. https://doi.org/10.1177/0022466900033004

Trainor, A. A., Morningstar, M. E., & Murray, A. (2016). Characteristics of Transition Planning and Services for Students with High-Incidence Disabilities. *Learning Disability Quarterly*, *39*(2), 113–124. https://doi.org/10.1177/0731948715607348

Troiano, P. F. (2003). College Students and Learning Disability: Elements of Self-Style. *Journal of College Student Development*, *44*(3), 404–419. https://doi.org/10.1353/csd.2003.0033

U.S. Bureau of Labor Statistics (2024). Person with a Disability: Labor Force Characteristics 2023 (report No. USDL-24-0349) Retrieved from https://www.bls.gov/news.release/pdf/disabl.pdf

U.S. Congress. (1990). *Americans with Disabilities Act of 1990*, Pub. L. No. 101-336, 104 Stat. 327. https://www.congress.gov/bill/101st-congress/house-bill/2273

U.S. Congress. (1975). *Education for all handicapped children act*, Pub. L. No. 94-142, 89 Stat. 773. https://www.congress.gov/bill/94th-congress/house-bill/6920

U.S. Department of Education. (2004). *Individuals with Disabilities Education Act (IDEA)*. 20 U.S.C. § 1400 et seq. https://sites.ed.gov/idea/

Vaccaro, A., Kimball, E. W., Moore, A. M., Newman, B. M., & Troiano, P. F. (2018). Narrating the Self: A Grounded Theory Model of Emerging Purpose for College Students with Disabilities. *Journal of College Student Development, 59*(1), 37–54. https://doi.org/10.1353/csd.2018.0003

Vaccaro, A., Kimball, E. W., Newman, B. M., Moore, A. M., & Troiano, P. F. (2019). Collegiate Purpose Development at the Intersections of Disability and Social Class. *The Review of Higher Education, 43*(1), 403–426. https://doi.org/10.1353/rhe.2019.0100

Vaccaro, A., Lee, M., Tissi-Gassoway, N., Kimball, E. W., & Newman, B. M. (2020). Gender and Ability Oppressions Shaping the Lives of College Students: An Intracategorical, Intersectional Analysis. *Journal of Women and Gender in Higher Education, 13*(2), 119–137. https://doi.org/10.1080/26379112.2020.1780134

Vaccaro, A., Moore, A. M., Kimball, E. W., Troiano, P. F. & Newman, B. M. (2019). "Not Gonna Hold Me Back": Coping and Resilience in Students with Disabilities. *Journal of Student Affairs Research and Practice, 56*(2), 181–193. https://doi.org/10.1080/19496591.2018.1506793

Vaccaro, A., Moore, A. M., Newman, B M., & Troiano, P. F. (2024). How Students with Disabilities Cope with Bullying, Stereotypes, Low Expectations and Discouragement. *Journal of Postsecondary Education and Disability (JPED), 37*(2), 99–112. https://www.ahead.org/professional-resources/publications/jped

Vaccaro, A., Daly-Cano, M., & Newman, B. (2015). A Sense of Belonging Among College Students with Disabilities: An Emergent Theoretical Model. *Journal of College Student Development, 56*(7), 670–686. https://doi.org/10.1353/csd.2015.0072

Vaccaro, A., Lee, M., Moore, A. & Kimball, E.W. (2024). "Am I Picking the Right Major?" A Grounded Model Major and Career Choice for Disabled College Students. A paper presented at the Association for the Study of Higher Education (ASHE) conference. Minneapolis, Minnesota.

Varino, S. (2024). A Viral Pedagogy: Undoing Things with Long COVID's Autoimmunities. *Catalyst: Feminism, Theory, Technoscience, 10*(1), 1–20. https://doi.org/10.28968/cftt.v10i2.40289

Wang, S., Rubie-Davies, C. M., & Meissel, K. (2018). A Systematic Review of the Teacher Expectation Literature over the Past 30 Years. *Educational Research and Evaluation, 24*(3–5), 124–179. https://doi.org/10.1080/13803611.2018.1548798

Watson, A. C., & Larson, J. E. (2006). Personal Responses to Disability Stigma: From Self-Stigma to Empowerment. *Rehabilitation Research, Policy, and Education, 20*(4), 235. https://doi.org/10.1891/088970106805065377

Watson, N. (2002). Well, I Know This is Going to Sound Very Strange to You, but I Don't See Myself as a Disabled Person: Identity and Disability. *Disability & Society, 17*(5), 509–527. https://doi.org/10.1080/09687590220148496

Watson, S. L., Hayes, S. A., & Radford-Paz, E. (2011). "Diagnose Me Please!": A Review of Research About the Journey and Initial Impact of Parents Seeking a Diagnosis of Developmental Disability for Their Child. *International Review of Research in Developmental Disabilities, 41*, 31–71. https://doi.org/10.1016/b978-0-12-386495-6.00002-3

Welkener, M. M., & Bowsher, A. (2012). Soul-Building: Students' Perspectives on Meaning, Purpose, and the College Experience. *Journal of College and Character*, *13*(3), 1–11. https://doi.org/10.1515/1940-1639.1881

Whittle, E. L., Fisher, K. R., Reppermund, S., Lenroot, R., & Trollor, J. (2018). Barriers and Enablers to Accessing Mental Health Services for People with Intellectual Disability: A Scoping Review. *Journal of Mental Health Research in Intellectual Disabilities*, *11*(1), 69–102. https://doi.org/10.1080/19315864.2017.1408724

Williams, A. S., & Moore, S. M. (2011). Universal Design of Research: Inclusion of Persons with Disabilities in Mainstream Biomedical Studies. *Science Translational Medicine*, *3*(82), 1–10. https://doi.org/10.1126/scitranslmed.3002133

Wondemu, M. Y., Joranger, P., Hermansen, Å., & Brekke, I. (2022). Impact of Child Disability on Parental Employment and Labour Income: A Quasi-Experimental Study of Parents of Children with Disabilities in Norway. *BMC Public Health*, *22*(1), 1813. https://doi.org/10.1186/s12889-022-14195-5

Wong, A. (Ed.). (2020). *Disability Visibility: First-Person Stories from the Twenty-First Century*. Vintage Books.

Zilvinskis, J. (2020). Using Large Survey Data to Understand the Engagement of Students with Disabilities. *Journal of Postsecondary Education and Disability*, *33*(3), 257–263.

For Product Safety Concerns and Information please contact our EU
representative GPSR@taylorandfrancis.com
Taylor & Francis Verlag GmbH, Kaufingerstraße 24, 80331 München, Germany